BIRDM

Thomas E. Gaddis, who died in 1984, had a lifelong interest in prisoners and prison life. A freelance journalist for much of his career, he wrote numerous articles and three books: *Birdman of Alcatraz; Killer* (1970), the case history of mass murderer Carl Panzran, which he wrote with James O. Long; and *Unknown Men of Alcatraz* (1977). He worked for some time as a probation officer and it was during this period that he began work on *Birdman of Alcatraz*. Gaddis received a Masters and Doctorate in Educational Psychology from the University of Oregon and was a practising psychologist. He headed a Ford Foundation project called NewGate which, offering college education to prisoners, was the first of its kind. He was also a teacher in criminology and in creative writing. Throughout his life, Thomas Gaddis was an active campaigner against capital punishment.

BIRDMAN OF ALCATRAZ

The Story of Robert Stroud

THOMAS E. GADDIS

Epilogue by Phyllis E. Gaddis

LONDON
VICTOR GOLLANCZ LTD
1985

To

my wife Martha

who saw it through

First published in Great Britain 1956
by Victor Gollancz Ltd
14 Henrietta St, London WC2E 8QJ

First published in Gollancz Paperbacks 1985

The names of the prisoner's birds and of several minor characters, are changed. Although literary licence is taken in dramatizing scenes, this book is documented.

British Library Cataloguing in Publication Data
Gaddis, Thomas E.
Birdman of Alcatraz.
1. Crime and criminals—California—San Francisco—Biography
I. Title
365'.44'0924 HV6248.S/

ISBN 0-575-03710-5

Printed in Finland by Werner Söderström Oy

NOTE AND ACKNOWLEDGMENTS

IT IS PROBABLY a form of presumption for a non-convict to write a prison book. Prisons exude a curious atmosphere. Those who have suffered in them—the keepers and the kept—can sense this background in the written word.

It seems to me, however, that this story carries a meaning far beyond the question of atmosphere. The feeling has persisted that this prisoner and his life are trying to say something about man; and the writing of this book became an independent pursuit of what it is. Such a pursuit is a step into the unknown. When the step is taken, it is exhilarating to note how people come forward to help in unexpected and unpredictable ways.

For this assistance, which was as varied as the book itself, I am indebted to the people listed below and also to those others—penologists and correctional personnel—whose help was no less invaluable because they cannot be named.

J. Frank Burke, Fred E. Daw, Laeta Bartlett Dunbar, Stanley A. Furman, Ardythe Hitchcock Gamel, Bertha Marie Hayden, Jess Herbert, Alex Hixon, Cam Harding Knight, Benjamin F. Levy, Dr. Lois G. Lobb, Ernest Spagnoli, and a staunch editor at Random House, Belle Becker.

T. G.

BOOK ONE

PROLOGUE

IN THE SLATE WATERS of San Francisco Bay, between the city and the Golden Gate, thirteen acres of grey rock thrust up like a clenched fist: the island of Alcatraz. Its prison buildings glint through the mist like stone knuckles under the eye of the sun.

There is a man living there today who has been kept by the United States in a solitary cell since 1916. When steel doors first shut behind him, Teddy Roosevelt was President. Wilhelm Hohenzollern was a hale man, and the shot at Sarajevo had yet to be fired.

This prisoner kissed his last woman (other than his mother) before the *Titanic* slid down the ways, and when Russia was still ruled by a Tsar. He was in jail before there were income taxes. He has never seen an aeroplane on the ground, never obeyed a traffic light, never changed the gears of a car. He has not broken bread with another human being since President Wilson adjusted his glasses and signed a declaration of war against the Kaiser.

Prison, in the Arabian phrase, is engraved on his eyeballs. He has been kept in isolation for thirty-nine years, longer than any Federal prisoner in history.

What manner of man is this? How does he live? What has he done? What has been done to him?

He is sixty-five. He wears a green eyeshade cap, like an ageing baseball umpire. His face is long and narrow and his penetrating blue eyes are enlarged by metal-rimmed glasses. His grey hair is close-cropped and although his shoulders are bent, when he straightens he is six-feet tall. When he went to jail, he was six-feet-three.

No one may visit him except his brother and a prison chaplain. No one is allowed access to his file. He is permitted to send and receive a letter each month from a mailing list of three: a brother, a half-sister and an old man in Florida. He is not allowed newspapers. He is forbidden to exercise in the prison yard. He cannot have a radio. He has never seen a television set.

"The writer," he said of himself in a recent court petition, "knows exactly as much about driving a car, or modern traffic regulations, as a Berkshire hog knows about the quantum theory. Unassisted, he would probably starve to death before he could get to the other side of Market Street."

As he pads in prison-felt slippers back and forth inside a locked white room, he can hear the intermittent moan of foghorns. Behind this sound, when the wind is favourable, he can hear the evening traffic of the West Coast's most cultured city two thousand yards away. When the fog rolls back on some evenings, he can see the neon garden of San Francisco's night life.

He had only three years of schooling. But he has written books. His best book, written fifteen years ago, circulates briskly today in public libraries, but this man is not permitted inside the prison library. He is allowed to read one volume at a time. Recently, he was refused permission to revise his own book for a new edition, although the request came from the publisher, and the book was about birds.

Is he insane?

The Federal Prison Bureau states that he is not psychotic. He receives no psychiatric treatment. Insane prisoners are lodged in the Federal hospital in Springfield, Missouri.

Is he violent?

The Bureau states that he has committed no act of violence since his life was spared by President Woodrow Wilson in 1920. Before that time, he killed two men. He was eligible for parole in 1936.

Prisoners sentenced to life are released after serving terms on a general average of ten to fourteen years. A Los Angeles judge stated recently that there are probably 200,000 persons walking free in the United States who have been convicted of murder in the first, second and third degrees.

This Alcatraz inmate has watched prisoners convicted of murder come and go for decades.

Is he dangerous?

Even in Alcatraz—the last outpost of the Federal prison system—he is kept apart and alone. He was behind bars before "the mad dogs of the Rock"—the killers, kidnappers and incorrigibles—were born, or out of knee-breeches. Before Alcatraz existed as a civilian prison. Before there were gangsters, before Prohibition, years before the Federal Prison Bureau existed.

The grandson of a judge, he is probably the only convict in the history of Federal prisons who defied a government bureau and reversed a policy concerning himself. The conflict was over canary birds.

Birds once stood upon his gallows; later, they stood upon his shoulders and tangled their feet in his hair. Barred from all people for all of his life, he found his greatest love elsewhere. For the last thirteen years, however, he has not been allowed near a bird.

When this man's name is mentioned among the keepers of men, anger and fear, hatred and contempt rise from the past in a dull red glow. His long confinement and curious life form one of the great enigmas of world prison history.

After four decades of extended and profound punishment, his spirit remains unbroken. He is one of the living dead: Number 594, Alcatraz.

His name is Robert F. Stroud. This is his life story.

ONE

IF OUR TROUBLES are those of our parents, Robert Stroud's began before he was born. Ben and Elizabeth Stroud had not been married long before friction developed between them. Part of the trouble stemmed from her family, and more from her unexpected pregnancy.

Ben Stroud was a tall, handsome, pleasure-loving Indianan of good family. He was sociable, he enjoyed life, and when times were good he made money. He had a roving eye and was not above sharing a bottle when the company was right.

In Elizabeth he married a woman older than himself by several years, a widow with two small girls. She must have attracted him deeply, because he undertook much by marrying her. Ben may have been somewhat appalled by the discovery of a third child so quickly on the way.

Elizabeth McCartney Schaefer Stroud was an attractive and formidable woman. First-born in a mixed family of twelve, she grew up in a virtual dynasty founded by a remarkable pioneer, Judge J. F. McCartney.

McCartney had risen to Lincoln's call, fought through the Civil War, retired as a Captain and settled in Metropolis, Illinois. He practised law, founded a bank and helped organize the Prohibition Party. Later becoming a judge, he left a million-dollar estate when he died at eighty-four. No one could recall that "J. F." ever chewed, drank or swore. His strongest epithet in anger was "Judas Priest".

This paragon must have set an impossible standard by which his eldest daughter would judge men. Elizabeth was married young to a serious farmer named Schaefer. According to family sources, Schaefer administered beatings to the self-willed Elizabeth. When he set upon her during the pregnancy of her second daughter, she ended the mismatch by leaving him. She developed a hatred of physical beating which spun a black thread in her thinking, and she later passed this on to her son Robert.

Against her family's will, Elizabeth persuaded Ben to go west. They hoped to escape their troubles by framing them in new surroundings. They chose Seattle and arrived in the summer of

1889, only to gaze upon a charred, still-smoking ruin. The town of 20,000 had burned to the ground two days before they arrived. Built entirely of wood, even to wooden pavements, the town had collapsed in flame.

Ben Stroud stood in the fringes of the 600 businessmen who planned a new city even as the last embers smoked. Ben found a tent, quartered his family and took a clerical job. He came home to a pregnant wife hiding her nausea and cooking clams over an open fire.

Ben shouldered his load, but Elizabeth later claimed that he shared it with the bottle, and became abusive and insulting. "He insisted I destroy the unborn child," she wrote. "Because I refused, his treatment of me . . . kept me in a state bordering on insanity the entire period."

The Stroud tent was exchanged for furnished rooms as Seattle swiftly rebuilt itself with a centre of brick and iron, allowing wooden houses only farther out. In one of these, at the cold end of a January night in 1890, Robert Stroud was born. Elizabeth's long boy-hunger was fulfilled in this baby, and she nursed him with fierce protective tenderness.

"When the child was born," she later wrote to President Wilson, "his father ignored it. As he grew, the father became abusive toward him and often beat him and threatened to kill not only the child, but the entire family, in his drunken frenzy. As a result the child was never like other children."

There is evidence that her picture of Ben was overdrawn. Elizabeth was to become a bitter and unforgiving woman, and she painted a dark picture in her subsequent fight for her son's life. Ben Stroud supported the family and came home to two cool stepdaughters and a wife who found him wanting. She hugged her baby ever tighter against Ben's indifference; and there is little doubt that Robert drew in father-hatred with his mother's milk. She called him Robbie.

She nearly lost Robbie when, at two and a half, he fell ill with pneumonia. Her daughters, Minnie and Mamie, left high-school classes to perform household chores while Robbie's mother clung to his bedside.

Even at four, however, he was remembered as an abstracted, lonely boy. Elizabeth kept him from other children; the neighbours remarked that her apron strings were too long.

While other boys were at marbles, Elizabeth taught him

American history. She read aloud "The Ancient Mariner", and Robbie learned this by rote. She dominated him utterly, and he gave her the whole of his brooding heart.

When she started him in school, his life became miserable. Thin and tall for his age, left-handed, and unaccustomed to other children, he sat apart at a corner desk. He seemed unable to raise his hand even to ask for permission to perform toilet functions. During recess, he ran home.

He was polite and respectful, but the teachers complained that Robert seemed "miles away" during classes. Reports from the school soon resulted in paternal discipline and fault-finding at home. In the third year, Robbie stopped going to school.

When he was alone with his mother, however, the boy was talkative, eager and worshipful. After a family quarrel, she would regale him with tales of her great father, until Judge McCartney loomed massively in the background as a family god. She forgot her unhappy teens and retreated to her girlhood, drawing her son into the glowing picture she created until they seemed of the same age together. Robbie resembled his mother and she considered him a McCartney.

Ben's little stepdaughters, Minnie and Mamie, sought escape from family friction by burying themselves in school affairs. When a quarrel developed, they learned to absent themselves. But Robbie stood at his mother's side. He may have sensed behind Ben's profane bluster a fear of his wife. She was the decisive force in the family. She found solace in her baby while Ben watched, an irritated outsider, the growing attachment between mother and son.

Ben was working hard and he became known as a "good mixer". He secured a good start in the coal business as the assistant to a shipper. The family soon moved into a home of their own despite the depression of the middle nineties.

Robbie's life during these character-forming years seemed to be a chequerboard of hostility alternated with mothering. The home, however, held together. Proof of this was Elizabeth's second pregnancy as the wife of Ben Stroud.

When the second son, Marcus, was born, Ben was pleased.

"He looks just like me," was his repeated exclamation as he peered into the crib of the chubby baby. He regarded this baby as a good omen, and felt his hunch confirmed when Seattle's depression ended abruptly in 1897. Rumours of a rich strike in

Alaska became as real as the bearded men who staggered over the gang-board of the S.S. *Portland* with bulging leather sacks in their calloused hands, each sack a small fortune in nuggets. When the city learned that the boat had brought a ton and a half of gold, with more on the way, Seattle went mad. It also became the outfitting centre for the Klondike and the Alaskan lodes.

Ben Stroud held out for months in the coal business, but the yellow lure finally overcame the black, and in 1898 Ben joined a hundred thousand other *chechakos* in the lemming-like stampede for the Yukon.

Later, like most of them, Ben returned empty-handed, with nightmares in his eyes and a story of dead men, frozen horses, and piles of spanking new equipment lining Chilkoot Pass, thrown there by armies of fortune-crazed tenderfeet.

Although the family door still opened to him, Ben Stroud ran into a psychological wall. Elizabeth was supporting the family. She was fast and proficient with the needle, a craft she had learned as the eldest daughter in her father's dynastic house. Her daughters helped her to fit, baste and sew, and her work pleased an expanding circle of customers. Baby Marc was now two, and Robbie ten years old.

The returning husband may have felt like an Enoch Arden looking in on a completed family circle as he stared into the strange eyes of his elder son. For Robbie now looked and acted like the father of the family. A photograph of him taken at this time shows him slim and straight, wearing a large watch-chain across his thin, waistcoated front, his face abstracted, proprietary and grave.

The bewildered Ben noted that his son had no jealousy whatever of his baby brother, despite the favour shown him. Robbie's attitude was wholly paternal, protective. Elizabeth treated him as though he were the man of the house.

Ben moved in, took up his old job in the coal business, and in a matter of months the little family began to experience good times in Seattle's gold boom.

Ben never gained ascendancy over his hostile son, however. The family managed well, but there was an atmosphere of armed truce at the top.

The conflict by-passed young Marc. The darling of his father, protected by his brother, he grew among his playmates as a happy, outgoing boy.

Many years later, Robert Stroud opened a window into his early life in a letter. "My mother was a dominating woman and my father was strong-willed and they never got on. But I never let them do anything to my young brother, never let them put a hand on him or tell him any lie. If they did, I told him the truth and was ready to fight for his right to be himself at any time."

When Robbie was eleven, he contracted a severe case of typhoid fever. His recovery was slow and he grew more seclusive and erratic. At this time he became enraged at Ben for threatening to spank Marc, nearing four. Their mother had virtually ordered Ben to leave discipline to her. Ben withdrew from the scene this time, punishing no one. A short time before, Robert had routed three boys his own age for picking on Marc. The boys had been cowed by the dogged finality with which he took them on. He was soft-spoken, quiet. In the words of his brother, "He never knew the meaning of fear." But his actions had begun to show how he had absorbed his mother's hatred of physical beatings. It was to become one of the obsessions of his life. He seemed unable to tolerate the sight of any weaker creature suffering from the hand of a stronger one. More dangerously, he felt impelled to intervene.

Now approaching twelve, he was shunned in the neighbourhood and was restless at home. Ben now favoured young Marc with an allowance his elder brother never had.

Robert began to drift toward the life of the docks and sea. He met sailors and lumberjacks and bums. Their freedom attracted him. They were strays, unwanted ones.

Young Stroud would come home from these forays to frowning parents. They did not approve of the waterfront life and Elizabeth worried about its women. But the boy's mother-bond and the sour taste of his home life had sealed him against them. When Ben showed affection for his wife, the son turned away, troubled by his inward unrest.

Marc was now old enough to remember the family life at that time and to him it was a brighter picture. "My dad," he states, "was friendly and genial. He talked a lot but was never the boss. I do not recall that he beat Bob. My mother would not stand for it and she was his backbone. They went to lodge meetings together and card parties and entertained at home. At one time my mother was president of their lodge.

"Dad was outspoken and windy. He swore a lot. Bob was

quiet and said little, and my dad, in order to justify his feelings, would not do anything for Bob in a financial way, whereas he lavished money on me just to show Bob he was the boss. It probably bolstered his ego."

Marc recalls how his brother watched card games on the waterfront and listened to tales of professional gamblers. Bob formed a boy's interest in card tricks. Scarcely able to read and write, he found a dog-eared booklet which described the difficult front and backhand palm. The gangling boy, sensitive about his left-handedness, practised the two passes in front of a mirror day after day, failing at them but refusing to give up. In six weeks he mastered them. He displayed a tenacity and persistence unusual in a boy; he was to display these qualities throughout his strange life.

Close on Robert's thirteenth birthday, the Stroud home cracked open. During a violent quarrel, Ben taunted his wife with a description of his affair with a woman of the neighbourhood. Elizabeth, goaded into fury, invited him to stay with the woman. The stubborn Ben thereafter lived openly "in sin", coming home only to bring money and to enjoy the company of Marc. Ben's coal business had prospered in booming Seattle. The open break pulled Ben into a "fast crowd and heavy drinking", as Marc put it.

Shortly after this rupture, Robert vanished. He left a crude note, telling his mother he loved her, not to worry, he would come back. He may have heard some inner warning. He may have wanted to avoid violence with his father.

Young Stroud stayed away for eight months. With a stripling's passion for freedom, he beat his way across the open face of 1903 America. He moved with hoboes and lived in "jungles", learned the art of riding the blind baggage and survived the perils of "the bindle stiff's iron armchair"—the rods underneath freight cars.

Late that summer he returned for a few days, kissed his mother, played with Marc and was gone again. For the next two years he survived in the hungry underbelly of the country, living the life of the road, wandering and searching for he knew not what. A place to belong, perhaps, or another home.

In 1904 he turned up at the home of M. N. McCartney, a school superintendent and one of the family uncles who lived in Sangamon County, Illinois. McCartney sensed trouble in the tall, quiet boy and asked him questions, but Robert vanished and returned to the road. Later, Stroud wrote a description of his life with tramps, "wobblies" and other wanderers into a huge prison manuscript. He titled the chapter "The Great American Bum".

Elizabeth had never wearied of scanning accident and ship casualty lists in the papers for news of her son. At sixteen, he returned, tall beyond her memory of him, lean-faced, seasoned and deceptively mild-mannered. When she gazed up into his strange eyes after their embrace, she was relieved. She knew he still was hers, this first-born son.

As Robert examined the prosperous furnishings, she told him about the family. His half-sister Minnie had been a schoolteacher and was now engaged. Mamie remained at home, her mother's docile helper. Little Marc, now nine, was doing well in school. Marc's worship of his big brother remained unchanged, and Robert soon learned how Marc was giving his small boy's effort to hold the family together. Their father Ben spent more time at home now, but his erratic living and heavy drinking went on. It was on-again, off-again for the stormy couple.

Robert went to work. At seventeen he was installing electrical fixtures in the growing residential section of new Seattle. Robert turned his earnings over to his mother, but Ben criticized his son's job and choice of companions, hardy youths in the building business.

After a violent quarrel with his father in the spring of 1908, the old hunger for escape surged through Robert and his thoughts turned to Alaska.

In May, 1908, he heard about a job. Section hands for a railway gang in Alaska were being recruited on the Seattle waterfront. Details were secret, but men were scarce and the pay was good.

Ben put his foot down when he heard of the project, which was enough to decide Robert to sign up. After a slow week in a noisome converted cattle boat, the green section gang was dumped at the frontier port of Katalla, Alaska.

TWO

THE MEN SOON learned why the mission had been secret. The Guggenheim Syndicate was pouring money into a railway thoroughfare from Katalla inland to Chitina. Controlling the fabulous Kennecott copper mine, they were fighting against time and rival interests for an outlet to the sea. A huge breakwater had been built in the Katalla harbour.

Young Stroud stood the gruelling labour, but work came to an abrupt end when a savage storm wrecked the Katalla breakwater and proved to the Syndicate that their choice of a harbour had been wrong. They abandoned the project.

The gang moved north where a fabulously daring engineer named Mike Heney was laying down, for rival interests, a spur inland to Chitina from the more sheltered port of Cordova. Stroud became one of the groaning crew which sank caissons 150 feet deep to the beds of roaring rivers, and stretched a four-span bridge across the face of a moving glacier. There the lanky youth met a man whose books he was later to read from the depths of solitary confinement. He told young Stroud that Alaska salmon interested him more than gold. His name was Rex Beach.

Cordova was a roaring boom town then. Twenty-six saloons lined its short main street. Money came and went fast—even on Sunday, when the Red Dragon saloon became a church. Stroud was one of those who watched an altar, suspended all week by ropes against the ceiling, lowered to the floor for services. While the minister talked, a beer mug was passed from hand to hand under the genial eyes but sharp ears of a bartender. The unique clink of a silver dollar in the mug was the only sound. It was hardly safe to give less.

In Cordova, Stroud's career took a fateful turn. His endurance worn thin under the driving work, he again developed pneumonia. He was cared for and nursed to convalescence by a dance-hall girl whose assumed name was Kitty O'Brien. In woman-hungry Alaska, almost any female under fifty in Kitty's business was called a girl. She was thirty-six, with dark blue eyes, a clear Irish complexion and a strong, honest face.

Hidden under flounces of her dance-hall satin was one of the most beautiful figures in Alaska—such were the whispered reports.

What Kitty sensed behind the pale, composed face of the youthful Stroud will never be known. The fascination, perhaps, of a much-used woman who sensed a door never before unlocked? No woman had entered the arena dominated by his mother.

Kitty evidently unlocked the door in the late summer of 1908. The youth, at eighteen, knew the joy and fascination of his first woman. Kitty was flattered and amused. He treated her gently and perhaps even with reverence when they were alone in the room they shared. Used and cheapened by men, she felt elevated in the company of this serious companion. Her feeling for him grew, and the maternal amusement she first felt turned a demanding enjoyment of his passion. In the Cordova cabarets Kitty was a "box hustler" but in Stroud's presence she escaped.

He was infatuated, and his infatuation floated him beyond the disturbing questions that arose. He was penniless. He had to make money somehow. The Alaskan day was shortening and the sea-wet winds of Cordova grew chilling.

One August day Stroud hit upon a way to make money in Cordova. With Kitty supplying the money, he rented a popcorn wagon. Wearing a large white Stetson hat, the lanky Stroud stood beside his glass cage and sold large sacks, flavoured with salt and lard, of the confection which reminded his customers of their distant homes. Occasionally he would get a nugget worth many times his merchandise from a homesick, drunken sourdough.

Stroud was stamping his boots one frosty afternoon in September when a husky, nattily-dressed man in a black hat, coat and tie approached his stand.

"Flip you double or nothing for a sack of that stuff."

"Charlie Dahmer!" Stroud exclaimed. "I thought you were staying in Katalla." Charlie's real name was F. K. Von Dahmer. Born in Russia of a German family, he was called Charlie because he dressed like a riverboat gambler. A long black moustache made him look older than his twenty-eight years. Rated as a hard man in a fight, Charlie had been a bartender when Stroud knew him in Katalla.

Charlie flipped a silver dollar and Stroud lost a sack of popcorn. They talked a while.

"Where you headed?" Stroud asked.

"Juneau. Tending bar at the Montana." Charlie gave Stroud a sly look. "Hear you're with Kitty O'Brien, kid." Stroud looked up quickly at the bartender's tone.

"Knew her well," Charlie added with a wink. Stroud quickly changed the subject.

"Look me up if you two come down to Juneau, Bob," Charlie said. He strode off, throwing popcorn into his mouth.

Later, Stroud asked Kitty about Charlie.

"I knew him," Kitty said. "It's all over."

As the Alaskan night lengthened and business fell off in Cordova, Stroud sold the popcorn concession and, after repaying Kitty, they discussed their plans. In November they boarded a boat for Juneau. They moved into the Clarke Building, and Stroud looked for work. He found even the saloon-sweeping jobs taken by stranded sourdoughs, many of whom had lost their "pokes" to whisky, gambling and women before they could leave with the gold they had sweated from the crowded strikes.

Juneau's great rainfall had turned to snow and white mountains closed in on the wooden-piled streets of Alaska's rough capital. Snow powder hissed against the town's double storm windows, driven by the *Taku*, the gale that blows up Gastineau Channel in the twenty-hour January dark. Tempers grew short; sickness and killings crowded Juneau's little graveyard; and the bars and dance-halls boomed.

Kitty found work in a cabaret. She tried to cheer her morose lover, who sat through the long dark with others who borrowed, waited and hoped.

At the Montana bar, Charlie Dahmer was making money, only to lose it at roulette and faro. When he saw Stroud, he invited him to visit the cottage which Charlie shared with a room-mate, Nels.

"Bring Kitty, Bob. Beer's on me," Charlie told him.

When Bob told Kitty about the invitation, she hesitated.

"Come on," Bob said. "Charlie owes me a few bucks I'll never get."

Kitty fingered the gold locket around her neck. "Charlie owes everybody, including me. It isn't that." She laughed and put her arm around him. "All right. What's past is past—but you have to look out for Charlie."

"I'm not afraid of him. He's good company."

Kitty did not tell him that Charlie's interest flowed from more than camaraderie. He had offered her money, which she refused, because of their past association.

Their first party was enjoyable. In the holiday spirit of lonely people far from home, Stroud noticed nothing unusual in Charlie's actions. Everyone toasted Kitty and the bartender kept looking at her, but so did Nels. They all parted friends, with Charlie insisting that they repeat the occasion soon.

On January 18, 1909, they met again. Charlie furnished beer from the Montana bar. Early in the evening, however, Stroud left for the Juneau docks. A sailor friend had promised him a sack of fish to add to the evening fare. Unknown to Stroud, Charlie's room-mate Nels also had other plans. They may have come from the bartender. In any case, Nels left, leaving Kitty alone with his room-mate.

When Stroud returned later with his food package, he found Charlie's cottage empty. A chair was overturned and Charlie's bunk torn up. Puzzled, Stroud returned to the room he and Kitty shared.

He found Kitty groaning on the bed. Both her eyes were blackened and there was a red line on her neck. Her locket was missing. Stroud poured her a strong drink of whisky.

"Kill the beast, kill him, kill him," she whimpered. Stroud bathed her bruises and plied her with whisky.

"Was it Charlie?"

She nodded. "He took my locket with my daughter's picture. Said he's keeping it until I come to stay with him."

In the smoking yellow lamplight she did not notice her lover's face. Then she heard a drawer opening and sat up drunkenly. She saw Stroud carefully examining her old .38 single-action revolver. His face was composed and pale. He flipped open the barrel and saw that the gun was empty. He rummaged through the drawer again.

"No!" Kitty wailed, swaying up from the bed, trying to focus her eyes on him. "I didn't mean it—no, don't go back there. He'll kill you!"

Stroud put the gun back in the drawer and closed it hard. He sat by her and smoothed her hair and waited for the whisky to work. He may have been thinking of childhood scenes and Elizabeth's tales of beatings, and the loathing of physical punishment stirred in him again.

When Kitty's breathing became regular he straightened her cover and kissed her. It was the last lover's kiss of his life.

Ten minutes later, the clerk of the Jorgenson store told a tall dark youth in a white Stetson that they did not sell cartridges in lots of five. Stroud purchased a box.

At six-thirty, Charlie Dahmer returned to his cottage and fumbled in the dark. He struck a match and lit his lamp. The light fell upon Stroud sitting in one corner with his hat on. He stood, the lamplight flickering against his long, lean face. The bartender watched him, his smile fading.

"Did you beat Kitty?" Stroud's long arms hung loose. His heavy overcoat swung open.

Charlie stared at the thin youth with the pale face and the absurd white Stetson. Charlie's eyes were measuring off the distance from the oilcloth-covered table to the corner.

"Why, no, Bob," he said placatingly. "Kitty fell down—you know. We were drinking . . ." His voice trailed off as he shifted his weight forward. He edged an inch closer.

"Stay there!" Stroud said, backing away beside a straight chair. "Get that coat off. Now you just bend over that table. Wait a minute. Let's have Kitty's locket and that money you owe."

Charlie's mouth fell open. He had never seen the quiet youth assert himself. Had he heard right? Charlie was used to beating men to the punch, the gun, the card. Men, not this love-sick stripling, in a white Stetson. Rage mounted in Charlie. His long, strong hands closed. He could almost feel them around Stroud's neck.

Suddenly he lunged, head down, arms outstretched like a tackler. Stroud's left hand dug into his belt. He got his gun out quickly. He fired and missed. Charlie bore down on him. Stroud fired again, point-blank. Charlie came on. Stroud slammed the gun against his head. The bartender crashed to the floor at Stroud's feet, one outstretched arm twitching on the rung of the chair.

Charlie was dead after the second shot. The autopsy showed the bullet entering high on the right temple and following a line down to his pelvis.

Stroud looked beyond his smoking gun to the dead man. His hands were shaking. Stepping to the table, he recognized Kitty's locket in a jam-jar. He picked it up and left, gun in hand.

A man ran out the door of the neighbouring cottage. "What's the matter in there?"

"Nothing," Stroud said. He walked quickly down Franklin Street and returned to the Clarke Building. Slipping in softly, he returned the gun to the dresser drawer, laid the box of bullets beside it, and slipped the locket with its broken chain into Kitty's stocking. He stopped and looked long at Kitty, asleep on the bed. Her hair rippled gold in the smoking light, contrasting strangely with her bruised eyelids.

Five minutes later he walked into the office of the Juneau City Marshal.

"I shot a man," he said. The Marshal took him to the Federal jail, where cell doors closed him in for the first time. It was forty-eight hours before the inauguration of President Taft. Stroud, except for his appearance at trials, has not been out since. This was January, 1909.

When the Marshal ascertained from Stroud where the gun was, he entered the Clarke Building, shook Kitty awake and informed her of the killing.

"I told him to go and kill the Russian," she said. Stroud told the deputies he and Charlie argued over money. He did not mention Kitty.

Stroud and Kitty O'Brien were both indicted for first-degree murder. The *Alaska Dispatch* speculated that Stroud had struck the bartender on the head with the gun and then shot him as he lay unconscious. Since there were no witnesses, with the bartender known in the town and Stroud a newcomer, the newspaper speculation caused feeling to rise in Juneau.

Stroud refused to notify his mother. Elizabeth, however, had formed the habit of scanning newspapers. She saw the telegraphed story before anyone could tell her. She scraped together passage money immediately, cabled a retainer to a distinguished attorney in Alaska, T. R. Lyons, and herself sailed on the S.S. *Jefferson*, the first boat out. Within a week her arms were around her son.

Ben Stroud stayed in Seattle. The stormy marriage between

the occasional husband and his imperious wife came to an end.

Ben's lifelong coolness toward his elder son seemed to increase his attachment to his younger one. The alert Marc, now eleven, had remained with Ben during Elizabeth's quick trip to Juneau. Marc loved the father who had been unfailingly kind to him. But he loved his brother Bob as well.

Now Ben asked him to choose. He promised Marc much if he would remain in Seattle. Marc's lips quivered but he firmly refused. "I'm going with Mom to help Bob," he said. It was the beginning of a brother's effort, through much of his life, to balance a scale he had not created.

When Elizabeth Stroud was informed of the role played by Kitty in the life of her Robbie, her reaction was one of anger and contempt. A prostitute had not only involved her son, but had placed him in danger of his life. She did not blame her son: he was only nineteen, and the "vile woman" was old enough to be his mother.

Visiting Robbie in jail, Elizabeth found him determined to save Kitty. About her innocence, he was adamant. Elizabeth was furious. She could do nothing, however, to change her son's decision.

Unfortunately for their defence, Attorney Lyons was appointed to a Federal judgeship shortly after both defendants had entered pleas of not guilty and the case had been set for trial. A new attorney agreed that a plea of guilty to manslaughter might be accepted by the prosecution. This would eliminate a trial, thus making a trial of Kitty very difficult to hold.

The defence attorney, experienced in Alaska criminal cases, had good reason to believe in a light sentence. There had been many killings in the open frontier. Manslaughter rarely drew more than three years. To the determined Stroud, two or three years was worth Kitty O'Brien. He sat out seven months in the Juneau "skookum house" with quixotic resolve.

A change of venue set the case for disposition in Skagway. The prosecution, in preliminary overtures, did not object to the idea of a plea of guilty to a lesser offence, should this be acceptable to the judge. It would have been a difficult case to try.

Fate, however, intervened in the person of the new Federal judge, E. E. Cushman, an appointee who arrived from the States with an announced determination to crack down on violence in Alaska. Stroud was his first case.

The Court duly accepted Stroud's plea of guilty to manslaughter. Kitty's case was dropped for lack of evidence. She was freed.

Her indictment for first-degree murder was omitted from later accounts of Stroud's life. The court file of Stroud's case has also been missing or misplaced from the Federal record vault in Juneau.

The time arrived for sentence. On August 23, 1909, the new judge looked at the young defendant and sentenced him to the statutory limit: twelve years in the penitentiary at McNeil Island.

The sentence opened two careers, that of a Federal judge whose stern sentences became legend, and that of a prisoner whose unbroken resistance formed a life without parallel in world prison history.

THREE

ROBERT STROUD WATCHED his last Alaskan autumn through the porthole of the brig of the S.S. *Jefferson* in September, 1909. The old steamer bulged with whooping, flag-waving passengers on their way to the Alaska-Yukon-Pacific Exposition in Seattle.

Stroud had his first look at McNeil Island from the bow of a sternwheel steamer *en route* from Steilacoom. Heavily wooded and decked in autumn colours, McNeil looked deceptively attractive: seven square miles of land set in the blue waters of Puget Sound. These waters were the outer wall of a prison.

Formerly a Territorial jail, McNeil came under Federal control in 1905. In 1907, a new cell block was built. Here Stroud was lodged, outfitted in prison grey and handed a booklet containing ninety-five old-line prison rules.

The silence system was enforced. No talking outside the cell, at meals or at work.

No pictures were allowed in the cell. No gazing about at meals. Bread crusts were allowed to be left only on the left side of the plate. Inmates were required to stand at attention, cap in hand, until any official, visitor or guard moved beyond sight.

Stroud studied the rules. He soon learned to place his shoes outside his cell door at the sound of a gong. He was awakened by the buzzing of bells. The guards carried clubs.

It was a hard prison. Serious violators were beaten and handcuffed to the cell door. More stubborn men rated the Hole. Occasionally, a prisoner was strung up by his thumbs.

The warden, O. P. Halligan, was a penologist of the old school. According to an old prisoner, he had a unique form of protection which prisoners called "The Burglar Alarm". Two little terriers were trained to run ahead of him around corners. If anyone lurked there, the dogs would bark.

Their desperate struggle to survive welded prisoners into a grey brotherhood. They had traditions, and "the code of the con" was an iron law unto itself. After six months, Stroud embraced it with fervour. His allegiance to the underdog deepened. He walked the chalk lines as his youth twisted under prison life.

He soon grew to hate "the hardrock hotels and the screws", and since these were the product of what he called the "Christian society" outside, his rejection of religion increased. He thought of his grandfather as a hypocritical bigot and he slammed the door on society, its standards and gods.

Distorted and toughened in these penal fires, his personality took on strength. He grew into a man, six-feet-three, rail-thin, taciturn and withdrawn, with eyes as hard as a blue china plate.

His father did not visit him. His mother, now settled in Alaska, saw him once in two and a half years. Elizabeth came with Marc, now twelve. They lunched with the warden and marvelled at the excellent fare. Marc tasted his first lamb curry. Their impression that the prisoners received the same delicately flavoured food was dispelled neither by the warden nor by prisoner Stroud.

Marc eagerly related to Bob his young life in Alaska. Marc was an experienced paper-boy by the time the family moved to Juneau. There he received the Mayor's permission to sell newspapers in a free run of the town. He appeared at the doors of dives and gambling halls with the *Alaska Dispatch* and with older editions of Stateside papers. He rarely pocketed less than a half dollar from gamblers and painted ladies. He remembered taking in sixty dollars from news-thirsty passengers over the rails of the *Admiral Watson* before gang-pipers set the board. Young Marc made $12,000 before he was fifteen.

Elizabeth's boarding house and her needle and her busy son did well for the family. Robert learned that his father had won a ribbon for top-quality coal in the Alaska-Yukon-Pacific Exposition. His mother and brother became memories, and he began to depend on his other link with the world—the post. With the sureness of sunrise, a letter came every week from Kitty O'Brien. Written in black pencil with a bold hand, her letters were assurances of loyal affection, and newsy ungrammatical comments about her wandering life. Kitty had continued as a denizen of the line, but Charlie's death and Stroud's long sentence put a mark on her. She left Alaska.

Early one afternoon in the second year of his sentence, Kitty came to visit Bob. As the tall, sullen convict appeared, she fell back at sight of his masklike face. Stroud, too, was surprised. The hot juices of his youth had been soured by prison life, while his mind had fired Kitty's picture into unearthly beauty. He was unable to relate the image to the woman sitting before him. For Kitty was matronly now, her lusty abandon gone to sedate fat and what were clearly the marks of the bottle.

"Glad you came, Kitty."

"Bob, you're different. Your eyes make me feel miles off." She blinked rapidly. "Bob, have you forgot your old Kitty?"

"No. Your letters mean a lot inside this joint . . ."

"I'll write as long as you're here."

He had come to depend upon her letters. Soon after her visit, however, they came to an abrupt stop. It was only in later years that he learned that his brother-in-law had requested the warden to terminate the correspondence. The family blamed Kitty for Stroud's crime.

After two years and four months of hard prison régime, Stroud began to break prison rules. Working in the kitchen, he secreted food and took it to his cellmate. A short-term prisoner who also worked in the kitchen observed this and waited for a chance to use his information. At a parole-board hearing, this inmate informed on Stroud, hoping thereby to increase his own chance for parole. He was turned down. When he returned to the kitchen, the word had gone ahead of him. Stroud termed him a "snitch" and a fight ensued. Stroud buried a paring knife in his shoulder. As a result, Stroud lost all privileges, and an additional six months were added to his sentence. His own hope for parole went glimmering. He would be in his thirties before the prison gate swung open. It was a grim prospect.

FOUR

FEDERAL PRISONS HAD begun to bulge with inmates. In 1912 overcrowding became an open scandal. Under the rising outcry for prison reform, nettled authorities made some shifts.

In Leavenworth, Kansas, where an enormous new prison had been under construction for years, a new cell house was completed. To fill it, prisoners were routed from the most congested spots, and fifty-odd "hard case" convicts from McNeil were among those tagged for the transfer. One of them was Stroud.

The prisoners enjoyed the short boat ride. It was Stroud's first in three years. He was to take another thirty years later.

After a long train ride, the shackled convicts stumped from a dusty chair-car to find themselves inside the huge double-gate railway portal at the east wall of Leavenworth prison.

It was this wall which caused the recently waterbound inmates of McNeil to gape and swallow. Rising sheer from a slight elevation of the friendly prairie, enclosing sixteen acres, the wall sat like a flat, square snake of brick and mortar, its face a front of granite centred with a nose-like dome and portico. Ranging from thirty to forty-two feet high, the wall had been erected by the prisoners themselves, working by the thousands in steady shifts since 1899.

They had kilned the clay for the red brick, and had dressed the stone they quarried from an adjacent hill. The wall's history immediately became known to the inmates and it was an ever-present and awesome reality to convicts and guards alike. The wall contained the encysted sweat of prisoners forced to slave under the rifles of guards. Periodically some guard would quit, saying, "The wall got me."

Leavenworth, a maximum security prison, was known as a "hard joint" to the convicts who educated their new arrivals in quiet, clam-faced whispers.

Stroud found himself celled with a temperamental safe-blower named Eddie. Eddie was a plump, pink-faced apple of a man with bleached eyes and a wisp of blond hair. He was thirty-five, the proud owner of a high-school education.

Eddie looked down his nose at his gangling new companion

as one of the illiterate unwashed from the West. Yet Eddie was to become the unwitting cause of a change in Stroud.

They got on. Eddie regaled his young cellmate with stories of the prison break of 1910, when convicts seized a locomotive and rammed it through the railway gate. He warned about pitfalls and rules and tough guards, and dwelt at length on the character of the warden. The tone and temper of any prison is a reflection of the warden, his deputy and the captain of the guards.

R. W. McClaughry was the last of the old-time prison wardens at Leavenworth—and the hardest. When he took over the unbuilt institution in 1899 he had already established his reputation as Chief of Police in Chicago, and warden at Pontiac and Joliet. A quiet, keen-eyed, decisive man with grey hair and an enormous pepper-and-salt moustache dominating a heavy, clipped grey beard, McClaughry was merciless when crossed. He dealt out an Old Testament justice, but his prisoners knew where they stood.

McClaughry built the Leavenworth wall and most of the prison. During his régime, guards were under orders to shoot any prisoner who came closer than six paces or moved farther away than twenty. The food was prepared and served like garbage. Prisoners were allowed to chew tobacco, but not to smoke. It was a serious offence to be caught with a pencil. The Hole cells and the chaining methods were man-breakers.

"Carrying the Baby" was a common form of punishment. Offenders were chained for months to a twenty-five-pound iron ball. In order to walk, they had to carry the ball.

Despite this baleful picture, McClaughry's experience led him to believe in "the indeterminate sentence". He held that a life sentence should be construed on actuarial tables and earned time be drawn from it. In these concepts he stood in advance of his time and his ideas were rejected by his primitive associates.

It was Eddie's disclosures about the prison's first deputy warden, however, which became a factor in Stroud's outlook. This official had developed a sadistic lust for beating prisoners. An Indian youth casually known to Stroud at McNeil had been transferred to Leavenworth after an attempt to escape. Eddie told how he was placed in the Hole and there, chained by his wrists to the door, was beaten to death by the deputy warden.

His resignation was forced after guards themselves testified that they could not stomach his cruelty.

"I will never take a beating," Stroud told Eddie.

In his letters to his mother, Stroud began to speak of convicts as "my own people". His rejection of the world beyond the wall gradually became total, and his keepers became symbols of that world.

The warden, however, surprised him. While on tour of the prison he was informed that one of the young "cons" from McNeil was drawing on the cell wall with a chalklike stone.

"He gets the Hole—right, sir?" asked the captain.

"What was he drawing?" asked the bearded warden.

"Why, triangles and squares it looked like, sir."

"Nothing obscene?"

"Nothing we saw. Had his cellmate's geometry book."

"Defacing walls is a violation, but this is unusual. Give me his number. I'll check his record."

"Yes, sir," said the startled captain.

The warden noted that Number 8154's record for four years of prison had been good with the exception of the McNeil knife fight. He reprimanded Stroud for using the walls, but permitted him drawing instruments and raised his grade.

Later a new guard spotted the drawing instruments and confiscated them without a word. Stroud said nothing. He reported the matter to the deputy warden. The drawing instruments were brought back to the cell by the smarting guard. He had been reprimanded. He confronted Stroud.

"Why didn't you tell me the warden let you have the drawing instruments?"

"You didn't ask me."

Prison reform came to Leavenworth with the appointment of Warden Thomas W. Morgan in July, 1913. A serious and idealistic younger man with a reputation to make, he was appointed by the incoming Democrats after Woodrow Wilson's election.

The new warden appeared in the prison's enormous dining-room and had a tray of food from the line set before him. He sat down to eat what the prisoners called billy-goat stew. His first spoonful he spat on the floor. He ordered a quart of it served in a large bowl, forced the prison steward to eat all of it, and fired him.

Morgan abolished prison stripes, permitted smoking, abolished the "Baby", expanded the library, instituted a prison paper, and made of Christmas a goodwill holiday for prisoners and guards alike.

He also encouraged correspondence courses, and one of the first prisoners to enroll was high-school graduate Eddie. The pudgy safe-cracker decided to shore up his superior learning with higher mathematics. He still patronized Stroud and harped on his mere three years of schooling.

Eddie's third school assignment, however, had him scratching his pink scalp. Stroud watched him. He had read some of the problems while Eddie was asleep.

"This here equation is abstruse—tough, to you," mumbled Eddie.

"Can I help?" Stroud asked.

Eddie took the pencil from his mouth and looked up grandly. "Thanks for your offer, son. You may sharpen this here pencil with one of our knives."

"I mean, help with that problem."

"Sure, boy. Get yourself five more school years and some high school. Then see me."

Stroud scowled. "Eddie, I can do that twice as fast without your goddamn learning."

Eddie handed him the book. "But could you spare the *time*, Bob? Or may I read it to you?"

"Just gimme the pencil and turn off the crud."

Stroud solved five equations before the "count bell" rang. Eddie concealed his surprise with a sigh about beginner's luck.

As a result, Stroud enrolled. He completed the regular ten-month mathematics course in four. His slumbering intellect came alive and he astounded prison officials and Kansas State College instructors by sailing through courses in astronomy and structural engineering with "A" grades. These courses are prisoner favourites. Astronomy gives the prisoner a roomy feeling; structural engineering is helpful in prison breaks. But Stroud's interest was more general. He worked out prerequisite background from the prison library. He grew absorbed in study and tore through books and scientific magazines with voracious curiosity.

Time suddenly acquired value to him; this tough, left-handed convict who could scarcely write, now blotted up lakes of knowledge. He could dimly remember his mother reading books aloud, before his school revolt had slammed shut those mental doors.

Stroud's most important door failed to open, however, in his new learning. He acquired knowledge, but his uncompromising rejection of all social groups except prisoners may even have been reinforced by his reading. He assimilated culture with a mind into which the con's code had soaked like a green dye.

His hatred of punishment grew with his reading and his pent-up ego swelled with the view of worlds he could not reach. He became grave and inwardly ardent. He studied and worked deeper into astronomy, seeing, in his mind's eye, the sky and its heavenly bodies swimming in limitless space. Avidly, he read copies of the *Scientific American*. When the magazine propounded a contest problem in astronomy, Stroud covered pages of paper with equations and sent in his answer. He won an honourable mention.

His aversion to what he called "Christian bigots" kept his mind away from religion. But now he discovered something truly illimitable, beyond astronomy, in the spacious metaphysics of the Orient. He stumbled upon theosophy.

One of his letters to his mother revealed that, even as a boy, he had held the persistent notion that he had lived before. It may have grown from early fantasies when his unhappy mother would hold him close; when Elizabeth would soar in memory to her own girlhood, and Robbie, her little man, would share another life in reminiscent dreams.

Enthralled by his reading, Stroud embraced the brotherhood of *karma*, thought-transference and reincarnation.

Stroud developed the prisoner's archaic faith in the power of the wish. Men long in Hole Solitary had claimed they could send their spirits beyond the wall. Fending off madness as their eyeballs rolled in the dark, they swore that Self, the real Self, was no longer with their bodies.

Eddie, too, was familiar with the rudiments of theosophy. The prison library included several books on the subject. In nearby Kansas City there was a strong theosophical current running in revolt against the babbitry of the Bible Belt. Stroud soon became identified with the Kansas City Theosophical

Society. Its members visited him and later advanced funds to aid him in his subsequent legal trials.

Stroud's twin pursuit of physical science and theosophy produced a heady mental brew. He noted one contradiction, however.

"I soon saw the two phases of theosophy," he wrote to his mother, "the theory and practice of occultism, and the holding of life with respect to the theory of brotherhood, *karma*. I saw wherein the first was of more danger than value, while the second was of the highest value attainable. I started to live by the second phase. I have treated all of the people of my own kind as the teaching would dictate, so long as they would live up to the laws of our world."

These ideas, growing in the distortion of prison, engendered in Stroud a judgelike, patriarchal ego. He began to feel responsible for "his people" and, with his already deeply rooted hatred of punishment, he set off an explosion that was unique even in prison annals.

FIVE

NONE BUT A CONVICT can comprehend a prison. Inside the Leavenworth wall there was the anarchic "freedom" of the jungle. No inmate's life was safe. No prisoner could "call cop" without incurring the deadly ostracism of convict society. Anything could happen and often did, because nobody could leave. A long-nursed vengeance, a murder for pay, a disturbed man suddenly turning psychotic, a jealous passion over a light o' love —any of these could burst forth at any time to destroy an inmate. As in most punitive bastilles, under the dull routine lay a bristling arsenal. But the prison knives, pins, hooks, knucks, sock-saps and garrotes of rope and wire were more for protection than for offence.

"Y' can git the Hole for that," a new prisoner said, watching an old-timer slide a piece of steel into his jacket.

"You'll find out, fish," was the typical answer. "How you gonna know when some ding-a-ling's gonna choose *you*?"

Among the "hard-case" prisoners, it was a mark of distinction to own a knife, and top prestige to make them. So Robert Stroud made knives. Between hours spent on structural engineering, physics, and odd creeds, the stoop-shouldered Stroud turned out razor-sharp weapons of distinctive design. Wrought from stolen kitchen cutlery, they had straight, parallel edges like Roman swords, and short leather handles.

Long-termers managed to conceal them with success. To them, the loss of a knife was a severe blow. They were all-purpose instruments: used for threats, protection, cloth- and paper-cutting, handicrafts, hair-trimming, whittling, nail-paring and sometimes even for shaving.

One day during the yard break, a young Dutchman who used the name Willie West approached his best buddy, Stroud. West was a nineteen-year-old Army prisoner under a fifteen-year sentence for assaulting an officer.

"Bob, will you lend me your shiv?" Stroud slipped him his knife without a word. Two days later a prisoner named Jones murdered a prisoner named Smith. Nobody told where the knife came from. It was confiscated as evidence, however, in the murder trial that followed. Through loss of the knife, Willie owed Stroud an important favour which Willie was to remember three years later.

In 1914, Stroud's long study hours and the prison food began to tell on him. He was seen walking with his hand always pressed against the small of his back. After several months his condition grew worse. He saw the prison doctor in the winter of 1915, and the doctor's diagnosis was mild nephritis, or kidney disease. Stroud was given medicine and advice about diet. Since the food had deteriorated steadily, "diet" meant omission rather than substitution. Stroud lost weight and grew morose. He used pocket money received from his mother to buy what was available from the prison commissary, but this consisted mainly of chocolate fudge. He wore away the hours with books and looked forward to the monthly visit of a teacher from the State Agricultural College.

Of Leavenworth's 1,200 prisoners, eighty were enrolled in extension courses. The instructor assigned to visit his convict protégés was impressed by Stroud's problem-solving ability and his hard work to better himself. He received high marks in a course known as Strength of Materials. Anything with endurance intrigued him.

The teacher later testified that completion of such a course required geometry, trigonometry and differential calculus. He found his student neat, polite and respectful; he may have failed to sense the prison-wrought oddness of the man underneath. He did not notice that even the smooth T-square Stroud was using had been fashioned with a knife.

In the spring, Stroud's cellmate, Eddie, began to change. He mourned about voices under the floor which called him a heathen devil. He began to inspect the cell carefully every day as Stroud watched, puzzled.

One day Eddie set fire to his mattress to get the devils out. He was taken away and Stroud lost a cellmate.

Stroud grew gaunt and pain-racked, and puffs appeared under his eyes. His letters to his mother lost their forced gaiety and he remarked that he did not expect to live out his term. Elizabeth had not seen him for five years. She became alarmed that he might take his own life.

In March, 1915, she sailed from Juneau on the long trip

south to see her Robbie. When she arrived, the sight of him filled her with dismay. After consultation with the prison doctor she was informed he had Bright's disease. He told her it might be incurable, and sometimes affected the mind in its acute stage.

In 1915, Elizabeth wrote a 2,000-word letter to United States Attorney-General Gregory. After outlining the early life of her son and the mitigating circumstances surrounding his crime, she continued:

> I had not seen my son for over five years until 1915 when I, having been told he was in poor health, paid him a brief visit March 15. In April I again called on him and on that occasion, had a brief consultation with Dr. A. F. Yohe, the physician in charge at the institution. He tells me my son has Bright's disease of over a year's standing. The boy, who now is just 25 years of age, is extremely thin with puffs under his eyes and is bothered very much with swelling of the feet and limbs. Has practically done no work at all for a year, he tells me, and is in the hospital a good portion of his time.
>
> I am very anxious to secure his release, hoping the change of surroundings and climate may prove beneficial to him, for my home is now in Juneau, Alaska. If this change does not prove a check to the disease, it at least will be a great comfort to me to be able to care for him in his last days. I have no desire to condone his crime. He certainly did wrong, and better to have starved or written home for help, but he has suffered six years of his life, and one might say the six *best* years of his youth have been given to pay for a moment's heat of passion. I've never rebelled or complained for I realize that such punishment is necessary for the welfare of society. But now I ask your kind offices in his behalf so I can care for him and, if need be, bury him when the call of Death comes. I just ask to be allowed to care for my firstborn son. . . .

Her last sentence contained a mother's premonitory warning:

> I plead with you to act. For I fear, unless he is released *soon*, our efforts will all be in vain.

Elizabeth Stroud's plea brought nothing. Destiny, however, drew its proverbial curtain of mercy over her, preventing foreknowledge of the future.

By 1915, the prison reform spirit had sagged to slow motion within the stone cage of Leavenworth. The warden's idealism had begun to wither and the capable deputy warden was transferred.

Living costs had risen sharply, due to the war in Europe. This ate into the buying power of prison budgets. The food grew still worse. Fewer guards were employed. The Harrison Special Tax Act was passed, and this suddenly turned thousands of drug-users into felons, who were duly prosecuted and thrown into Leavenworth. More narcotics found a way into the prison. A counterfeiting ring was also discovered in operation inside the wall. The Republican Party Press was amused, and ugly intimations of scandal touched close to high prison officials.

The careering prison régime cracked down. The Hole was kept full, rule-breakers were again shackled to the door, and prison reform gave ground as the prison pushed back like slow rubber into the old moulds.

All Federal guards still carried clubs: long hardwood truncheons with a thong looped at one end. Potent, with the impact of an axe handle, such clubs ranked second only to the wall as a symbol of punitive force to the inmates. It was a violation for a guard to strike a prisoner except under certain conditions. In operation, though, the use of the club flowed from the character of the guard.

Ironically, it was in June, 1915, while Elizabeth Stroud was inscribing her letter from Juneau on behalf of her son, that a new guard received a transfer to Leavenworth after less than a year at Atlanta Prison. The uncanny prison grapevine had bad news. Word raced through the sides of a thousand mouths that the guard had been marked for attack by some Atlanta inmates and was unsafe there. Right or wrong, the report was that he had fractured the skull of an old prisoner with his club. Further word had it that the Altanta convict, Harry Ferguson, had died six days after the guard was transferred.

Had the new guard been as gentle as St. Francis, it might have availed him little in Leavenworth. The long-term convicts, probably including the high-strung and ailing Stroud, hated him on sight.

The new guard, Andrew F. Turner, was a stocky, muscled, large-fisted man of thirty-nine. He was five-feet-eleven-inches tall and weighed 185 pounds. Arkansas-born, of limited education, he had worked as a crate-handler for groceries before becoming a guard. He parted his curly brown hair in the middle, and wore metal-rimmed spectacles which imparted a severity to his appearance, further accented by a large, straight mouth.

He soon became known among the guards as an aloof and moral man.

A month after Turner's arrival, Stroud fell seriously ill and was placed in the prison hospital, where he remained for twenty-six days. The doctor confirmed his previous diagnosis. He did not tell his patient about the high fatality of the disease, but Stroud soon drew his own gloomy conclusions from the remarks of the convict nurses.

The patient began to discourse learnedly with nurses and patients about the unimportance of present life. They had lived before, he told them. They could learn how to send out a powerful wish which would fly beyond the walls and do their bidding. Especially wishes that were not for good and not for the wisher's benefit.

Stroud came under the quiet notice of the head nurse. The nurse was a former minister who had received a sentence for technical violation of the Mann Act. The charge later was proved false. A convict on circumstantial evidence, he was made head nurse after two months in prison.

After several talks with Stroud, the head nurse spoke to the doctor.

"Doc, isn't that Stroud a bit off his base?"

"He's sick. Bright's disease. The pain and weakness to the system bring out queer behaviour sometimes."

"Might he break down? He seems under a strain. All that talk about wishes, bitterness, hatred. He's burning with it—psychopathic."

The doctor shrugged. "Not much we can do about that."

"I'd like to help him," said the nurse.

"Go ahead. He's here. We'll do what we can. I have my hands full and we can't coddle them all. I've taken him off the work list."

The head nurse was drawn by Stroud's razorlike intelligence. He did what he could for the stricken prisoner. Later this man came from a long distance and a successful life to testify for him.

When Stroud was returned to his cell, he walked stooped-over, with his left hand constantly pressed against his back. Every day he reported to the doctor's call and was marked for quarters. This caused remarks from working prisoners and drew the attention of some of the guards, including Turner.

"Who's this stringbean with his nose in the book?" he asked the guard on the range adjoining his, in C Block.

"Had him in the hospital; that's 8154, Stroud. Now the doc sends him to quarters every day." The small guard looked about uneasily. "Watch out for that type—nobody never laid no hand on him."

Turner shrugged. "He ain't my con. But he was dog-eyeing me the other day. Maybe he needs help." Turner fingered his club.

"Me, I don't push around here. Never know who's packing a knife."

Turner balanced on the balls of his feet. "Ah hope nobody pulls one," he drawled.

Unaware of Turner's casual attention, Stroud endured his kidney trouble and studied his books. But his dragging illness wore his patience thin. In despair he blamed his condition on the prison food.

He had no visitors now, and since his illness had forced him to abandon correspondence courses, the instructor's visits stopped. Elizabeth received bitter letters assailing her for failing to adopt her son's theosophical convictions.

On his twenty-sixth birthday, Stroud received good news. His brother Marc was coming to see him in early spring. To Stroud it was all-important.

In early February he watched an incident outside the dining-room which fastened his morbid attention on Guard Turner. A bandy-legged little prisoner named Kasellis stepped out of the food line after a rancid meal and walked over to complain to the Captain of the Guard. He had hardly opened his mouth when Turner bore down upon him, seized his arm and jerked him back. When the prisoner pulled away, Turner flattened him, then carried him from the dining-room, with Guard Rowe following. They took Kasellis to Isolation, according to the transcript of Stroud's trial.

Stroud kept watching Turner whenever he was around, in common with other convicts. Prisoners complained and later testified that Turner used his club to nudge prisoners along. The prodding made the inmates nervous in the laundry where Turner now officiated. It kept reminding them of their danger.

"His idea of running the laundry was not invoking proper

authority to discipline a prisoner by reporting him, but to do it personally," a prisoner named Wallace later stated. "He believed in personal contact with the man as a discipline. He loved the physical contacts."

Late in February, 1916, a nervous young prisoner whom Stroud liked stopped him in the yard.

"The screw from Atlanta is on me, Bob. Rapped me twice now."

"Did the son of a bitch hurt you?"

"Not yet. But he's on my tail all the time, fingering me with his stick. How's about loaning yer you-know-what?"

"That club-happy screw," Stroud said softly. "Somebody's gonna go out and take him with 'em. But not you."

"Come on, Bob. You got it on you. Gimme it."

"Not a chance, kid. You don't choose a club-wise screw like Turner. Take it easy."

March 24, 1916, was bath day. Between the shower room and main laundry room was an arched alcove. There Guard Turner sat, overlooking both rooms. He was approached by the prisoner named Wallace. Wallace was working as head prisoner in the laundry. He had a quiet, joking manner which enabled him to stay on the good side of guards.

He saw Turner staring intently into the steam-filled shower where naked prisoners were soaping themselves. Wallace peered into the steam and then back to Turner.

"Something wrong, sir?" he asked lightly.

Turner glanced at him briefly and his gaze returned to the shower. Wallace waited.

"Ah was watching that stringy con that keeps dog-eyeing me," Turner said. "If he ever makes a break at me, Ah'll club his brains out."

That night Stroud received a letter from his mother. He began an answer:

. . . I am sorry if I have made you sad. I guess I have done that very thing far too often by not showing my affection when I should. I cannot be hard hearted enough not to write to you after reading your letter, although it was my intention never to write again, when I sent you my last letter. Well, I may stop writing all too soon anyway. I am feeling so badly that I would end it all if I did not have my eye on the morrow. I got the money o.k. and am glad to get it but I sometimes feel much ashamed to take it and use it as I do, when it comes so hard to you. I guess you intend it to give me pleasure and I use it for that purpose. . . .

Mother darling, I don't blame you, you are as much a victim of circumstances as I am.

He left the letter unfinished, to resume later.

On Saturday afternoon, March 25, 1916, when Stroud returned from a visit to the library, he found a large basket of fruit and sweets in his cell. There was a note with it.

Hello Bob, I got here from Alaska but they would not let me see you so here's what I brought and will try to get in to see you soon.
Love. Marc.

Stroud stared incredulously at the note. He had missed a visit which he had awaited for weeks, months. Unable to eat, he paced, pausing sometimes to stare at the tiny green ribbon atop the basket. Marc, all the way from Alaska, kept out because of a Saturday afternoon rule! The week before, a trusty had been called out of the line to see a visitor on Saturday afternoon. But despite this luck, he would see Marc soon now, after years of waiting.

At the wordless evening meal, Stroud stared at the food, but ate little. Toward the end of the meal, the prisoner next to him leaned forward, hiding his words. "Hear ya got a basket, Bob. That why you ain't eatin'?"

Stroud started. "Never touched it," he said harshly. "They shut my brother out after he come all the way from Juneau."

A con hissed a warning. Stroud subsided and stared straight ahead.

"Gimme yoh numbah," drawled a heavy voice. Stroud looked up. Above him was Turner. His club was tucked under his left arm. He held a pencil poised over a small pad.

Stroud paled as the meaning of the violation sank home. He had broken the silence rule. If Turner reported him, Stroud would lose the visiting privilege. This would bar him from seeing Marc. Stroud twisted around to look up at Turner's face, an instinctive plea in his own. Then he remembered and stiffened. It was the Atlanta screw.

"Stroud. 8154," Turner wrote the number and walked on.

Later Stroud sent word through a friendly guard asking Turner to delay the report until after Marc's visit. The guard brought him word. "He can, but he won't."

Stroud continued his pacing. During that night, he seethed and tossed. The memory of Turner's physical nearness looming over him at mess pressed on his mind.

Sunday morning, March 26, 1916, broke grey and damp. A slow drizzle had started before dawn. Haggard and drawn, Stroud found his unfinished letter to his mother and resumed writing.

Sunday morning.

I have read your letter over many times and each time my breast chocks up with emotion I have been think all night and as a result I can only say that I am sorry, very sorry things are as they are but I can see no hope. If there was one person who cared enough for me to try to understand and help me I would make an effort but there is none and I am very tired. I am sending you an other poem of the same kind as the last please do with it as you done with the last.

Marc was over to see me yesterday and as it was Saturday they wouldn't let him in. He had some fruit and candy for me which I got tho. I guess if every thing goes well I will get to see him next week. The chance are I wont tho. It is raining to day and we wont get the yard.

Mother I should feel very badly if you were to pass away but do you know that I can see very littel left in life for either of us. You have had the best of me tho at that for you had the pleasure of your youth the satisfaction of a family. I have for years longed for a family and a home where I could be happy but that like everything has been denighed me.

I gues Minnie will never write to me again. I have tried my best to insult her in my last letter. She told me about Arthur K. standing a chance to get life in Walla Walla. She spoke of it as tho she thought it was just the thing. Well she know what I think. I have wished a piece of hard luck on to her which she hasnt a chance to avoid and that is that she will some day know what her word "life" really means. She will for the chance are 100 to 1 that that kid of hers will go wrong for neather of its parent know enough to help it go right. I feel sorry for the boy.

Say do you know there is something funny about me. What I wish when I am in a certain State of minde always comes to pass. I wished a Stroke of parallisis on a man last summer who was in perfect health. I was bound by my word that I would avoid trouble with him. 48 hours after I expressed the wish he was in the hospital with the Stroke. I have had the same thing happen fifty times with people and things. The funny thing is when I am in that state of minde I can never wish any thing good. Or any thing directly for my self. I must say good by Mother Darling

Your loving Son.

R. F. Stroud

A Kiss for my old sweetheart, who I love better than life.

I am weary, Life seems dreary
And the world is bleak and bare
I am lonely, Oh so lonely,
And there's none who think or cair
In my sadness close to madness
All the world has turned away
All is blindness there's no kindness
For the friend of yesterday.

Elizabeth Stroud did not receive her son's letter, or those which followed. They were confiscated for use as court exhibits by the warden, due to the fateful event which followed.

That Sunday noon, 1,100 blue-coated prisoners hurried into the enormous prison dining-hall, their shoulders wet from the March drizzle. Eighty prisoner-waiters hurried around the seated men as they dug into their food. At one of the 210 tables, at the far end of the hall, sat Stroud. Seventy-five feet away, at the front end of the hall on a two-foot platform overlooking the massed men, sat the Captain of the Guard, John Purcell.

Next to him, a fifteen-piece band drowned the culinary clatter of the great room in a blare of brass. Up and down the aisles, swinging their clubs, paced the guards.

Stroud had followed the bells and calls like a sleep-walker. He pecked at his underdone pork chops and stared at Turner as the guard strolled up and down the aisle.

Stroud held up his hand in the usual signal for prisoners to rise in case of sickness or personal need. Turner nodded, and Stroud rose. He edged by two men and stepped into the aisle. As he approached Turner, his movements were trancelike. Turner squinted over his glasses, watching Stroud come. His club was tucked under his left arm.

Stroud stood in front of him. From the sea of prisoners, heads bobbed up here and there, like corks. From his dais, Captain Purcell watched casually.

It was somewhat unusual to talk to a guard thus. Turner looked relaxed. He was standing in the presence of 1,100 men, his fellow guards ten seconds away.

Words passed between Stroud and Turner. Suddenly both Stroud's and Turner's faces grew violent. Turner's mouth worked and he went for his club. Stroud saw the club raised, seized it with his right hand. The guard jerked at it. Stroud grabbed for it with both hands. Then Stroud's left hand let go and vanished under his prison jacket. With one straight thrust he buried his knife in Turner's chest and stepped back. Turner's dying stare met eyes that were mad. He wavered, lifted his hand, and fell on top of his club. Stroud stood frozen, the knife in his left hand slowly dripping blood.

Captain Purcell grabbed his club and dashed from the platform. A freezing wave moved down the vast hall through table after table. Food-laden forks stopped and slowly sank back to plates.

The brass band played on. The name of the tune was "In Paradise".

Prisoners seated at tables around Stroud began to rise. Guards bore down on them. Captain John and four guards were now standing around Stroud, clubs in hand. After seeing his face, none moved. From his mouth poured harsh sobbing and cursing sounds.

Then Captain John walked over to him. "What's the matter?" he said casually, as though asking for the time.

"That man—I asked him a civil question—you stand back!"

"Come up here," Captain John said softly, "and possibly we can talk it over . . ." Then he deliberately turned his exposed back on the shaking Stroud and walked slowly away as though he expected the prisoner to fall in by his side. He was not the Captain for nothing; his "trouble sense" was proverbial in Leavenworth. Stroud stared at his back, dropped the knife and stumbled after him.

"Take this man to Isolation," he told a guard. Then he faced the hall.

Row on row, tense prisoners crouched in their seats, waiting. The great room was as tight as an unexploded bomb.

Finishing its piece, the band stopped. Through the dead silence, crockery noises filtered in from the kitchen. Captain John slowly wheeled, staring down a thousand pairs of eyes. Several guards and prisoners now carried away the body of Turner. A strange rustling stirred through the dining hall. It was like an enormous sigh.

The impassive Captain casually gave the accustomed signal. The men began to move. Nervous guards hurried the prisoners to their cells. Locked in, the convicts glared at the guards.

Both sides knew what killing a guard meant. A black river of hysteria and hate began to boil silently through the corridors of Leavenworth as the shock melted.

Shortly afterward, the prison shake-down began. Twenty-six knives were taken from prisoners that day. The twenty-seventh, wrapped in a bloody napkin, lay in the pocket of Captain Purcell.

The knife's owner watched from solitary confinement the powers that now moved swiftly, and they were focused on one goal: to bring Stroud's singular life to a close at the end of a rope.

SIX

NEWS OF THE KILLING staggered young Marc, now a darkly handsome, well-groomed youth of eighteen. First cabling his mother, he again took the train from Kansas City to Leavenworth. He read the Press reports over and over. Already he had concluded that he was the unwitting precipitant of the events which had snapped the string of his brother's control. Added to his early respect and love for Bob, he felt an obligation.

Now Marc was allowed to see Robert. The youth was appalled at the sight of the emaciated, drawn man with the burning eyes who smiled at him. Marc manfully hid his pity and concern and they bantered in the way of brothers. Robert insisted that his mother remain in Alaska.

Concerning his brother, he remained protective. "I hope you will never go the route I have," he wrote Marc. "I could not have done different. If I could I would, for you know I am a mild-tempered man." But to the prison authorities and in letters, Stroud remained defiant, impassive and unmoved.

The warden permitted the prisoner to write all the letters he wished. None of them left the prison. They were to become damning exhibits in the hands of the prosecutor in the trials to follow.

Letters were neither received nor required by Elizabeth Stroud. She immediately sold her rooming-house and her furniture. Once again, she sailed on the first boat that would take her to Seattle, a train and Robbie. Her pleasant and prosperous living in Juneau became a memory. Like her strange son, the mother seldom hesitated and never looked back.

Eleven days after the guard's death, she faced Warden Morgan in his office. He told her she was wasting her time.

"After inquiries by me as to the causes leading up to the tragedy," she later wrote, "and the statement I should employ an attorney to look after my son's interests, the warden begged me not to do so, stating he was sorry for me, but the prison officials had determined to make an example of Robbie for prison discipline and I would be wasting any money I used to employ an attorney, as it would do no good."

She retained General L. C. Boyle, one of the best defence attorneys in Kansas. His opponent was U.S. Attorney Fred Robertson, a capable and relentless prosecutor.

Both sides dug in to work up their respective cases in the short interim remaining before the trial date. Witnesses were sought and interviewed. The prison hummed with fast-breaking developments which broke its dull routine.

Since Stroud had killed Turner face-to-face in the presence of 1,100 men, his crime took on the character of a public act, a trial by combat between a prison-maddened convict and a feared guard. It held symbolic implications which did not escape the prosecutor. He was to portray it as a premeditated blow at the prison system itself.

Stroud's mental state was such that he believed that 1,100 "of my own people" had stood up in the dining-hall to support his fearful and fatal act. But the Grey Brotherhood now faced a stringent reality.

Within the walls, prison eyes narrowed and prison minds weighed self-preservation against the coming trial. Paramount with most short-term convicts was the overriding desire for release. Among the scores of witnesses to the killing of Guard Turner, each had ample time to "look at his Hole card".

The prison was like a roof ready to fall on any convict who aligned himself with a guard-killer. To testify as an eyewitness for Stroud was to challenge the furious determination of prison authorities to see Stroud hanged.

The prisoners reacted in character throughout the trials that followed. Before it was over, six convicts floated to freedom on the blood of Guard Turner. Others were placed in Isolation.

The guards reacted as a group. For them it was sudden ostracism to say anything in favour of Stroud while prison officials were nailing down an overwhelming case to destroy him. An example had to be made. To the warden, the case seemed cut and dried. He was already looking ahead to details of the execution.

The trial opened on a hot May day in Kansas, a state whose laws forbade capital punishment. But this was a Federal trial for a crime committed on Federal property.

The prosecution produced an array of witnesses, both prisoners and guards who established an iron chain of evidence supporting first-degree murder. A defence alienist testified that

Stroud was insane, but five government doctors swore otherwise.

In four swift days, twelve Kansans brought in a verdict of guilty to first-degree murder. On May 27, 1916, Judge John C. Pollock sentenced Stroud to be hanged on July 21.

The judge, however, had forgotten a law passed by Congress in 1911 which gave Kansas juries the power to state whether or not a defendant shall suffer the extreme penalty. Stroud's case was immediately appealed to the Federal Circuit Court. The Circuit Court affirmed error and promptly nullified the trial. This was in December, 1916.

Judge Pollock's instructions proved historic in another way. He instructed the jury to acquit Stroud if they believed the guard was trying to strike him with his club before Stroud stabbed the guard. Thereafter, Federal prisons restricted the use of clubs by guards, and later abolished clubs as weapons except in riots.

Stroud's successful appeal infuriated some prison officials, who expressed concern over its effect on prison discipline. One guard who had charge of the isolation cells told Stroud, "If we don't get a chance to bump you by the neck, we'll do it some other way and it can never be proved on us." Stroud informed the deputy warden that he would eat no food handled by that guard. Warden Morgan disciplined the guard, and took extraordinary measures to cherish the health of his doomed prisoner. The warden had plans for Stroud.

Stroud accommodated his keepers by eating. The special diet, ironically, produced an improvement in his health, which the guards observed with grim dismay.

Stroud stood foursquare and unrepentant on his act. Its terrifying success, his peculiar behaviour, the totally open character of the crime, had combined to protect him from savage reprisal in the tight hours after Turner was killed. Had the guard been better liked or longer there, Stroud might never have lived to face trial.

Shortly after the indictment, Stroud was visited by C. E. Edgar of Kansas City, a member of the Theosophical Lodge. This man of strange faith, some sects of which refuse to swat a fly, had one question to ask the embattled convict. "How do you reconcile your action with theosophy?"

"I don't," Stroud answered. "I can't. The best of men will break down under some conditions." Edgar gave him the lodge address and said they would do what they could to help him. Later, they donated sums for his defence.

Now the struggle between the convict and those determined to hang him deepened. Quarter was neither asked nor given on either side. Elizabeth Stroud complained that one eyewitness prisoner who offered to testify, without telling beforehand what he would say, was placed in Isolation, held there, declared insane, taken from the prison, and later found sane again. Another was placed in Isolation because a personal foe told the guards this man had given the knife to Stroud. Stroud flatly admitted he had made the knife and carried it for nine months.

On May 22, 1917, Stroud's second trial opened, six weeks after the United States entered the First World War. It was necessary to draw three panels of jurors because of a curious event.

The prosecution's death-penalty target had aroused critical comment in Kansas. No man had been hanged there since 1878. This sentiment ran strong in Kansas City, and Elizabeth's tireless effort on her son's behalf strengthened it. Letters appeared in the Press and resolutions were passed by women's clubs. Penal reform groups became interested.

When the Federal jury panel was drawn, circulars denouncing capital punishment were sent to every member. They were urged to refrain from the death penalty.

Learning of this, Judge Pollock was outraged. Already smarting because of the Circuit Court reversal, he urged investigation and prosecution of the senders of the circulars.

Defence attorneys asked Judge Pollock to disqualify himself. He did, and another Federal judge was assigned to the trial.

Both sides had made elaborate preparations. Elizabeth spent money she had inherited to retain two formidable attorneys, I. B. Kimbrell and M. J. O'Donnell. She also employed psychiatrists to examine her son. The fees were high.

Government doctors had stripped and examined Stroud, "looking for signs of the stigmata of degeneracy", as one of the Lombrosian alienists later testified. They found none.

The prosecution had stronger medicine to apply during the second trial. Alert U.S. Attorney Robertson had built the already overwhelming case into something that looked airtight. Two guards, the prosecution's own witnesses, had testified in the first trial that they had seen Turner's club in his hand,

and that Stroud had grasped it. Robertson had to seal his case against any reasonable doubt that Stroud had acted in self-defence. To do this, he needed prisoner testimony he could be wholly sure of. His specific problem was to secure five convict witnesses to testify favourably, and to prevent nine convict witnesses who were determined to testify for Stroud from reaching the stand. This was accomplished through use of the pardon power of the Government.

Defence attorneys applied for a writ to subpoena their nine witnesses. The Judge, J. W. Woodrough, refused to issue the writ, holding that convicted felons were incompetent to testify. The same writ had been advanced by the prosecutor, four days before. The judge had allowed the writ to issue, which brought the Government's prisoner witnesses as far as the courtroom.

On their way from the courtroom door to the stand, each prisoner was met by the U.S. Attorney and handed a pardon signed by the President. This made them free men, "competent to testify". Two other convicts had already been released from prison after the first trial, through pardons. They were saved a total of thirteen years in prison.

A witness seated yards away from the fatal stabbing testified to details of conversation between Turner and Stroud. Another stated that Stroud was "as cool as a cucumber". A third held Stroud was "very red in the face and angry". All held fast to their stories, nervously twisting their pardons in their hands as the defence attorneys worked them over.

The prosecutor's second problem was to bolster his case against any attempt to prove Stroud mad, irresponsible or mentally ill, anything that bordered upon insanity. An insane defendant might win an acquittal. An unbalanced one might sway the jury from the death penalty. For the prosecution, anything less than Stroud's death was a defeat.

The transcript of the second trial contains long passages of conflicting testimony by psychiatrists. Stroud's belief that he could send mental messages beyond the walls was marked by the defence and deprecated by the prosecution.

The opinion of the alienists varied beyond expectation. It became clear that Stroud's behaviour somewhat baffled them; it was difficult to evaluate this convict, using standards of the world outside. Stroud's actions had been taken under institutional stringency, a state often compared to that of war.

He was variously diagnosed as sane, competent, capable, mentally responsible, insane, hardly sane, mentally defective, victim of systematized delusions, psychopathic, possessed of mental obliquity, of unsound mind, a criminal degenerate, progressing toward insanity, morally defective, abnormal, mentally defective, intelligent, paranoiac and ethically twisted.

Defence witnesses from Elizabeth's family told of a number of relatives who had gone insane. The prosecutor met this by offering to produce testimony that there were as many or more insane relatives in Abraham Lincoln's family.

Stroud attentively watched the proceedings on which his life was suspended.

On May 28, 1917, the case went to the jury. After seven hours they returned their verdict. "We find the defendant Robert F. Stroud guilty as charged in the indictment, *without capital punishment*," Harold Short, Foreman, announced.

Prosecutor Robertson stared incredulously at the jury. Grim looks settled upon the faces of prison officials.

The defence attorneys shook hands and watched Elizabeth embrace Robbie. Used to seeing his life tossed through the million syllables of two trials, Stroud stood unmoved. He had been in a solitary cell for a year and three months, after eight years in prison.

Judge Woodrough imposed the life sentence immediately.

When court adjourned, the bailiff nodded to the prison guards to take Stroud away. But he held back. His attorney hastened over.

"They know I killed Turner before he could club me. They wouldn't let my witnesses testify and I will be in prison for life at the mercy of every screw. Nobody wants to die, but . . ."

Attorney Kimbrell stopped smiling. "Are you telling me you might want to appeal this?"

"I certainly am."

The lawyer shrugged. "You have your life."

"Was it a fair trial?"

"Well—no. I believe the judge let himself in for two reversible errors. But you have your life, Stroud."

"What kind of a life, Mr. Kimbrell?"

"But another trial opens up everything. It could go like the first one."

"They can hang me?"

The lawyer reflected. "They can—although I'm not sure.

You've had your neck on the block twice. Now you've won a life sentence. I don't know. There's something about double jeopardy, but it requires study."

"I'm through doing time. I want to go all the way. Let them acquit me or hang me."

With Elizabeth Stroud's dubious agreement, the lawyers drew up an appeal.

When U.S. Attorney Robertson heard about it, he could hardly believe his ears. He was delighted. Here was a new chance to stretch the stiff neck of the unyielding convict. He did not protest the appeal. Nor did the Attorney-General later.

Stroud's lawyers filed their assignment of error with the U.S. Supreme Court in August, 1917. It was unconstitutional, they asserted, to deprive a man on trial of equal right to subpoena witnesses. They also asked that letters written by Stroud immediately after Turner's death be returned to him and excluded from evidence under the Fourth Amendment, which prohibits unreasonable searches and seizures. Confiscated by the warden, these letters contained aggressive and defiant statements by Stroud.

Attorney-General John W. Davis filed a confession of error on behalf of the Government, and the Supreme Court quickly nullified the verdict and ordered a new trial. They did not rule on the letters. It was now February, 1918.

Everyone seemed satisfied except Elizabeth Stroud. She had spent all she had and much of her son Marc's earnings to defend Robbie. It was her job to raise more money.

The months rolled around to May, 1918, and Stroud was again taken from isolation, out beyond the great wall of Leavenworth to the Federal court. Manacled but cheerful, he filled his lungs with free air and was brought into the third trial of his life for the same offence.

Sixty prospective jurors, farmers and storekeepers and rustics from tiny hamlets in Kansas sat in the courtroom awaiting the judge.

All the local Federal judges had disqualified themselves. The Court reached across country to Denver, Colorado, and now presiding was the Honourable Robert E. Lewis.

The judge had hardly arranged his black robes when he became aware that Stroud was there, but his attorneys were not. Elizabeth sat near her son, looking tired and bewildered.

The steadfast prosecutor, who now knew the case like the alphabet, signified that he was ready for trial. After a short wait, the Court delivered some sizzling remarks about Stroud's attorneys. He appointed forthwith three new lawyers to the defence, and set the case over for one day. Stroud was trotted back to prison.

On May 23, the prosecution again announced itself ready.

"Are you prepared to empanel the jury?" the Court asked.

"No, Your Honour," answered one of the new defence attorneys. "I have an affidavit here for a continuance that I am filing at the request of the regular attorneys for Mr. Stroud."

"I don't consider those gentlemen any longer Mr. Stroud's attorneys in the trial of this case," said the Court.

Behind the acidulous remarks of the judge was a unique situation. The original defence attorneys were now working for a defendant whose resources had been exhausted. In addition, they had taken on a lucrative out-of-state trial that fell on the same date as Stroud's. They had visited the prosecutor and proposed that he consent to a plea of guilt to second-degree murder, with the understanding that he receive a life sentence. This, at least, was Prosecutor Robertson's understanding. He had refused.

Stroud was dumbfounded. He rose from his seat, protesting. He stated he had never under any circumstances authorized such a proposition "for the reason that he was not guilty of the charge contained in the indictment or of murder in any degree."

Judge Lewis looked down upon the legal tangle. Coldly incensed, he accused the absent lawyers of unprofessional conduct. He concluded, however, that a continuance of the case had to be granted. To do otherwise would be "an abuse of discretion". The new trial date was set for June 23, 1918.

Stroud's original defence attorneys, hearing of the judge's remarks, re-entered the case with angry determination. Since the judge had appointed the two new attorneys, Stroud now had four attorneys in his corner.

By the time the trial finally opened on a stifling morning late in June, the nerves of the participants were frazzled, with the exception of those of the defendant. He seemed to enjoy every brief respite from his lonely cell, even with his life at stake.

Prosecutor Robertson kept on hand six doctors to testify regarding the sanity of the accused. They were never called to the stand. Since the defence was nearly bankrupt, there were no medical experts to testify for Stroud.

The defence argued that Stroud's letters written after the Turner killing and not posted by the warden should be excluded. The petition was denied.

Read aloud to the jury, these letters alone appeared sufficient to place Stroud's neck in the noose—if the jury believed they were written by a sane man. Stroud had berated the "Christian warden" for telling young Marc that his brother had committed an awful crime. The defendant had characterized his grandfather, a pillar of the community, as a hypocrite and bigot. Stroud stated he, Stroud, was looked upon as the kindest and most charitable man in prison; that his conscience approved of his action entirely and would disapprove of any other manner of action under prison conditions as he lived them. Finally, he stated that unless he fought for himself and his fellows he would be a coward; and that the dead guard was no good before he was given "heart trouble".

Whether the jury would believe all this the product of a sane or a prison-shattered mind, was now a problem.

The drama of death settled into the stifling air of the hot courtroom. Horror, madness and an ache for retribution were like an electric charge released anew for a crime more than two years old.

Now the perspiring defence attorneys opened their case. The U.S. Supreme Court had affirmed the right of unpardoned prisoners to testify. Stroud's attorneys asked for the prisoners.

"You have the writ," Judge Lewis said. "Insert the names."

This writ brought from the bowels of Leavenworth eight prisoners who had waited long to testify for Stroud. They were of different calibre from the pardoned Government witnesses.

They were brought in, a manacled group in prison denims: Murphy, Stratton, Duffey, Wallace, O'Dell, Ryan, West, Coates and McGrath. Their presence startled the courtroom. Rebels and hard-case men, they came knowing how their testimony would affect their lot in prison. The prosecutor was ready for them; he had their records in his hand. Bank robbers, counterfeiters, yeggmen, their testimony favoured Stroud—but after cross-examination their past actions loomed larger than their sworn words.

One of the younger prisoners was Willie West, the blue-eyed, yellow-haired soldier. He still owed his friend Stroud a favour for the knife he had borrowed from Stroud years before. West testified that he had been kept in isolation for twenty-five months after volunteering to testify for Stroud. The prosecutor asserted that West had tried to get his mother to mortgage her property to help save Stroud's life. It soon became clear that Willie was more of a loyal friend than an informative witness. He had lived by the inmates' code and had balanced his account. Stroud stood up, bright-eyed, when West was taken away.

The final witness for the defence was not of this group. A free man, he proved the most unusual.

This witness had been head nurse of the prison hospital during Stroud's protracted illness. An ordained minister and later a businessman, he had proved his innocence and gained a pardon. A large, clean-cut man, he held a degree from the University of Chicago. He was well established in the trucking business by the time of Stroud's last trial. He had offered himself as a witness after telephoning Elizabeth Stroud, and had come at his own expense from Peoria, Illinois, as an eyewitness to Turner's death. In the partisan welter of testimony, this witness appeared the least involved.

"What is your business now?" asked the defence attorney.

"The motor truck business. Making motor tractors for the Allied armies."

"Are you in easy circumstances now?"

"I am not in needy circumstances."

"Worth about how much money?"

"Possibly sixty thousand dollars."

The jury came to life. The witness was a farmer's son who had made good. He was far removed from the hard-core convicts who had stood for Stroud.

"Were there any marks against you while you were there?"

"I think at one time I was reported for not keeping my quarters clean. I was not a good housekeeper."

"Did you, while you were there, meet the defendant in this case?"

"Many times."

"Was he an inmate of the hospital while you were there?"

"A great many times."

"How long a time would he be in?"

"One, two days, sometimes quite a bit longer. Marked in as having the grippe, sometimes for observation."

"What do you mean, for observation?"

"I understood for observation as to his condition. I understood in Stroud's case it was psychopathic, but I could not say it always meant that."

"What do you mean by psychopathic?"

"They wanted to know whether he was right mentally or not —what symptoms he had would develop."

Many faces turned toward Stroud. He had started when the witness had mentioned "psychopathic". Stroud looked away from the witness and stared ahead, wooden-faced.

"How often was he there for such observation?"

"We looked upon Mr. Stroud as a patient that should be observed at all times."

The defence attorney drew out the witness's account of the killing. He had been seated at a table fifteen feet ahead of the death spot, and off to one side.

The witness testified that the pork chops were underdone, and he had turned to signal for another portion when he noticed the unusual circumstance of a prisoner talking to a guard in the aisle. He testified that Turner had raised his club first, that the prisoners were in fear of Turner, and that Stroud was nervous and probably mentally ill.

The prosecutor's case had been rock-solid to this point. He had reduced the effectiveness of every defence witness by impeaching his status and record. But this witness was more of a problem.

"Do you have a kind of fear of the record?" the prosecutor inquired, referring to the witness's statement that hospital records were made by prisoners and not entirely reliable.

"I assure you, not," the witness said. "I am not sure of anything but what I know is the truth."

"You say you are on entirely friendly terms with the officials at the penitentiary."

"I have not said that. I said I had no grudge against any official."

"Do you remember when you went out of the prison, you published a series of articles?"

"I do."

"Attacking the institution and the officials of it?"

"No, sir, attacking the prison system."

"Some of them were published and then they ceased, didn't they, after a bit?"

"Those articles were merely a portion of a book of mine."

"Why did they cease to run?"

"Because they were gone over by a cub reporter and the first one was so full of egregious mistakes that I didn't want them run under my name."

His questioner could not resist a parting shot. "You are very careful about your name?" he sneered.

"I am," said the witness.

At this point, the defence rested its case.

Prosecutor Robertson, who had correctly foreseen defence moves except for this last witness, now scurried to produce witnesses in rebuttal. The prison doctor testified that Stroud had not been under mental observation. Atlanta prison officials testified that Turner's reputation had been good. They were unable to recall the death of a prisoner named Ferguson. He may have died; they couldn't recall the matter. Leavenworth guards added testimony in praise of the dead guard.

The trial drew to a close and the jury retired to consider its verdict. Some hours later, the jury foreman brought in the verdict. They found Robert Stroud guilty as charged, and recommended that he be hanged. It was June 28, 1918.

Judge Lewis immediately passed the death sentence, ordering that Stroud be hanged on Friday, November 8, 1918, within the walls of Leavenworth.

The surprised murmur that filled the courtroom soon expanded into a louder outcry over the state.

"A Kansas jury will never order a man hanged even for murder," opponents of capital punishment had told Congress in 1911. A Kansas Federal jury now had ordered a hanging by Federal law in a state where execution was forbidden by state law.

During the week following the sentence of death, prison officials watched the mounting reaction with dismay. On July 1, 1918, Warden Morgan issued a statement: "If Robert F. Stroud is not hanged, he will be kept in solitary confinement all his life. If life-termers can murder guards without fear of further punishment, sixty men cannot control eighteen hundred prisoners."

Defence attorneys appealed to the U.S. Supreme Court,

alleging an improperly selected jury from prejudiced veniremen, prejudiced instructions, and some legal technicalities.

A stay of Stroud's execution was granted. Robert Stroud lived to watch his second date for death pass by him on November 8, 1918. Three days later Stroud was one of the 1,200 prisoners who cheered themselves hoarse from the depths of Leavenworth as the Armistice ended the First World War.

The tall, thin Stroud was nearing his twenty-ninth birthday. He had lived in isolation for two and a half years, his life suspended by delicate legal threads. One by one they were being snipped as he waited and watched.

Since the authorities were determined to keep him ripe for the gibbet, Stroud received better care than other convicts. A new and different kind of life opened up for him. He had ample correspondence privileges and visitors. The complex legal defence, the affectionate visits of his mother and the sinister prestige of his case, combined to ease his gnawing awareness of impending death.

As the months became years, Stroud utilized his mathematical ability in a study of music. He learned counterpoint and mastered the elements of harmony. One day a visitor brought him a battered violin.

Stroud, who had heard little more than waterfront nickelodeons and his mother's lullaby hum, now composed music. It was strange and mathematically exact; and when he scraped the weird tunes upon his instrument, the sounds grated upon the ears of the troubled prisoners in isolation.

During this time, Stroud began to watch the detail of prison life with a maturing mind. He carefully stored impressions in his fantastically retentive memory and later recorded his observations.

He wrote of the bravery of the former world heavy-weight champion, Jack Johnson, when the Negro was threatened with death. Stroud added that Johnson had paid $7,000 to keep from being assigned to the prison stone works. Stroud wrote with affection of the prison Christmas programme, noting its force for good. He characterized the Captain of the Guards and a Deputy Warden, both of whom were sworn to see him hanged, as the bravest men inside the wall, and he cited incidents to prove his contention. He predicted the arrest and trial of a prison official for graft, and lived to see the forecast verified.

And then, on November 24, 1919, the Supreme Court affirmed the death sentence imposed upon Stroud. His attorneys petitioned for a rehearing. Governor Capper made a formal request to Washington that Robert Stroud not be hanged in Kansas.

The U.S. Supreme Court studied the appeal brief of Stroud's attorneys, Kimbrell and O'Donnell. Since their client's life had been spared in the second trial, they contended that he had been placed twice in jeopardy for the same offence, "putting the constitutional guaranty in barter".

On January 19, 1920, the Supreme Court refused a rehearing and reaffirmed the death sentence. Stroud, the Court held, derived no immunity from a trial nullified by agreement of prosecution and defence because of error.

Stroud had gambled his life for a possible acquittal and release from prison at the expiration of his original twelve-year sentence—in 1922. He had lost.

SEVEN

DURING THESE YEARS, how did Stroud's imprisonment affect members of his family? His death sentence was fixed after ten years in prison and four years of public trials.

When Elizabeth took her family to Alaska, shattering the unstable home, Ben Stroud's downward course accelerated. The desertion of his son Marc was a blow. The family prospered in Juneau. Elizabeth and Ben were divorced. Heavy drinking and fast company floated Ben out of the coal business. He drifted, like a ship which had lost anchor, down the Pacific coast. He squandered a small fortune. He found work on a ranch in California, and there he received a letter from Elizabeth telling of the Turner murder and asking for help. In later years, Marc wrote:

"My Dad wrote back, 'Let him die. He's getting what he deserves.' My brother forgave Ben, but I did not. I refused to write to him the last twelve years of his life. He died a pauper on a California ranch."

When Elizabeth's plea was rejected by Ben, her bitterness grew. She held Ben responsible for Robbie's tragic life.

Her elder daughter Minnie had become the mother of a baby girl. They came to Robert's second trial; he dandled his niece on his knee as witness after witness described his crime.

Mamie, the second daughter, remained unmarried and stayed with Elizabeth throughout her life.

After her arrival from Juneau, the mother lived with Marc in Kansas City, where he taught for a while in an engineering school. Marc was darkly handsome, personable and gifted with a quick mind; he had already made more money than youths of his age often do.

Over the years of his brother's imprisonment, Marc had developed an odd hobby: slipping handcuffs and rope ties. After hours of practice, he learned how to release himself in seconds from what his friends, after much labour, assured him were their best efforts to truss him up. Soon he was offering cash to anyone who could tie him in such fashion that he could not escape. He released himself, without untying a knot, with great dexterity.

When his act was perfected, he changed his name to L. G. Marcus and in 1917 entered vaudeville: The Great Marcus, Escape Artist. He slipped handcuffs, leg-irons and rope chains, and extricated himself from strait-jackets before gaping vaudeville audiences from Chicago to San Francisco.

"In 1918-1920 I was in movies, working for Mack Sennett, the old L.K.O. lot, National, and the old Bronton studio and others," Marcus recalls.

While his brother Bob waited in isolation in Leavenworth for the decisions that meant life or death, Marc was breaking through confining bonds in his headline act. He sent money to Elizabeth, who used it to fight for Robbie.

She had thrown a $12,000 legacy and her life savings into the battle for his life. She received more from opponents of capital punishment in Kansas. Then she borrowed.

When death leaped toward her son over the final hurdle of the U.S. Supreme Court, the stricken mother sought and gained an interview with the new Governor of Kansas. There was only one man in the world who could save her son from the gibbet. Elizabeth asked Governor Allen to intercede with President Woodrow Wilson.

The Governor signed a petition and members of the Kansas legislature followed suit. The petition stated that the death penalty had not been inflicted for twenty-two years, and that no person had been hanged for forty-two years.

"My son is the victim of his father's degeneracy and is paying the penalty for it," she pleaded. "I pray that it not be an execution."

In February, 1920, the haggard mother, dressed in black satin, visited her son, kissed him fervently and told him not to worry. Then she left for the nation's capital.

Judge Robert E. Lewis of Denver arrived in the city of Leavenworth to pronounce sentence for the last time on Robert F. Stroud, and, on March 5, 1920, the prisoner made his final trip to court as a defendant. Judge Lewis sentenced him to be hanged April 23, 1920.

Stroud received his ticket to death without emotion. After the sentence he requested permission to speak. He thanked the

Court and the attorneys who had worked hard in his defence. He spoke dispassionately, as though talking about another person.

"I have had a fair trial," he said.

One person present wept for him—his half-sister Mamie. Elizabeth was in Washington, Minnie on the Pacific coast and Marc headlining in a Chicago vaudeville house.

His destiny sealed, the tall, thin convict became an exhibit. He was the object of quiet visits by guards, trusties and prison officials. Some showed a tired sympathy, but most said little and watched the prisoner with satisfaction.

"Get your eyes full, screws," he told three guards who stood staring at him one afternoon. "But you nor nobody is gonna see me hang." His words carried along the grapevine as fast as the report reached prison officials. The convicts speculated whether Stroud's fateful luck would hold. Short-termers laid bets, but the "hard-case cons" sensed the import of his words. They did not know what method the condemned man might find to cheat the gallows, but they took no chances. Before the week was out, Stroud had three razor blades secreted in his cell.

On the following Saturday, the first death watch ever placed over a Leavenworth prisoner was set up. It was six weeks in advance of the execution date. At that time, Federal death watches were normally begun the week before execution.

For four years, Stroud's execution had been planned and abandoned. Now U.S. Marshal O. L. Wood advertised for bids on scaffold materials, located gallows blue-prints, and set about learning how to hang a man. With Leavenworth's new warden, A. V. Anderson, Wood walked the prison grounds, as prison eyes watched them move and surmised their mission.

These officials soon chose the spot for the erection of Stroud's gallows. It was in the exercise yard of the isolation unit, about twenty feet from Stroud's cell window and in full view of the condemned man.

Later, a loud crash brought Stroud jumping to his barred window, which overlooked the west side of the yard. He saw dust rising from a pile of fresh pine lumber gleaming yellow against the grey March snow. A guard pored over a large blueprint. As Stroud watched, fascinated, the guard measured and marked planks, and began to saw them.

Hour by hour, Stroud watched the slow construction of the

machine designed to take his life. He watched until his neck grew stiff. Unable to contain himself, he hissed through the window bars to the guard, a good-natured former carpenter named Brewer. Hammer in hand, the lanky guard sauntered over. He squinted curiously at Stroud's shadowed window. His breath made a cloud of steam and he slapped his arms.

"So you're making it," Stroud said.

"Tailor-made," Brewer said. "Ain't you six-foot-three, weight about 140?"

"One-fifty now. They're fattening me."

"Somebody's gotta build the thing. They promised help, but nobody'll come near it."

"Take your time, Brewer," Stroud said. "You might as well work on a treadmill. I'd never worry about it if it was me."

"Whatya mean, treadmill?"

"That trap will never drop me. You might as well saw out a three-holer."

Later, when Brewer was constructing the step rail to the trap, Stroud called him over again.

"Why so slow on that railing?" Stroud asked.

"I want it smooth," Brewer said, holding up a piece of sandpaper. "Don't want no slivers in it."

After the rope was hung to cure, officials gathered early in April for a ceremony. U.S. Marshal Wood, Warden Anderson and other officials stood surveying the scaffold. Stroud, glued to his window, watched Brewer truck up a large sandbag. Brewer tied the sandbag to the noose, mounted the platform and pulled the bag up through the open trap. He closed the trap, placed the bag on it and climbed down. The Marshal pulled out a stop watch as the officials waited, gazing up at the bag. The Marshal yanked a lever. The trap opened and down hurtled the sandbag. Its fall was broken by the noose and it rocked crazily back and forth like a living thing, as Stroud watched. It was dropped three times during the test. Stroud turned away. He stared at his wrists.

Stroud noticed that the death-watch guard was gone. Soon the guard was back on his stool.

"Tired of watching over me?" Stroud asked.

"Naw." The guard smiled lazily. "Just had to take a peek at the—er—rehearsal." Unknown to Stroud, this same guard had filled a tobacco sack with sawdust from the scaffold as a souvenir.

Despite his stoic manner, Stroud was unable to hide from the death-watch guards and visitors the signs of an inner change. He was entering into an experience which has altered the outlook of every man who ever faced it: the imminent certainty of his own death by execution. Stroud's letters reveal fragments of his reaction to the shock of the death-wait. He felt his obligation to his mother intensely. At the same time, he wrote that he saw deep into himself and discerned the obscure and massive tie that bound him to his mother.

"I was twenty-nine years old and nearly gone from this world before I got myself straight in the matter of my mother," he wrote. "I found the defect within myself that made me kill, and took steps to correct it and rebuild my life along constructive lines as I listened to the construction of my gallows."

He was under the shock therapy of impending death. Did he see and mark the dark fountain of an inner hate? He knew his life as an accumulation of misdirection, harm and waste. Was there a basic change in his view of his father? There is no evidence that he bore any ill will to Ben Stroud after this time.

When the chaplain came, he found Stroud civil and impersonal. After several visits, the minister asked the condemned man whether he wished spiritual consolation.

"I have never professed religion in any form," Stroud said. "Why make a farce of it at this late day?"

He wore out the hours staring at the gallows that loomed outside his window. He said that the sombre yellow structure rising from the grey slush of the bull pen began to look three stories high. He was determined that this would not be his legacy to his mother—to be dropped from its rope in that twisting, convulsive disgrace.

He paced and hungered for word from his mother. He knew that Elizabeth had gambled a final visit with him against the remote hope that she might win his life in Washington. If she failed, his body would be dissolving in lime before her return.

EIGHT

ELIZABETH STROUD had written to President Woodrow Wilson a 5,000-word petition for Executive Clemency. By letter, she had polled the jury of her son's last trial and had received five replies. Two were neutral, one opposed any change in verdict, and two expressed a willingness to change the verdict from death to life imprisonment.

She secured letters from the Alaska judge who was Robbie's first attorney and from the Alaska marshal who first placed him behind bars.

Painstakingly penned in her own handwriting after many drafts, her petition was a heartfelt and well-organized document. Building her plea around a conviction that her son was insane at the time of the killing, she quoted the testimony of psychiatrists from court transcripts and their private conversations with her. She stressed her husband's role in the early life of her son and contrasted this with the splendid service to the country of her distinguished family, dating from Civil War days, and the crushing disgrace it would suffer if her son were hanged.

> As a man of family you will be able to partially realize the humiliation and disgrace his large circle of relatives have suffered because of his offences against the law, and that in all these years the only grain of comfort I have ever been able to extract from the crushing disgrace felt by myself and other children was the knowledge he was not to blame, but was paying the penalty of his father's sins.
>
> I am his mother and am responsible for his being and am to blame for the father he had.
>
> Twice representatives of the Government came forward and confessed error and I've had to pay heavily for these errors.
>
> You have made a world-wide name as a humanitarian, Your Honour. I feel you will not ignore the plea of the most humble, heartbroken mother of this vast country of ours. I plead for the sake of myself and my innocent children to commute this death sentence to one of life imprisonment, and may God's choicest blessings rest on you and those dear to you.

Then she wrote a desperate note to the President's wife, Edith Bolling Wilson.

Dear Madam:

Pardon me for addressing you.

I have a son under sentence of death and am striving to have this sentence commuted to life imprisonment and have come on to Washington hoping to be able to present my sad case to the President for Executive Clemency.

Would I, a heartbroken mother, be asking too much of you, the first lady of the land, when I ask for a brief interview that I may state my case to you, who are nearer to our beloved President than any other?

If you will grant me this great privilege I shall be glad to call when it least interferes with your other duties and obligations.

A human life is at stake. Time is limited and I a distracted mother am pleading for help at your hands.

Your most humble and heartbroken well-wisher,

Mrs. E. J. Stroud.

In Washington, the tearful but determined mother was turned away by kind but equally firm secretaries. She came again and again. She pleaded, wept and begged for her son's life. Then, grasping at a wild hope, she found the secretary of J. Hamilton Lewis, the Illinois Senator. Her family's roots in Illinois were deep. Senator Lewis saw her and took her through to Joe Tumulty, the President's secretary.

"Joe," he boomed, "will you see if you can get this heartbroken woman a hearing?"

Mrs. Stroud then met Edith Bolling Wilson. Mrs. Wilson herself was busy shielding and nursing a shattered and broken man. The President, with the Nobel Peace Prize in his trembling hand, had seen his ultimate dream destroyed while he sat paralysed in his wheel-chair. The Senate's "wilful men", headed by Henry Cabot Lodge, had smashed his Treaty plans less than three weeks before. Edith Wilson would not permit Mrs. Stroud to see the stricken President. But she took the mother's desperate plea and the papers to him.

When Mrs. Wilson returned, she had the sentence of death in her hand. Across the face of the order was a great scrawl: "Commuted to life. W. W." Elizabeth Stroud saw the words glistening with ink still wet. It was April 15, 1920, eight days before the scheduled execution of Robert, her first-born son.

NINE

BACK BEHIND THE Leavenworth wall, the atmosphere had become more tense after the testing of the gallows. Convict resentment imperceptible to an outsider was felt by the guards—a subtle change in the inner climate of the place—the sum of a thousand tiny changes in the stirrings, subdued voices, the rhythm of the footfalls and a thousand stealthy sounds.

On Friday morning, April 16, Stroud rose from his bunk, suddenly wide awake, sensing an inexplicable change in the prison. He looked for the death-watch guard. His stool was there, but the guard was gone.

The guard's absence unnerved him. Unable to contain himself, he began to rap questioningly on the wash-basin pipe. The answering raps grew into a steady, rhythmic pounding, like the tolling of old broken bells. Gradually, they died away.

Stroud soon had news from the grapevine. The cell-tender had got it from a trusty, who had brought it to the Isolation Building with a bucket of soap, having heard it from another trusty around the sally port, who had overheard the gate guard deliver a telegram to the warden's office, where a clerk prisoner had overheard the warden phone his deputy.

The cell-tender swept along by Stroud's cell. Stroud was tense against the bars.

"What's up?"

"They commuted you."

"You sure?"

"Sure. The President commuted you. Warden's comin' over later with the news."

Stroud retreated to the end of his cell. His throat swelled and tears scalded his eyes.

When the warden arrived, accompanied by his deputy and a guard, Stroud had recovered himself. The warden pulled a yellow paper from his pocket and read Stroud his visa for living in a hard, nasal voice. Stroud showed no emotion as he thanked the warden.

"Don't thank me for doing my duty," the official told him. He peered in at the prisoner. "I have a hunch that you'll live to regret you ever heard this telegram."

Stroud met his eyes. "I heard about it already and was just thanking you for coming over."

"Your privileges are revoked as of now and you will remain here in deep lock."

"Yes, sir."

The warden walked off, followed by his party.

U.S. Marshal Wood, who had set up Stroud's appointment with the noose, remained sceptical. "My orders," he told the Press, "are to hang Stroud Friday. I know nothing about the order of clemency except what I read in the papers. If he is not going to be hanged, they'd better tell me about it before Friday." Marshal Wood soon received his wire, too.

Tested, ready and waiting inside the prison wall, the gaunt machine made to kill one man now stood abandoned. Its new yellow rope swayed idly in the April breeze. Along its beams perched the spring-returning birds of Kansas, and they soon limed and whitened it with their own living.

Later still, two thousand pairs of eyes watched the gallows razed to kindling. Stroud heard the cries of the startled birds and the shriek of the tearing wood. He shivered, and moved slowly to his barred window.

He watched his gallows go down.

BOOK TWO

TEN

"UNLESS OTHER PROVISION is made," Warden A. V. Anderson told the Press after President Wilson's commutation order, "Stroud will be kept in the segregated ward during his sentence, which is for life. He will never be permitted to associate with other prisoners. He will be allowed only the customary half-hour each day for exercise in the court. . . . He will not be permitted to see visitors other than members of his immediate family."

Behind the enormous stone façade of Leavenworth, past the great cell blocks, the Isolation Building huddled alone. On the first floor, the rear half of the structure held eighteen segregation cells, nine on each side. It was a prison within a prison.

Stroud's cell was twelve feet long and six feet wide, and the thick plaster walls were painted grey. At the rear was a small barred window. The door was of heavy steel bars covered by wire netting. There was a second door of solid wood which could be swung upon the steel door, shutting out light and air. In the cell stood a lavatory, washbasin and a narrow bed. From the high ceiling dangled a twenty-five-watt bulb.

The eighteen segregation cells were separated from the rest of the building by a barred, locked partition resembling a bank vault. Here sat a guard. Beyond the partition lay the large office of the deputy warden, a captain's office and a guard's room. On the floor above were the open cells of "trusties".

In this setting, Stroud faced indefinite solitude. Endless days, months, years, until he would become a grey, stuporous hulk; until his blood slowed and his breathing stopped.

During his four-year tilt with death, there had been visitors. The trials had provided interludes in the monotony and changes of scene. There was hope, despair and hope renewed: always some date, some blinking landmark in the sea of prison time. Now it was over. Stroud was changed from Number 8,154 to Number 17,431, legally dead, hated, feared, isolated and without privileges.

Oddly, Stroud was a man in debt as well: the recipient of his own life as a gift. He felt a need to justify the largesse, and he looked forward to the return of his mother from Washington.

Elizabeth Stroud had not unpacked her bags from her Washington trip when she read the warden's statement in the Kansas City *Star*. To her it carried a sinister meaning. She felt that her son, already teetering between madness and ill health, might well cross the line into both. At her insistence a conference was held in the late spring of 1920. Flanked by Stroud's attorneys, she met with the deputy warden and a representative from the office of the U.S. Attorney-General. The prisoner was brought from his cell to the deputy warden's office.

Elizabeth was determined to secure a transfer for her son to Atlanta Penitentiary. The attorneys were ready to take to court some of the internal ambiguities they had discovered in laws relating to treatment of prisoners.

Stroud, the prison officials maintained, was never held for any length of time in solitary confinement, but was, rather, placed in Isolation—"on the shelf", in prison parlance. He was sequestered for his own protection, they insisted. But the prospect of a legal tangle, with the redoubtable Elizabeth on the other side, did not appeal to harassed officials. A new President had been elected. Under the political spoils system of the day, government employees in the correctional field had no job security. They wanted things quiet. The best way was to keep Robert Stroud on the shelf.

The conference wore on for nearly an hour. Stroud had not been consulted, but he had been thinking.

"Can I have a word here?" he suddenly asked. The conferees looked at him, startled. "I'm not sure I want to be released from Isolation. I can stand being alone, if allowed to study and improve myself." Stroud's attorneys stared at him, open-mouthed.

"It is true that many men here hate me, especially the guards. But they all know me, good points and bad. If left here and given a chance I can overcome ill will. This is the best way to show the world I'm worthy of my life being spared."

His listeners were too surprised to speak. Mrs. Stroud rose.

"Robbie," she said softly, "I want to talk to you." She bowed slightly to the warden. "Please excuse us for a moment."

She hurried her son to a corner of the large room. "Robbie,

you don't know what you're saying! Men go crazy in solitary confinement."

"Mother, I've thought about this. If I'm released to the general prison, I become a cog in a machine. I can be framed there, easy—and if I raise a hand, I'm done for. Every guard on the make, every snitch looking for favours, I'm their meat."

"But, Robbie," she pleaded. "You should be transferred to Atlanta. You're not to be penned up alone. Mother knows best."

He was unmoved. "Atlanta would be the same. Turner came from Atlanta. Mother, in Isolation I will be able to figure out some way to help you. I know there must be a way. But there is no way outside of it. You don't have hope and you *don't have time.*"

"*Time?*" Elizabeth Stroud peered at her Robbie. Tears started down her iron face. He bent and kissed her warmly.

The compromise which followed proved the prisoner's notions to be less illogical than they seemed. Nor was this lost upon the deputy warden who ran the prison. Stroud had evinced a desire to make something of himself. The authorities granted a few concessions. Elizabeth was allowed to visit more often. Her son was allowed writing materials and such other privileges "as would permit him to occupy his mind". He was granted one hour daily in the open air instead of thirty minutes.

Stroud had learned some lessons well. He had done all kinds of time—from the lockstep to the gallows-wait. He sensed that liberty is a complex and relative thing. Everyone was in a prison of some kind. With characteristic resolution, he prepared to make the best of a bad bargain.

For four years, Elizabeth Stroud had borrowed, begged, written hundreds of letters, interviewed politicians, travelled, worked, cried and cajoled on behalf of her son. As a result, her son still lived.

Stroud felt the obligation keenly and wanted to pay her back. Two years earlier, he had received a box of water-colours, and with the help of an aged widow's correspondence lessons had learned to draw and paint. In order to do something for his mother, he must create something that might make money. What was easy to sell? Small cards. Seasonal cards.

During his mother's next visit, he asked her to get him some sheets of bristol board and a larger set of water-colours.

With these, his stolen razor blade, pencils and a ruler, he started to work, turning out Christmas and birthday cards. Some of them carried verse. Elizabeth soon sold a few among her friends.

Stroud went back again and again to the drawing lessons sent him by the sixty-year-old widow who had taught him art by post. Mrs. Grace Miriams of Trinidad, Colorado, had worked hard to help him as he waited for death. Stroud was to return this favour to Mrs. Miriams many years later.

He became impatient with the poor quality of his few brushes. One day he arranged to provide a guard with birthday cards in return for a request which had the guard laughing.

"I want a good fistful of hog bristles," Stroud said.

With these, the convict made brushes. He began to use oils.

Stroud's awareness of his own limitations as a painter drove him to copying. From this he learned a good deal about drawing. As autumn darkened into winter, he toiled on, working under a twenty-five-watt light. Soon his mother's apartment walls were covered with chromos depicting standard subjects—Cherry Blossoms, Indian Maidens, and copies of the Wolf on the Hill. From memory, he tried to paint a bowl of nasturtiums. The result was weird, and he seemed relieved when Elizabeth admired it and took it away.

Stroud was fascinated by a print of Queen Louise of Prussia. He worked long hours painting a reproduction in oils of the work. He made a good copy. This painting he later gave to Cora Peck Finney, a bird fancier. It was hung in the Sabetha Mary Cotton Library in Sabetha, Kansas.

Enforcedly a celibate, Stroud used his hard mind and resolute will to force himself through eye-wearying hours in his tedious card work. But Elizabeth, now entering her sixties, was unable to maintain herself by sewing and her son's painting. She received occasional aid from her son Marc. Marc wrote to his prisoner brother that he was always ready to help from a distance, but that he had his own life to lead since his marriage in 1922.

During one of Elizabeth's visits, her son received with a grim smile her ironical news. She had found a job, working for twelve dollars a week in a casket factory, where she sewed the satin linings that coffined the dead. With this and the help of her sons, Elizabeth supported herself and her daughter Mamie, a partial invalid.

Stroud left his mother on a note of hope, but in his cell, a small despair nibbled at him. He could not admit the futility of his card work, because there was nothing else. He had, at this time, no idea that his ability to draw would cause thousands of readers to study his sketches in another field. He only knew a need to find something. Unexpectedly, an event reshaped his solitude, adding to the fateful pattern of his life.

ELEVEN

EARLY IN THE afternoon of a June day in 1920, Stroud threw down his brush and stood away from his bed and drawing board, stretching and rubbing his eyes. All day the prison had been locked to stillness under an oppressive, humid heat. He waited impatiently for his exercise hour.

Adjoining the cells was a separate, cement-paved "bull pen" about forty feet wide and 120 feet long. It was shouldered in by walls: on one side by the high wall of Leavenworth, on two sides by a fifteen-foot siding of brick and on the remaining side by the Isolation Building. Prisoners were allowed to run, exercise and play handball.

The guard finally opened his cell door and walked the prisoner to the open pen. From there Stroud could see the top of one tree, the roof line and his individual slice of sky.

The sky had darkened and a small breeze whipped around the bull pen when a guard finally led Stroud into the open.

He looked with dismay at the lowering sky. A storm was on the way and he broke into a fast run to get as much exercise as possible. He played a game of hand-ball. Although it was Stroud *versus* Stroud, it became a spirited affair.

A light patter of rain started, and then he felt the sudden onslaught of a Kansas thunderstorm. The vast stone buildings of Leavenworth resonated the thunder like a giant drum and it rolled and crunched deafeningly around the walls of the bull pen.

Stroud retrieved his ball and dogtrotted to a corner of the yard where he watched, fascinated, as the oncoming storm drove in with increasing intensity.

Newspapers and broken branches tumbled over the great wall. The prisoner saw a large sparrow diving and fluttering and then whipped away by a gust of wind, only to return to a corner of the yard. He buttoned his grey denim tight and hunched over to the spot.

Near a fallen branch he detected slight movements. There in the corner were the shattered remnants of a nest. He saw four baby sparrows, obviously fledglings. They looked more like mice than birds. One was still, three were moving. Stooping, the prisoner stared at them. A sudden fist of wind pushed him over and he slipped, sprawling on his hands and knees. The cold, wet cement chilled his kneecaps. He looked at the sparrows, then quickly picked them up and placed them in his handkerchief.

Cupping the tiny birds in his two hands, he hurried through the pelting rain to the shelter of the doorway. Then he jumped back, startled. A large sparrow, twittering angrily, flapped against him.

"It's all right, Mother," he cried. "Your babies are adopted."

Back in his cell, he quickly placed a sock around the light bulb to warm it, and groped in the dusk for another to dry the forlorn baby birds. Then he placed them in the warm sock and brought them to his bed.

Watching the fledglings with a slight distaste, he wondered what had prompted him to bring them in. Several times over the years he had picked up birds which had fallen into the natural trap of the bull pen, but his only impulse had been to let them escape, and he had thrown them over the lowest-fifteen-foot wall.

It must have been his own feeling of cold wetness as he crouched on his hands and knees on the rain-pelted concrete of the yard. He remembered vaguely the stray dogs he kept bringing home as a child.

The storm settled into a steady rain. He bent over his bed to observe the nestlings. They looked inert and dead, like trapped mice.

When his evening tray was brought, Stroud fell to hungrily. Through the corner of his eye he caught a slight movement near his arm. All three baby sparrows were surging and straining with gaping beaks in their warm sock-nest, like a tiny chorus singing in inaudible song.

Stroud dipped pieces of bread in his lukewarm vegetable soup and dropped soggy crumbs into the babies' mouths.

He knew nothing about birds, but sensed from watching them that their requirements were immediate and swift. Whenever they opened their mouths, he filled them. This proved to be much more often than he anticipated. Later in the evening, to his amazement, he discovered that the bread he had set aside was nearly gone.

Anyone peering in then would have been surprised to see the convict crouched in a corner of his cell, a rag in his hand, his eyes fixed on a crack in the cement near the washbasin. Suddenly his hand swooped to the floor and a large cockroach was ground to bits inside the rag then dumped on to a piece of toilet paper. Within half an hour, Stroud had five or six cockroaches and a beetle. He mixed them with the remaining wet bread, grinding it into a mash of feed with his heel. The sparrows found it good. Later, Stroud was to write about the rich vitamin content of insects as bird fare.

Stroud did not know then that a bird must eat half its weight each day in order to live, but he did know next morning that the birds were making inroads on his breakfast. He improvised a nest from cardboard, toilet paper and cloth and fed them with a toothpick. Stroud began to observe them with increasing interest.

Two of the sparrows were hopping about, but the smallest one clawed helplessly with one foot. Stroud examined it carefully. Its leg was broken. Using a match and thread, he improvised a splint. The little bird recovered with amazing swiftness, but its broken leg remained shorter and bent. It became the prisoner's favourite.

"What in hell you doin' in there, Bob?" the muffled growl of a convict—call him Feto Gomez—came from the recesses of a cell twelve feet down the corridor.

The cell block was less than half-filled, and two of the inmates were in Hole Treatment, with the wooden doors closed. Another inmate was stuporous. Still another had conceived a hatred for Stroud and refused to speak to him.

"Hey, Bob, what you doin' in there? I heard you up all night there. What you doin'?"

Stroud thought for a while. He knew that Gomez wanted a pet. He had tried a cat several years before.

Stroud went to the cell door.

"Got a surprise for you, Feto," Stroud said. "When you hit the bull pen, check around. You're gonna be a father."

"Listen, con," rumbled Gomez. "Why smart off? Guard—Guard!"

The elderly guard left his chair at the end of the corridor and walked down to Feto's cell.

"What's wrong with Stroud, eh?" Feto asked.

"I don't know," said the guard, stretching lazily. "Was he ever right?" The guard walked over to Stroud's cell and peered in at him. "You all right in there?"

"Sure," Stroud said.

"Feto worries about you."

"Don't worry about me. I would appreciate one little thing, though."

The guard looked suspicious.

"Save all your food scraps from your lunch for me and Feto. We'll need them."

The guard looked in at him. "What for?"

Stroud had gone to the far end of his cell.

"What for?" repeated the guard, louder.

"These." Stroud held up to the wire netting a cardboard nest. Its ends were joined like a suitbox. Three wide-open mouths protruded.

The guard gaped. Then he smiled.

"O.K. I'll save 'em."

"This one is for Gomez," Stroud added. "Let him find it out." The guard nodded.

Another rumble came from Feto's cell.

"Stroud. What was that you said?"

"You follow me to the bull pen, don't you?" Stroud called out. "Just look around. It'll still be there when you get there!"

During his exercise period, Stroud picked up bits of grass and leaves which still littered the bull pen after the storm.

When the burly Gomez took his turn for exercise, he found a small white basket topped by two black eyes and one enormous mouth, which opened as soon as he made his presence known.

Later, Stroud heard Feto rapping for him.

"Stroud, why is the bird's mouth open all the time? Is it sick or something?"

"No, it's hungry, stupid. Keep putting food in it. Mash up some bugs and bread."

Stroud's sparrows were soon making experimental forays from the bed to the floor. In six weeks they were in full flight. He watched them with a growing wonder, mingled with occasional irritation when they splattered his art work.

Feto grew disgusted because Stroud had first chance in the bull pen. When Feto's turn came, he looked in vain for the occasional grasshoppers, crickets and butterflies which fell there.

Stroud's best sparrow he named Percy, after a Captain of the Guard for whom he entertained respect. The other was his tough little cripple. He named him Runt.

The prison librarian was startled one day by a request from Isolation for bird books. Stroud read everything he could find about birds.

Percy and Runt developed a fancy for the beetles which propagated in the wall cracks of the Isolation Building. Stroud would mix flies with bits of beetle in a small glass jar. Holding out morsels of beetle as a reward, he worked by the hour teaching tricks to his sparrows. It was a pleasurable diversion from the tedious hours of decorating cards.

One day in September Stroud talked to the guard, an old farmer who had lost his property. He was fascinated by the two convicts with their sparrow pets. It reminded him of better days when he was growing living things.

"Tell the deputy warden I'd like to see him if he'll step in some time," said Stroud.

The guard picked at his stubbled teeth, regarding Stroud.

"All right," he said. "Mr. Fletcher loves birds."

"I know," said Stroud.

Two days later his visitor came.

The deputy warden was a tall, thin man with an erect bearing. He wore authority with a natural air, and relaxed with his hobby, which was birds. He kept two warbler canaries.

"Hello, Stroud," Fletcher said, studying him through the door's wire mesh. "What is it?"

"Just a little something to show you, Warden," said the prisoner. "Want to come in?"

The deputy knew his man well. He regarded him with reserve, the memory of many events in his mind.

"All right. Open up, E. N.," he told the guard. Stroud's door swung open and the warden walked in, looking at Stroud intently.

The prisoner snapped his fingers. There was a tiny rush of wings, and two sparrows came from nowhere and perched upon his hand. They balanced well, jerking their little heads about. The smaller one looked comically crooked in its stance.

The deputy gasped. "Well," he said, smiling. "Where did you get those?"

"In the bull pen during a storm," Stroud said. "They were lost babies."

Stroud turned his head to one side and whistled. Both sparrows made a dive for his shirt pocket. They clung and fluttered there, pecking inside, and then flew away with small black objects in their bills.

"Why, that's—that's great," exclaimed the deputy staring into the cell shadows. "What did they get from your pocket?"

"Beetles," Stroud said casually.

"But where are the birds?"

"In their nest. Up there." Stroud pointed to a structure suspended high in the corner of his cell. He snapped his fingers again and the sparrows returned. He closed his fingers and they perched upon his wrist. Stroud grew slightly nervous as he tried his next and hardest trick.

He snapped the fingers of both hands twice, rapidly.

The small sparrow hopped immediately to Stroud's bed. The larger one appeared to hesitate, then followed. There in the middle of the bed, on which Stroud had spread a white handkerchief for better visibility, both sparrows lay still, on their backs, with their toes in the air.

The deputy broke into a roar of laughter.

"How in hell did you get them to play dead?" he asked.

"Well, Warden, it took time," Stroud said, relieved that his birds had performed and that the deputy liked them.

"I guess there is plenty of that," the deputy said. It was the oldest joke in prison. He chuckled. "Now there's a trick I'd give anything to teach my canaries. I haven't got time now but later I want to learn in detail how that was done. But I guess," he continued expansively, "you want to know whether you can keep the birds. Well, I see no harm in it. Go ahead." He turned to leave.

"Thanks, Warden," Stroud said quickly. "But I'm worried about their health. They need more than what I can save from the jail grub. I wouldn't ask for myself, but these jailbirds would appreciate some birdseed."

"Well, I'll say they deserve it." He laughed. "Yes, they could have it if I had any." He started out of the cell.

"Thank you," said Stroud. "I was confident you'd say that, so I've already had some sent here. It is now impounded at the storeroom and I would like an order from you permitting me to get it."

Fletcher stopped. His face grew red.

"I'll be damned," he exclaimed. He stalked out of the cell and turned around. He glared at Stroud, who was smiling. The sparrows now were standing on his shoulders. They stared at Fletcher with the side-eyed inquiry of birds. To the deputy it appeared that three people were watching him.

"You don't know whether you can have a bird at all," he growled, "yet you order birdseed in advance. . . . All right, you have my word. I'll requisition it."

Back in his office, Fletcher scrawled an order and sealed it in an envelope.

"Take this over right now," he told his trusty.

Later, a short, nervous storekeeper came to see Fletcher.

"Warden, this here O.K. for Inmate 17,431. I can't make it out. Looks like 'seeds'."

"It *is* seeds."

"*Seeds?*"

Fletcher's face reddened.

"*Bird*seeds, dammit! You impounded 'em. Look up your stock."

"Uh—*birdseeds?*" The storekeeper's mouth hung open. He looked at the deputy's face. He fled.

Before long, Feto Gomez secured official permission for birdseed, too. He based his request on the precedent set by Stroud. As the Kansas winter deepened, both convicts worked hard to keep their tiny charges in good health.

Gomez named his bird Pancho and he enjoyed watching and training his sparrow hour after hour.

The prisoners in Isolation listened with amusement to the troubles of the two men with their birds. Some of the banter angered Gomez. Stroud seemed impervious.

Late in January, Stroud was heartened by news that his mother had sold one of his paintings. During the Christmas season she had made a few extra dollars through the sale of cards. He redoubled his efforts, bending low over his table under the dim light of the twenty-five-watt bulb.

One early afternoon Percy and Runt were pecking at his abandoned meal tray. Guard Smith stopped by and peered in for the count. "How are the birds?"

"O.K.," said Stroud. "They're getting more restless with spring coming. The way they're jumping around today must mean a storm. It's dark enough."

"What do you mean, dark?" asked the guard.

Stroud blinked, trying to focus his eyes.

"What gives you the idea it's dark?" persisted Smith. "It's a fine day."

"You mean it isn't dark like before a storm?" Stroud asked.

The guard shook his head. "Nope."

Stroud turned away and stared a long time at the drawing table. He put his hand to his eyes then opened them and stared at the outmoded light bulb. The burning filament wrote itself across his eyes in its little twist that looked like the bottom of a safety-pin. When he turned away the burning loop remained in his eyes and, wherever he looked, it was there, with woolly darkness around it.

The following morning he asked to see the prison doctor. The doctor was a tired old man who had been a prison physician for many years. He knew Stroud well, having testified as a witness in his trials after treating him.

"Your eyes are very bad," the doctor said after a careful examination. "What've you been doing to them?"

"Painting greeting cards and chromos. I've got to go on with it."

Stroud's spirits sank as he watched the doctor shake his head. "Your eyes are no longer in condition for such work. The lighting in the cells is very poor."

"Can you write an order for a brighter light? Maybe a fifty-watt bulb?"

"I have no authority. You'll have to find other ways to occupy your time."

The convict stared at the worn eyeshade in his hands. The doctor shrugged and took the prisoner back to the locked waiting-room.

"Maybe things will change," he said, not unkindly. "Some new supplies are coming. Later we'll see about a new pair of glasses."

Elizabeth remarked during her next visit that she had

received fewer cards. Her son changed the subject. He said nothing about his eyes.

Spring was breathing delicately around the corners of these cold weeks: the frost was beginning to disappear from the rimed walls of the bull pen. Spring and better light gave Stroud new hope, and added to the enthusiasm of Feto Gomez as well.

Gomez, who had killed a guard years before, was subject to black moods of depression which used to assail him for days at a time. But the responsibility of his sparrow Pancho had changed him. His heavy black eyebrows would ride high over his huge broken nose in a vast satisfied contemplation as he watched by the hour the quick movements of his bird. He became friendly, especially to Stroud, and he leaned on him for advice. Prisoners unused to the cell block could scarcely tell whether Feto was talking to his bird, to himself or to Stroud. His heavy voice rumbled constantly.

Feto was permitted to attend religious services—a privilege Stroud had declined. Feto now showed increased interest in his Sunday respite. He wanted the priest to come and bless his bird. He had noticed that his sparrow seemed to prefer the warmer spots of his cell.

"Hey, Bob," he called one morning. "My bird is cold all the time. What's the matter, eh?"

"Don't know, Feto," returned Stroud thoughtfully. "What else does he do?"

"Well, I know he ain't sick because he eats more than he ever did. Now he's taken to holding on to the light cord close over the light."

"I don't know. Wish I knew more about birds. But if he likes it there, why not tie a loop or make it easy for him to stay there? Fix up a stick for a perch if you can get one. Or hang a cardboard box under it."

Several days later, Gomez called to Stroud, "Bob, he's sleepin' all the time with his feathers puffed out. All he does is sleep."

"Sounds to me like he's sick, Feto. What you can do for a sick sparrow, I don't know."

On the following Sunday, the chaplain answered Feto's plea. He came to see the prisoner for a brief time, and to please the importunate convict, he blessed the bird.

Whether it was Feto's imagination or heavenly intervention, Pancho seemed better for a day or two.

A new prisoner across the corridor heard Feto's talking to his bird in a crooning rumble.

"No bird could live on this lousy grub," the new man said. "Why don't you get him some worms?"

Feto's burly form hurled itself to the cell door.

"Where do I get worms, lazy con?" he said.

"Dig 'em out of the concrete," answered the prisoner.

Feto's roar of profanity echoed through the cell block. But he did prevail upon the guard to bring him some.

When the guard came to his cell next morning for the breakfast count, there was no movement in it. He saw the convict sitting on the floor with dazed eyes. In his hands he was cradling the sparrow. Pancho was dead.

"I've got the worms for you," said the guard.

Feto made no response.

The guard gave the worms to Stroud. The cell block was silent at the news of Feto's loss.

The muscle-bound, two-time killer was heartbroken. The uncouth black stubble on his battered face stayed wet with tears for days. He would not talk about his loss even to Stroud.

Several weeks later Gomez wrote a letter to his friend, a stenographer in Washington, D.C., who was on his approved correspondence list. He told her about the dead sparrow and she wrote to the warden asking for permission to send the convict a canary. She received a curt refusal.

The woman in Washington appealed to her bosom friend, the lifelong secretary of a senator, who dispatched a stiff letter to the warden.

In the meantime, another prison shake-up had taken place. When the letter arrived at the prison, it was opened, with surprise, by a new warden.

The senator's letter informed the warden that his attitude in refusing to permit a man serving a life sentence in solitary confinement the consolation of a canary bird was cruel and barbarous.

The new warden, William Biddle, made a hasty search for the correspondence and circumstances of his predecessor's problem. He had no desire to inherit what he considered unnecessary trouble.

He wrote to the ruffled senator. The senator was assured that the lifer could have all the canaries he wanted. The warden regretted this embarrassing situation—even though he, the new appointee, had not created it.

Thus no face was lost. The new warden was a politician, assuming charge of a Federal prison under the spoils system of the Harding régime.

TWELVE

"GOVERNMENT BY CRONY" had not spared the Federal prisons. A relative of the Attorney-General had been appointed as the new Superintendent of Prisons in Washington. He, in turn, ousted the capable warden of Atlanta Prison and replaced him with an Ohio politician.

But Atlanta's loss was Leavenworth's gain. The ousted warden, Fred Zerbst, was a capable penologist with thirty-three years of experience in prison work, many of them in Leavenworth. Warden Biddle made Zerbst his deputy, and turned over the operation of the prison to him.

Leavenworth's new warden, W. I. Biddle, was a former newspaperman. An able and experienced city editor, he believed in good public relations. He was not, however, unacquainted with prison work; he had been director of the state prison and had been a pioneer in creating a workable parole system.

These qualities of the versatile warden were unknown to Elizabeth Stroud as she frowningly scanned the headlines announcing his appointment. She knew him as city editor of the Leavenworth *Times*, and it was this paper which had led the state in its editorial demands for the speedy conviction and execution of her son.

Dismayed, she hurried to the prison. It was a hot Kansas July day.

Visits between the mother and son were held in the office of the deputy warden in the Isolation Building. After an affectionate kiss, Elizabeth Stroud looked at her son gravely.

"This warden business is terrible news," she told him. "Do you think he will make things worse for you?"

"Good afternoon, Mrs. Stroud," said a pleasant voice. A portly, amiable man had entered noiselessly. He wore pince-nez spectacles and a carefully cut grey moustache. Although he wore no jacket, he carried a cane.

"Please excuse my lack of jacket," he continued, seating himself. "I am the new warden here—and I assume you are worried about this son of yours."

"Well," said Mrs. Stroud carefully, "I . . ."

He interrupted her gently. "Let me assure you that if Robert co-operates, we will all get along extremely well. I want that made very clear to you," he said, looking at Stroud.

The word "co-operate" started a train of thought in the mind of the convict.

"You don't expect me to be a stool-pigeon, do you?" Stroud asked.

The warden's face tightened, but his tone remained cordial.

"No. Not that." He looked at Mrs. Stroud. "Your son rates as a dangerous prisoner, but recently his record has been good. It's important for my administration to keep it that way. From you, Mrs. Stroud," he smiled, "all I ask is that you leave my administration alone."

She smiled at him. "Why, Mr. Biddle, I'm no politician."

"You're modest, Mrs. Stroud. Some powerful men opposed you when you fought for your son's life. You're a good politician. That's why Robert's alive today. As warden of the largest Federal prison in the world, I want co-operation. We must have good public relations here."

"I would give a lot for a fifty-watt light," Stroud cut in suddenly.

The warden's courtly air did not change. He turned to his deputy warden, who was writing at his desk in the corner of the room. "Fred, what's the light in Stroud's cell—twenty-five watts?" The deputy nodded.

"Please order a seventy-five-watt light for Stroud's cell."

Stroud was surprised and shaken.

"Thanks," he whispered.

The warden nodded, picked up his cane and left. Elizabeth was watching her son's face as the guard came for him.

"What's wrong, Robbie? Aren't you feeling well?"

"I feel good, Mother." He kissed her and left.

Elizabeth shook her head. She could not understand Robbie's reaction to the promise of a light bulb.

The new warden was determined to make his prison the most respected bastille in the country.

One afternoon in July the key grated in the Isolation cell block's vaulted door. Warden Biddle peered in, nodded to the guard, and drew back. A well-dressed woman and two portly, red-faced men with wilted collars walked in. They looked apprehensive despite formal smiles.

"Even the most vicious heart responds to kindness," the warden was saying. "In these cells are some of the most dangerous men in the world. They are kept under lock and key at all times."

They were accompanied by the deputy warden, an orderly and an extra guard, an imposing cordon.

The entourage stopped at the cell of Feto Gomez. The heavy-browed convict was still despondent over the death of his sparrow, but had received word from his friend that permission had been granted for a canary, which was *en route*. He was back at work on his hand-illuminated mottoes. He looked up from his bed and stared at the guests, who peered through the cell door.

"Now Gomez here, and Stroud—down there, are both double killers. But they are returning our kindness in letting them occupy their minds and hands."

Gomez's large jaw dropped; he looked stupefied.

"Gomez here draws some very beautiful mottoes on fine paper, and then paints the large letters and borders. . . ."

Feto began to scowl. This was quickly noted by Biddle, who drew his visitors away and proceeded to Stroud's cell.

The warden turned to his visitors. "Do not fear: we always provide extra protection in cases of this kind." He signalled the guard and orderly, who stepped up to Stroud's cell.

The warden peered into the wire-netted door.

"How are you, Robert?" he called.

Stroud, who had been watching the proceedings carefully, came to the cell door.

"Fine, Warden," he answered cheerfully.

"I want these good people to see your art work and your birds. Do you mind?"

"No, sir," said Stroud.

"Open this door, please," said the warden to the Isolation guard.

The door swung open and the visitors involuntarily stepped back.

"Have no fear," said Biddle. To Stroud he said, "How is your mother? Has she been around recently?"

"She is very well, sir. She was up last week and we had a good visit."

"That's fine," the warden said. In an aside to the visitors he whispered, "Stroud has a very devoted mother. A wonderful woman!"

The visitors peered over the warden's shoulder into Stroud's cell.

"Robert is an accomplished musician and painter," he went on, "self-taught. He had only three years of education. See that mural painting on the wall? That is an oil painting of former Warden Morgan. Robert, may we see some of your cards?"

"Yes, sir." Stroud hastened to the rear of his cell. There was a sudden flutter and whir of wings. The lady drew back and started to run down the hall. The deputy brought her back.

"Don't blame you for being startled," Biddle said, chuckling. "Those sparrows perched back there are Robert's constant companions. How're the birds, Robert?"

"Fine, Warden. Want to see 'em perform?"

"Oh, yes," Biddle said.

Stroud handed his greeting cards to the warden, who passed them to the visitors.

"Are these for sale, Warden?" the woman asked.

"Indeed they are," Biddle said. "This boy draws them to help earn a little for his poor mother. Of course," Biddle added, "there's a regulation about selling anything in here, but I'm sure Robert will be glad to *give* you some." Both men glanced at each other and nodded. One of the visitors casually reached into his trousers pocket.

"All right, Robert," the warden said. "We're ready."

Stroud snapped his fingers. There was a sound of wings, and Percy settled on his shoulder, followed by Runt. The smaller bird immediately had the visitors laughing because of his crooked stance. Stroud put the birds through their tricks.

"Well," Biddle said finally, "we're late—must be running along. Thank you, Robert. Good work! By the way, do you smoke?"

"Yes, sir!"

"Here! My compliments. Don't forget to give your lovely mother my regards."

One of the men visitors handed the warden his cigarettes. "Give him these, too."

The cell door was locked and the delegation left. When they were at the door, Biddle turned back to Stroud's cell door.

"Do you see that I mean by co-operation, Stroud?" he said in a low tone.

"Yes, sir," said Stroud quickly. "Thank you very much, sir."

When they had gone, Stroud reached into one of the packets for a cigarette. His fingers encountered something papery and smooth. It was a five-dollar bill, rolled up. He stared at it and grew thoughtful.

The Isolation guard came back to Stroud's cell and opened the door.

"How about a smoke, Stroud?" he whispered.

"Sure." Stroud handed the guard one of his two packets. "Give some to Feto, will you?"

The guard nodded. "Got good news for you. You get extra time in the bull pen now."

It was a red-letter day for Stroud. He fondled his sparrows and fed them an extra portion of birdseed.

Shortly after, Gomez received the canaries. The sender had wisely chosen ordinary warblers noted for their hardiness. She had taken the warden at his word—"all the canaries he wants"—and had sent Feto three. They delighted the sentimental prisoner, and he tended them with lavish care.

One September afternoon Stroud stood still for a moment in the bull pen enjoying the weather. The sky wore an autumnal hue and seemed to wait, indefinably, for change. Stroud could see the red-and-yellow branch of a tall tree thrust up above the stone wall. He could smell, faintly, the aroma of burning leaves. The prisoner smiled. In the hush and the clarity of the atmosphere time seemed suspended.

He began to walk around the yard thoughtfully, then accelerated his pace as a fantastic idea took form in his mind. Why couldn't he raise canaries?

The precedent had already been set. True, they were pets, like his sparrows. But once he had them, if they were male and female. . . . His mother could sell them for many times the price of a Christmas card. The thought settled like a balm over the aching place in his heart that held his obligation to his mother.

In the 1921 depression outside every penny counted. His mother toiled in the casket factory, visiting him with unfailing regularity, trying in her spare moments to sell his work. He had now learned enough about drawing and painting to know the limits of his talent. What he was not yet aware of was the vast reservoir of ability which lay within him as a tireless worker in the field of science.

Stroud began to plan. How to acquire canaries? He could have his mother ask the warden's permission. But such an apparently easy way was fraught with psychological obstacles to the prisoner. To be allowed canaries as pets and then have them multiply, would have placed him in the position of taking advantage of a privilege. Such gains could easily be cancelled with corroding results to the spirit and endurance which enables a "hard-case" convict to survive.

After several weeks of patient planning, Stroud persuaded another prisoner to ask for a pair of canaries. This prisoner acquired two, but his nervous disposition was not adaptable to caring for them. Exasperated, he finally begged Stroud to take them off his hands.

Stroud casually agreed, and the guard turned the birds loose in his cell.

Stroud now had four male birds—two sparrows and two canaries. Inwardly excited, he watched his cocks by the hour and tended them like a father his four sons. He saw them through their moults, and mediated their fights like a referee.

He hastily made a small stock of greeting cards and then put his materials away and abandoned his drawing. From now on his time was to be taken up elsewhere.

The care and feeding of two sparrows had introduced many problems; the addition of two canaries more than doubled them. The simple physical wants, without the equipment available to the poorest citizen outside the prison, kept the prisoner busy. Food, water and disposal of waste were already a challenge to his ingenuity. To provide water, he improvised a stop for his washbowl. This became a temporary waterer and bath for his birds. A man of meticulous personal habits, he was forced to clean his basin before using it himself.

One day Stroud called to a guard who was passing by with a bottle of orange pop and his lunch. The guard was fond of the pop and would leave the empty bottle standing beside the soap box which he used as a lunch table.

On his way from exercise, Stroud noticed that the bottle was half full. It was a close, hot day.

"Say, can you spare that pop?" asked Stroud.

The guard was a temporary replacement for Guard Smith, who was on vacation. He was unsure of himself and was surly with the Isolation prisoners.

The guard regarded the prisoner coldly. It was too trifling a request, however, to refuse.

"Go ahead. Drink it if you're that thirsty," he said, shortly.

"How about me drinking it later?"

The guard hesitated. This meant losing the bottle for the refund. While he hesitated, Stroud murmured thanks, picked up the bottle and handed the guard three cigarettes, his back to the cell block.

"O.K.," grumbled the guard.

Back in his cell, Stroud poured out the liquid and went to work on the bottle. He found the hardest metal in his cell—the cell door lock—and carefully scratched the bottle against it until he had a straight groove in the glass two inches from the bottom. Later, over a tiny blaze, he heated the bottle, dropped water on the groove, snapping it off clean. The bottom became a small cup. The rough edge he rubbed against the stone floor until it was smooth. He filled the little cup with water for his birds.

The other end of the bottle formed a natural handle. He secreted this for later use. It became an efficient wood-scraper and the sharp contour of one jagged edge he later discovered would bore holes in wood, on the principle of a punch blade.

A week later the guard rapped on his door.

"How about my bottle?"

"It's in use. Want to see?"

A canary was drinking from the water cup, elevating its tiny head to let the water slide into its gullet.

"This is it," said Stroud. He picked up the smooth glass and brought it to the cell door. A sparrow flew after it, chirping.

"Well, look at that! How did you do that?"

Stroud explained.

"Well, goodbye bottle," the guard said, walking away.

Later he came by Stroud's cell door and unlocked it.

"Here are a couple more and a milk bottle, too," the guard said, gruffly. "Take 'em! This is my last day here."

"They won't forget it," said Stroud. He snapped his fingers and put his sparrows through their entire repertoire for the benefit of the guard.

From the bottles he made feed and water cups. When he had finished with the milk bottle, it was an efficient bird bath.

Stroud held a stubborn faith in his plans. Somewhere, somehow, he would acquire a hen. To contain it he would need a smaller cage than the cage which was his cell. How could he get a cage?

Stroud was allowed nothing of metal within his cell, not even a steel pen. Like most of the prisoners, however, he had managed to keep concealed a safety-razor blade.

The librarian-trusty at Leavenworth now scanned with irritation the repeated requests from the Isolation Building for anything and everything on birds. He located and sent Stroud a thin book which had escaped notice, an old text on care of pets. In it, Stroud found what he was looking for: a picture of a bird cage.

He read the text carefully.

"Today," the book said, "practical cages and appliances can be obtained ready-made or to order, and unless one is an adept at carpentering or cabinet-making, much time and expense is saved by placing one's orders with a cage-maker."

Stroud's birds must have fluttered at his harsh laugh. He remembered the wooden soap box the guard used as an improvised table for his lunch.

Casually, Stroud talked to the guard about the box.

They made a trade, and when Stroud returned from his exercise period, the box lay in his cell. Four packets of cigarettes had made it a costly transaction, by ordinary prison measure. But to Stroud the box held his hope, his future.

Determination hummed like a tireless motor inside of him. He lost no time in dismantling the box, working carefully until he had the nails loose. He pulled them out with his teeth and hid them. Each nail was handled like a jewel.

With pencil and a ruler, he began to draw diagrams of a bird cage. He worked hour after hour without rest, until he worked out a sketch that pleased him. Then he withdrew the razor blade from its hiding-place, a tiny slit in the stiff peak of his cap.

He studied the grain of the wood with meticulous care, and made calculations. Tense, but with infinite patience, he punctured the wood along the grain. It took him hours until a long thin piece of wood fell away from the board—a twenty-one-inch strip like a kite stick. He smoothed this by scraping it back and forth against a sharp spot on the steel support of his bed. He could not afford to blunt the razor blade as a scraper.

Two weeks went by—the fastest two weeks he had spent in eleven years in prison. In his drawing the sticks of the cage rose two-thirds of its height to a wooden cornice. Atop this, another tier of sticks rose the remaining third to a flat roof.

According to his drawing, the cage would require 128 separate bar-sticks, plus roof boards, floor platform, tier-bars, gate-pieces, and a roof handle. For this, he had a soap box, a ruler, a razor blade and his fingers.

He kept his materials concealed, and he hid the diagram and sketch of the cage between sheets of bristol board.

During this time, Feto Gomez had been busy with his three birds. The letter had told him that two of his birds were male, and one female.

"Bob, how come they don't sing more, hey?" queried Feto. "Only one sings."

Feto was afraid that one of the birds, which had been shivering a little, was becoming sick. He was more worried about this than the lack of song, but he did not want to reveal this. He made Stroud an offer.

"Birds *like* you, con," Feto said. "You want to take my bad bird—maybe you can make him sing? Maybe you can have him not for keeps but for a year, hey?"

"You worried about your bird, Feto?"

"He won't sing."

"You sure it's a cock?"

"Why not? The letter said it. He's the one with the grey under the green. How do you tell?"

"That's not so easy," Stroud said.

A sudden wild hope surged up in him. Did the sender make a mistake? Even experienced bird fanciers occasionally mistook sexes. Perhaps Feto's bird was sick—some communicable disease might be lurking in his cell—the same disease that killed the sparrow. Gomez was careless and less resolute than Stroud, who had never seen the canaries.

If the bird was sick, would it infect the others? Or was all this imagination? Were canary diseases communicable? He did not know. He felt helpless before his ignorance.

Feto rapped again, and Stroud hurried to his door.

"How about it, Bob—will you take him?" There was a pause.

"I'll take him," Stroud said.

Between their stints in the bull pen, the exchange was completed.

Stroud held the tiny bird lightly in his hands, and watched its fear gradually dissolve under the low tones of his voice. He released it after careful examination and turned to the sketchy descriptions in the canary chapter of his book on pets. While he was studying, there were sudden shrill notes from his canaries, a chattering of rage and alarm. Looking up in his cell, he saw his two male canaries engaged in the most vicious battle he had ever seen.

His new bird perched quietly.

On the basis of his notes and observations of the birds, Stroud was now sure. This was not a sick male canary. This was a fat little hen who was merely acting like a lady.

Feto had named the bird Jack.

"Welcome home, Jacky," Stroud murmured. Here was the first female, aside from his mother, he had known for thirteen years. He was captivated.

He was a man in his thirties, barred from his fellows, lost for ever from the rich and varied life outside. A man in a steel cage inside a stone prison, itself secured behind a mighty wall.

Ironically enough, this triple-caged man had willingly constructed yet another cage. And through cages, he crowded his solitude with the hottest and most amazing vitality on earth—that of living birds.

THIRTEEN

STROUD'S ATTENTION SHIFTED from Jacky to the scale drawing of his cage. He had started it weeks before on faith. Now he attacked the project with renewed vigour.

With his piece of broken bottle he scraped by the hour to smooth each slender stick. He built tiny fires from the shavings to harden the ends. He worked out a method of squaring them for joints. As he eyed his diminishing supply of wood, he spent days figuring out how he would make the cage-gate. Exhausted, he would lie back and relax, letting his eyes and mind dwell for comfort on his birds.

As autumn deepened into winter, an ominous quiet hovered over the Isolation Building. The prisoners began to sense trouble. The tension broke one day and news flashed through the grapevine. A pitched battle had broken out in the prison yard, short, quick and deadly. Captain Leonard was run through with a home-made cutlass. Another guard was virtually disembowelled and others were sent to the hospital with torn bodies. The convict with the cutlass was run down and killed on the spot. Hundreds of prisoners were jammed back into their cells and three were hurried into the Isolation Building. Huge wooden doors crunched shut on three cells, locking their occupants into Hole Solitary.

Some older convicts, including Stroud, were troubled and sorrowful about the death of the Captain—a rare feeling when tragedy befalls a guard. The convicts remembered the years of good food, carefully seasoned and well-served under the supervision of Leonard. He had received a deserved promotion, but his reward proved his misfortune. Word had gone around that the guard had not welcomed his elevation to the difficult post of Captain. He was literally promoted to his death.

"Leonard had no 'trouble sense'," Stroud wrote later. "His gift was more with good food than caged men. He lacked resource and resilience."

The tragedy was hushed up with remarkable speed, but it constituted an early blot on the new warden's administration.

Years later, Stroud inscribed the details of the story in a

prison history which officials still hold under lock and key. . . .

The sharp, stiff Kansas winter shaded toward spring. The prisoners watched with grey, winter-stunned faces, and waited for the change. Stroud's life, however, was veering far from the grooved routine. He was engaged in a desperate battle against time. His birds were beginning to chirp and sing with the urgent, unmistakable note that signals the approach of mating season.

He scraped and punched and cut during every unwatched minute. He now had more than a hundred of the 128 sticks required for the bars of his cage. He had the floor and ceiling nearly finished. He was carefully grooving out the slide bars of a cleverly constructed cage door.

There was no partial solution to his project. Unless the cage was complete, it was no good at all. He discovered he did not have enough wood. His razor blade had broken and even the pieces were dull. Tiny cuts from using the broken blade covered his hands. He watched for every chance to find new supplies.

Even the friendly guards, however, were nervous and hostile following the death of Captain Leonard. The prisoner across from him was now blocked into solitary by the wooden door. Feto Gomez refused to barter or dicker, or even tell whether he had a razor blade or wood. Surly and irritated, he blamed Stroud for the discovery that "Jack" was not a sick male, but a fit female, although he held to his bargain.

Desperate, Stroud remembered an old counterfeiter friend in cell block B. Mal was a "trader" who knew everybody and had matters much his own way. Stroud finally smuggled a note to Mal through the cell-tender.

One evening after the count bell, Stroud heard a rapping on the pipe. It came insistently, gently, between the murmurs of his birds: a "Notice" tap. It seemed to come from the "Trusty Hotel" on the floor above the Isolation cell block of the three-storied building. Stroud rapped back and waited. Soon he heard a faint sound outside his window. The screen had long been broken. Stroud took off his own improvised wicket, reached out and felt a string. He pulled, cautiously lifted in a foot of string and his fingers encountered wood. He out-ended a light thin bundle, edged it into his cell, and broke the string. There were the long sides of two boxes, the wood straight-grained and smooth; a dismantled cigar box carefully tied together, the nails pushed between the paper lining and the wood; and a rigid-backed, one-edge safety-razor blade. On one of the cigar-box pieces was a large pencilled letter M. The bundle had been constructed to clear the interstices of the window bars by a quarter of an inch.

Working fast, Stroud pulled off the cigar-box paper and dropped the precious pieces among his store.

The little hen Jacky was now giving unmistakable signs of her sex. Her slightest motion aroused the other birds to a frenzy of preening, swooping and fighting. Stroud acted as mediator and drove the sparrows, particularly, away from his canary hen. His plans called for baby canaries.

Stroud had long since made his birds finger tame, and he kept his little hen close by the head of his bed.

"You're the second female," he would say to her, "who ever slept in my bed." Jacky would ruffle her feathers and jiggle daintily on his finger.

Stroud named the two male canaries Ape and Petey. Ape was a full-bodied scrub canary warbler with yellow-green feathers. Petey was a mottled, mustard-coloured bird.

One morning Jacky flew to his finger. She had in her bill a yellow-green feather.

"Looks like Ape is making the grade," Stroud murmured to Jacky.

Returning from exercise period one afternoon he found Jacky perched on a ledge above his cell door. Near her, preening and strutting, was Ape. From his swelling throat came a song of triumph. The other birds were at the other end of his cell. If one of them tried to cross the line—there seemed to be an invisible line four feet into the cell from the ledge—he had to reckon with an angry bird. Ape had staked his claim, and won his mate.

Stroud, hardened convict, felt enriched and abashed as he watched Nature's imperious drama. Some part of him that had been starving was richly fed. He felt enormously protective as he paced up and down his cell, warm and blazing with new life himself.

The large sparrow, Percy, kept flying to the window and pecking at Stroud's improvised wicket—additional wooden bars for his cell. "Jailbird," he muttered. "Jailbirds. All right, Percy —go find yourself a mate," he told the bird. Removing the wicket, Stroud watched Percy fly away quickly over the north wall. He contemplated his canary, Petey, and the bandy-legged little sparrow, Runt. He snapped his fingers and Runt flew to his hand.

"Don't you want to go hunting, too?" he murmured as he released Runt through the window.

"You'll have to stay and suffer," Stroud told Petey as he fitted the wooden wicket back into place. "We'll have a young lady for you before summer's out."

The prisoner now set up his cage and hung it in broad view to one side of the window, away from draughts. In it he placed his feed and watering cups. He had forgotten to build an auxiliary perch. He put Jacky and Ape in the cage and then set to work to whittle a perch. He added a little nest pan fashioned of cardboard and wood and then placed within the hen's reach bits of dried grass, string, shavings and cloth.

"Go to it, folks," he commanded. "You're married."

"What you got in there, Stroud?" Feto's deep voice rumbled.

"Oh," Stroud said, "nothing that you can't make in a year."

Guard Smith stopped at Stroud's cell.

"I saw it as soon as you hung it up," Smith said, speaking low. "I got to report it, but not describe it," he added. "So I told the deputy warden you made a bird cage. He let it pass."

"Hope they let us alone for a couple more weeks," said Stroud.

The warden's public relations tours had ceased after the November riot. Now, with the prison loosening up again and running smoothly, the tours resumed. The Isolation cell block was not included, however, because of the prisoners in "the Hole". However necessary to prison discipline, the sight of closed wooden doors with living men behind them was not conducive to thoughts of rehabilitation in the minds of visitors.

This situation suited Stroud. He bustled around his cell, eyeing the mating canaries, pouncing upon insects for food, sifting birdseed, filling watering cups, studying his books, watching and waiting.

Whenever he rested, doubts assailed him. He felt helpless before the mountains of his ignorance. He worried about lack of sunlight, but felt there was nothing he could do about it. Then he wondered whether there should be "green food" for the mating pair. He secured a limp piece of lettuce from the guard and placed it in the cage.

He watched Jacky as she exhausted the supply of nesting materials. She had lined her nesting box with an intricate weave of string, grass and cloth.

Late one night, a week after the first mating, Stroud was awakened by a rustling sound. Jacky was restless and kept pecking at different bits of food in the cage. Ape was quiet. Stroud filled the empty watering cup and returned to his bed.

In the morning Jacky's look had changed, somehow. She was sitting on her nest, and when he put his finger in the cage she gave it a savage peck. Later he noticed Jacky, now off the nest, busy cracking seed. He looked in the nest and smiled.

There was one tiny, very pale blue egg with exquisite black markings on the round end. In a fever of excitement he uncovered his drawing materials and made a sketch of the nest with its single egg.

Each morning for five days, a new egg appeared. Jacky was restless in the night, and Stroud concluded that the eggs were draining her of minerals. He remembered, then, how wild birds had collected around a certain spot on the prison wall.

The guard in the watchtower was alerted later by the sight of a prisoner jumping and touching a white spot on the great wall side of the Isolation bull pen. To the guard, another prisoner had gone "stir-bugs".

Stroud was collecting a pocketful of salt crystals from the wall rock. When he placed these, with tiny pebbles, in Jacky's food cup, she ate them hungrily.

Thirteen days later, after an eternity of watching and worrying, Stroud noticed Jacky pecking at the bars of her cage. He opened the door and she flew out, closely followed by Ape. He watched them fly around in his cell and concluded they were enjoying some exercise. He went to the nest to look at the eggs. One of them was moving. Stroud blinked and rubbed his eyes and looked again. Almost imperceptibly the tiny egg was moving.

Peering closer, he saw a tiny hole punched through the blunt end of the shell. Then came another. Then two more. Stroud was later to learn what was taking place: the unborn bird was cutting its way out of its own egg with a sharp tooth growing from the outside of its bill—the egg tooth of the baby bird.

Suddenly the end of the egg fell off and the miniscule beak and head of the baby bird poked through. Exhausted, the baby lay panting.

Stroud grimaced. He had never, even in prison, seen anything uglier in his life. Mottled blue and pink, naked, soft, cramped, ungainly and blind, the nestling lay in a daze of exhaustion.

Later, a second egg moved and broke open. Then there was a rush of wings, and Jacky was brooding her nestlings. Fascinated, Stroud watched her throw out the egg shells.

Now Ape also fluttered into the cage. He had a fly in his beak. Jacky daintily received the fly and it disappeared into her gullet.

"Greedy little mother," Stroud scolded. But Jacky had ingested the fly and other food, only to regurgitate it. She nudged the hatched nestlings until their mouths opened, and pushed a milky, curdy bolus of food into their pink gullets.

Four days later there were five healthy nestlings and one unhatched egg. Some instinct told Stroud to leave this egg in the nest. It never hatched, but it served to protect the nestlings from the fretful activity of Jacky, who cleaned the nest, received food from Ape, foraged herself and brooded her ravenous progeny.

Stroud hovered over the cage like a paternal shadow, ready with all manner of food and material, much of which was of no use to his little family.

Feeding the five nestlings took an incredible amount of food and work on the part of Jacky, Ape and Stroud. The babies consumed more than their body weight daily. Jacky cracked seed and pushed it down their open gullets. She nudged and pecked among them to clean the nest, Ape flew back and forth, fought with Petey, and brought in crumbs and flies. Unbelievably, his little prison family thrived.

Elizabeth Stroud listened with amazement to her son's excited talk about his birds and the cage he had made.

The prisoner now had good reason to expect more than one nest from Jacky. She was most encouraging to her nestlings, and within two weeks, one by one, she nosed them out. Stroud watched her progeny become fledglings and by June they were fending for themselves.

Stroud looked at Petey, the bachelor.

"You'll have your pick of some girls yet," he promised.

FOURTEEN

WHEN WARDEN BIDDLE, his deputy and visitors got around to touring the Isolation Building, Stroud had completed a small carrying-cage of cardboard and wood and Jacky had laid four eggs in her second nest.

The entourage heard Feto Gomez's birds and stopped while the Isolation guard opened his cell. Manuel this time wore a wide grin and hopeful co-operation shone from his large face. He listened proudly while the warden explained the efforts of these dangerous Isolation prisoners to better themselves.

Warden Biddle left the visitors to his deputy and walked to Stroud's cell.

"How are you, Robert?"

"Just fine, Warden."

"That's good. How are the sparrows?"

"I let them go. They were males and got restless this spring."

"But I hear birds," Biddle said.

"They are canaries, sir."

The warden's eyes had accustomed themselves to the darker light as he peered through the wire mesh. What he saw made him jump back.

"What is that big thing hanging there?" he expostulated. "Is that a cage?"

"Yes, sir."

"Who in hell let you bring that in?"

"Nobody, sir. I made it—in here."

Biddle had a sudden vision of steel tools and other contraband. Flabbergasted, he glared in the direction of the deputy. "Well—I'll—I'll be back," he muttered.

He hurried his party on to other cells, where several of the prisoners displayed their handicraft work. The warden soon shepherded them from the Isolation cell block.

Stroud took deep breaths and paced up and down.

Later the warden and deputy returned. The warden went straight to the cage.

"Would you mind closing the cell door?" asked Stroud.

"Petey might escape." The warden nodded and the guard pulled the door shut.

The fledglings fluttered about Stroud's cell in alarm. Ape and Petey flew high to the window-end of the cell. The smaller birds skittered along the floor.

"Now, Robert," said Biddle, "who gave you this enormous cage?"

"Sir, I built the cage."

The smaller, wiry deputy exchanged glances with the guard.

"Let me see your tools—and tell me exactly where they came from. You know that knives will lose you your privileges."

Stroud's tall thin frame moved over to his washbasin. He picked up two broken pieces of razor blade. He lifted his mattress and brought up his scraper, made from the glass bottle.

"These are my tools, Warden," he said, simply. "And a small nail," he added.

The warden scrutinized the cage closely. He ran his hand along the wooden bars. He examined the joints and felt the roof. He spoke to Stroud but looked at the guard.

"Where did you get all that lumber?"

"From an old soap box."

"Guard Smith, did you give him the box?"

"No, sir," said Smith.

"Where did you get it, Robert?"

Stroud said nothing.

"One of the vacation replacements gave it to him," said the guard.

Biddle peered into the cage and lifted the door.

"That's Jacky," said Stroud.

The warden poked his finger at the bird, and jerked it back. Jacky had pecked it savagely.

"She's setting, Warden," said Stroud regretfully. He moved to the cage. The warden backed away. Stroud quickly lifted the hen from the nest. Jacky scolded him as he freed her.

"Incredible!" exclaimed Biddle. His grey head nearly touched the cage bars as he stared at three tiny eggs in the nest. Suddenly he smiled. "Unbelievable—but there it is—a cage with eggs in it, laid by a bird in a prison cell. I wish my visitors had seen this."

The guard exhaled with relief. The deputy relaxed.

"But, Robert, you can't have all these birds running loose in here."

Stroud spoke quickly. "I want to give some of them to my mother. She'll bring a cage. With your permission, I can take them to her when she visits." He reached under his bed and brought out the cardboard carrying-cage.

"Ah, yes—Mrs. Stroud—Mrs. Stroud," murmured the warden.

Suddenly Petey began to sing with the melodious burble of a male warbler. Ape, whose love life was too complete for arduous song, joined with an occasional note. The fledglings began an insistent cheep.

"We've had very little trouble in the Isolation cell block recently, Warden," said the deputy.

"Men don't make trouble when they have something they like to do," said Stroud. "Sir," he added quickly.

The warden straightened and looked at the thin, grey-faced convict.

"It looks like you want to be a family man," he said, and laughed.

Stroud's hand opened and he extended the broken pieces of razor blade. Nobody made a move to receive them.

"I'd like to build another cage," said Stroud.

"Don't abuse any privileges," said the deputy.

"Yes," said the warden quickly. "You are doing well, Robert. You co-operate and we'll get along fine."

"I always keep my word," Stroud said.

As they were leaving the cell block, the deputy warden eyed the guard severely. "Stroud has a very tough beard. He might need two razor blades to shave with."

"He might, at that, sir," rejoined the guard, straight-faced.

These events were not lost upon other prisoners. Word travelled fast throughout the great prison. Tensions eased. Stroud was Leavenworth's notorious hard case, a guard-killer. He was living on a commuted sentence, in solitary for life. Yet he had built a cage and filled it with singing birds. This gave hope to many other prisoners with less grim prospects.

This was an altogether different feeling from that of "getting ahead in prison" by becoming a "co-operator". It was not a matter of be-oming a trusty, stool-pigeon, or preacher. Every old-line con sensed that Stroud, for better or worse, was incapable of this adjustment, regarded by them as a form of spiritual death.

Prisoners who passed by the Isolation Building on a quiet, sunny morning could hear the pleasant warble of Stroud's canaries.

"Listen at them birds," some prisoner would exclaim, with a wondering smile. "It's that crazy bastard Stroud. Let's 'em love up and hatch out chicks right there in his cell. Had 'em growed before the warden knew it and the old man let it go."

In the Isolation cell block, Stroud became an information centre of advice on birds. Feto Gomez followed in the footsteps of his fellow prisoner, and his hen was soon hovering chicks before he could contrive a cage.

Creative enterprise had taken hold of many prisoners. The custodial authorities quietly slackened the reins. They did not openly encourage the activities or make the fervent announcements which, to prisoners, are the hallmark of "phony reform". Had this been done, the collective prison ego would have cast it off.

"The Isolation Department," Stroud later wrote, "which for years had been the hottest trouble spot in the prison, was transformed into the least troublesome." Through force of personality combined with their dangerous records, Stroud and Gomez exerted a calming influence on many isolation prisoners. Their profitable spare-time activities gave prisoners a stake to protect, and for each a privately tailored, individual hope.

The warden's public-relations tours became more frequent. He had that ability to mix brummagem with truth which is characteristic of good public relations. He soon discovered that the more dangerous he painted Gomez and Stroud, the more dramatic their "rehabilitation" seemed to visitors. The warden developed his tour to a point where timid women visitors, fearful for the warden's safety in Stroud's cell, would pull him away. The prisoner, in turn, would receive cigarettes and gifts. Stroud sold scores of birds, met many distinguished visitors and made several lifelong friendships, as a result of the prison tours.

Stroud may not have realized that "the act" was double-edged. It added to an enduring legend of himself as a Jekyll-Hyde criminal at the same time as it credited him for excellent use of his time with birds.

Stroud watched his birds come again into breeding condition. The male canaries' song took on a hard, ringing quality. As time passed, Stroud separated his males and females in different cages.

He studied them carefully—birds confined with others of their own sex, and anxious to mate. The canaries reacted like imprisoned men. Stroud loved to open the breeding cages and let nature take its hot, avian course.

The bird prisoner wrote his observations, later incorporated into his bird book. Of the fit canary males, he said:

"When caged with other males, he will try to make love to them. Fights follow the repulsing of his advances. He often masturbates, using any convenient object for his purpose, even the finger of his owner."

He wrote of the hens, that their breeding condition is indicated by their loud, ringing calls, ceaseless activity and energetic efforts toward nest-building. "When caged together, female canaries make use of each other in the gratification of their sexual desires, sometimes piling up four high. There is less serious fighting among the females . . . but usually more actual damage is done by them, since they are interested in nesting material and have no compunction about using the feathers of other birds. . . ."

He noted a parallel between jailbirds, avian and human. Long before he had seen a canary, he had watched the merciless yaffling of young prisoners by older ones, by cajolery or at knife-point. He had seen the wolves and the lambs, the pathetic and fantastic "marriages" between prisoners.

Most convicts were no more homosexual than his canaries. An instinct greater than themselves flowed and broke around them in a thousand guises. Stroud may have wondered as he watched his canaries how men could be reformed or improved by a system which twists and debases their most vital instinct.

The bird and pet proclivities of the convicts produced a more friendly relationship with the guards. It has long been known that policemen and guards incline toward cultivating flowers and pets as a way of "getting unwound" from the tension of the big house. In the Isolation cell block, the guards became covertly helpful. They would give food scraps from their lunches, pieces of wood, string and other materials to the prisoners. It was a friendly guard who gave Stroud pieces of liver and wood glue on which he cultured his first experimental smear of bird-disease germs.

In the years which followed, Stroud constructed scores of bird cages. Made at first of wood, the cages later had bars of wire as the birdman's privileges were extended. The cage roofs he made from large tin cans supplied from the prison kitchen.

Elizabeth Stroud proudly carried out of the prison four healthy warblers in a cardboard cage improvised by her son. She took the birds directly to a pet shop in order to purchase a cage. When the owner heard the mother's story, he immediately offered to buy them, offering her credit to buy the cage for the next lot.

Back in the bull pen, Stroud's exercise routine changed.

He jogged around the pen, eyes alert for any living thing that moved. Watchtower guards amusedly watched a tall, round-shouldered man chasing stray grasshoppers with deadly concentration and flailing at butterflies with his cap.

One afternoon a tiny shadow streaked through the air and fluttering wings braked to a stop. A decrepit little sparrow found his wrist and perched upon it.

"Runt!" Stroud exclaimed. Thrilled, he extracted a dead fly from his pocket and fed the game-legged bird. "Who but you'd ever come back here?" He took the sparrow to his cell, where Runt engaged in an exploratory battle with Petey, and then perched contentedly in its old spot on the ceiling radiator pipe. Stroud regarded Runt as a lifer like himself.

Jacky's second nest yielded only two nestlings from a five-egg clutch. The perplexed convict renewed his hunt for information. As the nestlings grew, they looked ungainly. Their little beaks and legs appeared too long. They were weak, and their feathers grew in scraggy patches. Jacky, too, seemed to have lost her brimming vitality. Stroud concluded that the one element his birds—in fact, all the birds kept by prisoners—lacked was sunlight.

He built a smaller cage. Then when his turn came in the prison yard and it was sunny, he simply took his canaries with him and set the cage in the sunniest spot in the yard. The guard looked, but said nothing. No such behaviour had ever taken place in a prison, and there were no rules for it, pro or con. Where his birds were concerned, Stroud had learned to move between interstices of rules.

His birds improved with the sunlight treatment. He did not know why, until later. Then he wrote the following:

". . . all young, growing creatures need large amounts of [sunlight] and it does not matter a bit whether they wear fur, feathers or diapers. . . ."

During the following year, 1925, Stroud raised fifty-three canaries. Gomez followed with a few. Mrs. Stroud sold them all.

She also subscribed to a canary magazine for her son. He was allowed to receive it on condition that the magazine became the eventual property of the prison library. By the time the magazine cleared Isolation, however, it was worn, underlined and dog-eared beyond recognition. Soon they remained with Stroud. Nor did the editor of this magazine, the *Roller Canary Journal*, dream that every issue was read word for word by a convict in Leavenworth with hardly any formal education and who was eventually to become his leading contributor.

Stroud had been unaware that there were periodicals devoted exclusively to the care and breeding of canaries. He had seen only two books on pets which contained chapters on bird breeding. He also located a Government bulletin on canary diet, which later was to cause difficulty for a new Isolation guard.

FIFTEEN

THE NEW Isolation guard became worried about Stroud and Gomez during the following spring. Whenever he spoke to the two prisoners, they merely nodded in response. Their mouths kept moving, but they said nothing whatever. Yet, as he watched them covertly, they did not seem to be eating, because he could not discern that they swallowed anything. Their chewing was secretive and strange.

The guard took an irregular step. He went to see the prison doctor.

"Doc," he said, fidgeting, "is there a kind of stir-simple where cons won't talk and keep doing the same thing over and over?"

"Why—yes," said the doctor. "Sounds a little like the stereotyped behaviour associated with schizophrenia."

"Well," the old guard returned sagely, "Stroud and Gomez is both off their rocker. Would you maybe take a look at 'em?"

The doctor glanced up at the unusual request. He had not visited the Isolation cell block for some time, however, and he was intrigued by the guard's description.

"Does Stroud still have his birds?"

"Both of 'em have birds."

"Well, that's strange. Yes, I'll go over with you—unofficially, you understand."

They tiptoed to Feto's cell and looked in. The big convict was looking abstractedly at the wall. His huge jaws were moving and grinding constantly. It looked as though he were eating. The doctor watched patiently, waiting in vain for him to swallow.

The guard looked at the doctor. They moved to Stroud's cell.

Stroud was facing the window. His birds were singing. When the guard peered in they churred with alarm.

Stroud turned around, blinking. His jaws were working away. He nodded and went on chewing. He had not seen the doctor.

"How are you, Stroud?" said the doctor suddenly.

The convict started at the sound of the doctor's voice.

"Fine," he said thickly, from a full mouth.

In the meantime the deputy had received word that the doctor was in the Isolation cell block and had hurried in. He joined the doctor and the guard. They all stared into Stroud's cell.

"What's the matter, Stroud—aren't you feeling well?" pursued the doctor.

Stroud removed from his mouth a rag with a lumpful of material in it, placed it carefully on his table and hurried to the door.

"I feel fine," he said clearly, facing the group. Then he added suspiciously, "What's wrong?"

"That's what we wanted to know. Are you sure you and Gomez are feeling all right? Getting enough to eat?"

"No less than usual, sir," Stroud said.

"Well," said the doctor, "if you're sick or have a toothache—I'll try to help you."

"I'm not sick," Stroud said. "I feel all right."

The guard grew exasperated.

"I seen you and Feto moving your jaws all day long, don't seem to swallow nothin', don't talk. Like prison simps."

Stroud reddened. It was the first time they had seen him at a loss.

"Ask Feto," Stroud said.

The deputy's voice cut in suddenly. "We're asking you, Stroud."

"All right." Stroud picked up a bound booklet and brought it forward.

"We're just following instructions of a Government bulletin on canaries," he said, in a forced, off-handed tone.

His interrogators were dumbfounded.

"What are you talking about?" asked the doctor gently.

"Well," said Stroud, "some of our baby birds are weak. We're hand feeding 'em. You have to chew up the food yourself—masticate it," he said sharply, feeling better as he got off the word, "then we give it to the birds like the mother hen does."

The deputy, disgusted, looked at the sheepish guard. The doctor smiled.

The guard spoke up. "Why didn't you tell me what you was doing?"

Stroud looked at him, unmoving. "You didn't ask me."

"Think we wanted this to get around?" Feto's voice rumbled

out. "Ain't there no privacy here? Now we get the laugh from every con in the joint."

The deputy's eyes lifted heavenward.

"Everybody is crazy around here," he said. With a quick glance at the guard, he stalked off. The doctor joined him. Feto's deep voice kept rolling in an undertone about no privacy in the joint.

As the guard opened his mouth to say something to Stroud, a high, thin voice from one of the cells sang out. "Hello, hello, Mother Gomez? Won't you please *feed me*?"

Gomez roared out a series of biologically impossible instructions which he admonished the prisoner with the high voice to perform forthwith.

Oddly, the expected ribbing was not repeated. The report of two tough convicts under life sentences for murder chewing up bird food and assisting tired mother hens by feeding their babies ten times a day caused comment. But the reaction was one of disbelief.

Although both prisoners experimented with many mixtures, they were unable to hand-feed with success. They even chewed rape seed, "which does not appeal to the human palate, in fact, becomes nauseating when it is chewed ten times every day. . . ."

Stroud's persistence at hand-feeding caused him to discover a simple answer.

"The difficulty," he wrote, "was to be able to tell what ill effects were due to the food itself and what were due to the method of giving the food."

He found that the metabolism of nestlings is so high and hot that cold food retards their development.

Later he used a chemist's watch glass on a piece of heated asbestos from which he toothpicked hot food into the open mouths of his more forlorn nestlings. His babies prospered.

Living in a small barred room with a tame sparrow and a score of warbling canaries, Stroud was forging obligations and responsibilities that kept him busy day and night. He fed his birds, talked to them, built cages for them and studied their habits. He made a schedule and within the bounds of his tiny empire, he rose, washed, ate, worked, exercised, rested, studied, read and slept like a citizen of the world outside. Since he was excluded from people, his people were his birds. Birds were his family, wife, children and afternoon matinée.

Hours sped away on the wings of birds. He had the shortest distance from avian theory to avian life of any bird breeder in the world. He need only look up from his book and snap his fingers, in order to place his hands upon a living bird.

Examining his birds with sensitive fingers, he verified, detail bv detail, their external parts. Where others took for granted the amazing thing known as a feather, Stroud studied the intricate structure of feathers—the million-pointed hooklets of the barbicels and their assembly into barbules; nature's ingenuity in constructing an effective airfoil. When his birds moulted in August, he watched the process as though it were a drama.

He asked permission to get a hand-glass, and was thrilled by new horizons looming before his tired eyes. He put his new glass on Runt's game leg and compared it with the good one of that surprised sparrow.

Stroud began to apply his two outstanding characteristics, often associated with genius: an accurate memory, amounting to almost total visual recall; and limitless patience.

The more he discovered about birds, the more absorbed he became. With the prisoner's fascination for something which can fly away, he investigated these hot-blooded wonders of the skies until he could name their parts and features in his sleep.

Around him, other lifers were sinking slowly into vacant-eyed stupor. But Stroud became deeply engrossed in the cycle of mating, birth, childhood, courtship, parenthood, sickness and death in the short, quick life-spans of his canaries. He was witness to some tiny drama each day.

Beginning as a prisoner seeking a way to improve himself and help support his mother, Stroud was gradually being transformed into another man—a man with an overwhelming passion to know, and to know why.

Each day brought new problems, unanswered questions. Why did sunlight eliminate the ungainliness of his baby birds? What had killed Manuel's pet sparrow? Why and how did birds moult their feathers? What was the structure of birds that enabled them to fly—and thereby capture the fancy of every prisoner since the beginning of rooms with bars?

When one of his nervous warblers somehow broke both a wing and a leg, Stroud was forced to release the sufferer from its misery. This was an opportunity to learn how to dissect a bird. Carefully, he made incisions into the tiny body with his razor blade. One by one, he freed the organs from their fascia and laid them neatly on white drawing paper. His best instruments were his only ones—long, sensitive fingers with sharp, uncut fingernails. Stroud verified the internal organs from anatomy drawings in his books, and wrote his observations. He could not have known how these drawings would prove of help later.

A steady procession of biology books now passed from the prison library to Stroud's cell. He read avidly all chemistry, physiology and zoology he could find.

As his knowledge increased, he found himself growing indignant whenever he discovered mis-statements in the bird journals.

He shook his head dolefully when he saw a round cage recommended in a bird book. Caged himself for fourteen years, he sensed rather than reasoned a truism. Years later, grown grey in a cage, he wrote:

"I want to go on record against that very popular and very stupid abomination, the round canary cage. That a bird is able to live in one of these contraptions says a great deal for his adaptibility. . . . Birds like corners for the same reasons that you like them; they give a sense of protection. This may be a throwback to the time when both of us crawled out of the sea and hid under a rock, but it is so very real that a large proportion of humanity would go mad if compelled to live in round rooms."

When the time came for Stroud to return his beloved Jacky to Gomez, he made a proposition. He told Feto that Jacky, now an old bird with many nests to her credit, might give him trouble. Would Feto want Jacky back, or would he like to have a new bird, one of Stroud's best warbler hens? Stroud extolled the virtues of the bird. Gomez grumbled assent, and the deal was consummated between exercise periods in the bull pen.

One day early in the following spring, Stroud found a baby sparrow in the yard. He placed it in a nest box for Jacky. She hopped around the baby inquiringly, cast a pert eye at Stroud, and quickly hovered over it. The nestling lay exhausted.

The heat of Jacky's bosom, however, was insistent. After a while the baby moved a little. Jacky would nudge it gently. It soon opened its mouth, took food, and eventually grew into a lusty fledgling.

Stroud was gleaning valuable information from the *Roller Canary Journal*. He began to write letters, raising questions and carrying on discussions in the letter columns. Why, he asked, were many canaries born dead? Why did sparrows grow white wings in captivity?

In this manner, Stroud made the acquaintance of Cora May Finney, who conducted bird contests, and of Howard and Nola Fogg, editors of the *Canary Journal*—national figures in the world of the canary breeder. Through letters, Stroud was entering a realm of people as passionately absorbed in birds as he was. Perhaps for the first time in his adult life, he could feel kinship with a group other than prisoners.

His correspondence privileges were extended. Although as yet unaware of the extensive bird literature in England and Germany, he was surprised by the hit-or-miss methods recommended for treatment of canary ailments in American journals.

From the Kansas City bird breeder who bought warblers from his mother came several books and Government bulletins which Stroud was permitted to keep in his cell. When conditions were right and no complaints came from other prisoners, Stroud would sometimes read aloud to Gomez from the bird books.

One afternoon Stroud chuckled and called to Feto.

"Want to hear from a new book?"

"Sure," Feto said.

" 'The best room for canaries,' it says here, 'is a well-lighted spare room where windows can remain open from May until October.' "

"That so?" Gomez said.

" 'And which does not get intensely cold and dull during an ordinary winter.' Got it?"

"You know what I got—same as you," Gomez said.

" 'Now the bird room is preferably not less than nine feet wide and at least fourteen to eighteen feet long, for one needs room to move comfortably in such a place for many obvious reasons.' "

"He don't say!"

" 'Dampness'," pursued Stroud, " 'and a tendency to mould should be avoided at all costs.' Got that?"

"How's about a man moulding?"

"Now here it says, 'It is very important that the roof does not leak.' "

"We got a chance, Bob," shouted Feto. "Our roof sure don't leak!"

"For nesting material, the book says 'white cow hair and long moss. The nest box should be lined with felt, or swans'-down lining.' " Gomez's rubbery lips exploded in a wet noise.

"He means can paper, don't he?"

"Now as to mating, he says, 'In March the pairs can be put together, when possibly a little harmless quarrelling may occur.' "

"Ain't that somethin', Bob, huh? Whoever heard of a harmless quarrel in here? Are them birds gettin' ideas from the—what's that word with iron in it?"

"Environment."

"Yeah. From that."

"Now it says, 'Experienced breeders, even old hands, have paired up two cocks in the spring due to a silent male or some other mistake.' "

"Guy must've been a warden," Gomez rumbled.

Stroud slapped the book shut. "Now we know what the good book says, you can go back to your birds."

One of Stroud's books recommended sawdust over sand for sprinkling on the floors of bird cages. He sent out a call over the grapevine for some sawdust. Two days later the cell tender looked up from his mop and whispered there was something for Stroud in the bull pen, pressed into a crack in the wall near the Isolation door. When Stroud found it, he put it into his pocket. It was a tobacco packet full of sawdust. Back in his cell, the prisoner sprinkled the small amount disgustedly over the floor of one cage. The bottom of the sack crackled faintly. He shook out a note. "This stuff is three years old," the note said. "It's from your galoos.—M." Stroud learned that Mal had traded it from a disgusted guard. The guard had held it for a souvenir of Stroud's once-pending execution, years before.

SIXTEEN

THAT SPRING OF 1926 Stroud gleaned bits of valuable information from the occasional asides of visitors. In common with other astute inmates, he watched events carefully inside Leavenworth and the politics outside which affected affairs behind the walls. He knew that the whims of prison officials, on the spot or remote, could make a prisoner's life intolerable.

Stroud was familiar with Thomas Mott Osborne's crusade to improve prison conditions. Later he wrote about Osborne's attempt to introduce self-government among prisoners, and he described the failure of a similar attempt locally in 1919 which he termed "the Sovietizing of Fort Leavenworth Military Prison".

In 1925, prison reformers of the Osborne Society nosed into Leavenworth, only to receive a cold stare from the political appointees who manned the Federal system. Turned from Leavenworth after a perfunctory tour, the Osborne penologists issued a sizzling report. They termed Leavenworth the most overcrowded prison in the country, housing 3,000 convicts in a plant whose capacity was 1,640. They condemned conditions in Federal prisons, and criticized the attitude and policy of a prison system kept under the jurisdiction of the Attorney-General, the prosecutor arm of the Government. Making one of the most far-reaching recommendations in modern penology, they recommended that Federal prisons be placed under the Department of the Interior.

Persistent reports of corruption combined with noisome scandals in Atlanta prison to build up pressure in Washington.

Eventually this pressure led to a complete reorganization of the Federal prison system and the establishment of a new bureau. It was to enter fatefully into the life of Robert Stroud, its most amazing prisoner.

Meanwhile, however, Warden Biddle used his political know-how and publicity sense to the limit, holding fast to his crowded bastille. Late in 1926 there was a muffled political explosion. The prison doctor resigned and a chief clerk committed suicide.

Stroud, hearing grapevine rumours about a new acting warden, tensely awaited signs of change. Although prisoners wield more power than is realized, it is of a negative kind. Prisoners are forced to trade what they can learn and what trouble they can cause, for the small dispensations which can spell survival.

Warden Biddle had not forgotten the good record of his prisoners in Isolation. One afternoon, Stroud had visitors.

Warden Biddle still commanded the prison, but in name only. The new warden was due for formal appointment in a few days. These men, together with the deputy and another official, stopped at Stroud's cell.

"Hello, Robert. Are you in there? All I can see and hear is birds." Stroud hastened forward. Warden Biddle's appearance had changed. He looked flabby and, although he still carried his gold-topped cane, his jaunty air seemed forced, and his eyes haunted.

"Robert, I want to thank you for sending me that nice warbler for Christmas. Everything going all right here?"

"Fine, sir," said Stroud. He looked at the new warden, who stood off to one side, flanked by his deputy.

"I am glad," Biddle resumed, "that Mr. White has decided to continue my policy for Isolation. This used to be the Number One trouble spot, but we've had practically no difficulty here for years. I think you're chiefly responsible, Robert. There isn't a single black mark on your record as I go out of here and I hope you'll keep it that way." He wiped his forehead and drew closer.

"You gave me my chance, sir," Stroud said.

"Let me see your sparrow, Robert," said Mr. Biddle, in a low voice, "this is my last round."

Stroud snapped his fingers and Runt swooped upon his wrist. Biddle smiled.

"Goodbye, Robert," Warden Biddle said.

"What are you going to do now, sir?" interposed the prisoner suddenly.

"Back to the newspaper business," Biddle smiled. "Hungry for the smell of it. Write me some time, so I can keep tabs on you. And"—he laughed half-heartedly—"don't believe everything you hear."

The officials left. Stroud turned to his birds. Nobody escaped the prison's embrace; it was merely a question of how it got you.

The prison, however, proved fortunate in its new warden, T. B. White, who assumed formal control in March, 1927. A meticulously groomed, spectacled, businesslike man, he did not look like the former officer of the Texas Rangers he had been. A courageous man facing impossible prison conditions, Warden White knew that the idleness rife in Leavenworth was the most vicious spectre a warden faces.

Warden White continued to encourage individual enterprise among his charges, and he left the activities of the Isolation cell block alone. As a result, Stroud's delicately balanced card-house of privileges was allowed to stand; he was allowed more time in the bull pen—frequently an entire afternoon.

The early spring found Stroud cheerfully planning for an all-out breeding season. His health had wavered several times but he had found one cause in the prison food. The men confined in Isolation were fed the same food as more active prisoners who worked in yard and shop—sedentary persons fed a labourer's diet. Isolation prisoners were allowed to purchase small amounts of fruit and vegetables. Stroud had learned the virtues of Seidlitz powders, supplied by the hospital.

For his birds, Stroud had now acquired several antiseptics: dilute carbolic acid, iodine, cresolis and a small amount of potassium permanganate. Two small, battered white-enamelled hospital pans had drifted into his hands. He had a thermometer and a supply of soap. He had a scrubbing brush and some small bottles. For nesting pans, he had acquired a dozen strawberry boxes sent his way from the kitchen after a banquet for prison officials held the previous summer.

The attitude of the new warden had put his mind at ease. White had met Elizabeth Stroud and commended her for her co-operation. The previous year's receipts from the sale of her son's canaries were $235.00.

Stroud's six-foot-wide cell was lined solid with cages and equipment. He had calculated to a nicety every available inch of space in his narrow, high-ceilinged room, itself blocked like a bird cage. He had perfected his cage-making technique and had invented a non-sag suspension device which he considered patentable. From the cages came the cheerful sound of 125 chirping, chittering, churring warblers.

He had several empty cages to spare. He counted them, and chuckled. Counting was such an important part of prison routine—the morning count, after-meal counts, all run by the mechanics of bells and whistles, like some odd combination of a walled factory and a primary school—that the prisoner felt relief in having something to count himself. Stroud went over his lively little prisoners one by one. He scrutinized their feathers and their droppings, and watered them.

In a hastily improvised place of honour was a small cage containing two imported pedigreed warblers given his mother by a sympathetic Kansas City banker. He had never seen birds of this quality before. They were a deep, rich yellow and he admired their regular grey-green wing markings and their smooth texture which distinguished them from the others. The male sang constantly. His song had been hard and ringing. Now it was lower and softer. When the hen trilled, it seemed to the prisoner that her notes were lower, too.

Stroud watched these birds uneasily. They seemed peculiarly nervous. He was inclined to put this down to some possible higher vitality of pedigreed birds reacting to new quarters. The hen appeared closer to breeding condition than his other birds. The male held his wings away from his body and, between songs, seemed to pant a little.

Stroud filled their feeding cups. Both birds had excellent appetites.

He decided to give them exercise and opened the cage door. The male immediately flew ceilingward, and there met the monarch of the radiator pipes, the sparrow Runt. The two males, after some chippering and scolding, engaged in a brief tussle. The warbler retired in a huff and flew to Jacky's cage, where he clung to the side to catch her attention. He perched near her and preened. Jacky watched him with the unruffled dignity of a dowager.

When Stroud returned the new warblers to their cage, both were panting heavily.

His male birds, fed upon the prisoner's special mixture which included rape seed, were rounding into breeding condition. It was a grey, blustery day and Stroud debated whether it would be worth-while to move his birds to the bull pen at noon. They would have, if not a sunning, at least an airing.

After a morning of hard work, he carried his birds to the yard. To expedite this operation, he placed twice the accustomed number of birds in one of his two large cages. He included his two pedigreed warblers.

Several days later his pedigreed warblers began to mate.

They were far ahead of his other birds. Observing them closely, he could not get over his uneasy feeling about them. They were lively enough. At the same time, their song was softer, gentler.

Then he noticed their droppings on the cage floor. They were ochre-coloured, looking as though squeezed from a tube of paint. Birds vent their waste products in a combined form, a white paste from the kidneys and blacker faeces from their bowels. Stroud had never seen droppings like these before.

Frowning, he leafed through his books. What he read made him jump as though he had grasped a live wire. Under "Diseases" he had found:

> Most dreaded among breeders is a highly contagious disease . . . sometimes called septic fever. Its actual existence can only be surmised and determined by immediate post-mortem by a veterinary surgeon trained in bird disease. Death may be rapid or delayed. The faeces are abnormal and the main diagnostic sign is a distinctive dropping, always ochre in colour . . . *There is no practical remedy*. . . .

Stroud's hands shook as he opened the door of the large cage. The imported birds were still in it; he had been unable to transfer them to their small cage because of visitors. He moved them quickly, placing their cage as far from the others as his cell permitted. Then he washed and scrubbed his hands. He returned to the large cage and cleaned it. He found a few ochre-coloured droppings and assumed they came from the imports.

He remembered the male warbler's fight with Runt. He called the sparrow and placed him alone in a cage. The second large cage of birds was moved to a corner. Jacky was put in a cage by herself.

The walls of the crowded cell never seemed closer. Stroud braced his shoulders and tried to think. . . .

Using carbolic acid and soap, he methodically scrubbed and cleaned every inch of the cell. As he worked, a premonition of disaster took hold of him. His evening meal lay untouched and he stayed awake far into the night.

Gomez and another prisoner called out to inquire into the unusual activity they sensed. He gave them short, noncommittal answers.

During the night he inspected the birds again. The imports looked and acted the same. There were no changes in the others, except for one. A thin warbler in his large cage was sitting with puffed-out feathers, head turned back, sleeping. Stroud noticed that its breathing was shallow and rapid. He took the bird from its cage and placed it in a smaller one. The bird looked frightened; it was so hot it stung his hand. He was later to discover that a clinical thermometer whose top reading was 113° F. did not record the fever peak of this disease.

The little bird would not eat or drink. Its abdomen was enlarged and looked black between the feathers. Even as he watched, the bird began to shake. The shaking increased and it panted desperately for air. Suddenly it fell to the floor of the cage and went into convulsions. After a spurt of droppings, the bird lay still. The droppings were now a bright, savage green. He detected a faint, not unpleasant odour.

Stroud crouched on his hands and knees, his face a mask of horror. The prison lay quiet in the deepening March cold. He could hear the faint hiss of a radiator pipe over the muffled sleep sounds of his birds.

Bright green was to become the colour of death to the harassed convict. Whatever it was, this dread disease, the imported birds must have been loaded with it. He wrapped the dead bird in paper, washed his hands, turned out the light and lay staring for hours.

He could not call in a veterinarian. If the disease was incurable, as the book stated, it would do no good anyhow. He could not remove his birds to other quarters. There were no other quarters. He dared not complain to the prison officials: it might end the enterprise which held all his hopes.

Helpless, himself caged, he waited for the next lethal blow from an assassin he could not see, feel or even define.

Next morning he arose red-eyed, dreading for the first time in his life to look at his birds. The imported birds seemed lively as ever. Then he noticed that the hen's bill was open as though she were singing, but there was no sound.

Stroud wrote a series of urgent letters to bird journals, to the Government Printing Office and to his brother Marc.

Then, his face set like a rock, he opened the paper containing the dead bird and pulled off its feathers and started to dissect it.

The bird's abdomen was distended, the skin drum-tight. The organs of a healthy bird can be seen through the transparent skin of the abdomen. The prisoner saw nothing under the skin of this bird but a cloudy black mass. He cut open the abdomen and recoiled. The swollen liver of the bird leaped out at him.

Instead of the smooth, greyish red of the healthy avian organ, it was five times normal size, blue-black in colour. There were bumps the size of hobnails on it, resembling a huge, rotten mulberry.

Hours later, he placed serous fluid from the abdomen of the bird in a small bottle, and begged the guard to send it to the hospital laboratory. And always, he kept washing his hands.

For the first time in his life, Stroud lost all thought of self.

Two days later the imported hen laid an egg. Stroud was astounded. There was something obscene about it. It was as though this tainted pair, in this atmosphere of hovering and suspenseful death that they had created, were acting out a little play. They might continue to live and breed long after his flock was a writhing mass of death.

Runt was unused to cages. Stroud was forced to release the bird lest he kill himself smashing against the cage spokes. Since Runt was a sparrow, he might escape the infection. Yet, flying around the cell, he might contaminate the other birds. But Stroud could not bring himself to kill Runt, nor to turn the bird out, a source of infection.

Runt almost seemed aware of the problem. He stayed on his perch.

The report came back from Stroud's hospital contact. "We find *Bacillus pasteurella* in large quantity. Condition of white blood cells indicates other poisons, possibly a filterable virus. No other indication. Statements made are guarded. We are not familiar with bird bac."

Stroud flew to his books. *Bacillus pasteurella* was the germ associated with fowl cholera. He dug further for descriptions of that disease. It sounded vaguely like the "septic fever" in canaries.

Stroud closed the books and studied his birds.

The worry and suspense began to unnerve him. He was now convinced that the swift death of his one casualty was not the regular form of this disease, but a galloping type which had consumed one of his weakest birds. He marvelled at the intensity of the fight for life of these small, hot-blooded creatures.

As the days dragged on, he counted them from the time of the initial contact. His imported hen had now laid three eggs. Now she began to sit.

The ochre droppings began to appear in his large cage.

During the fourteenth night Stroud's fitful sleep was interrupted by a commotion. Three birds were dying in convulsions on the cage floor. He wrapped the birds in paper, cleaned the cage, and noticed that seven others were fluffing their feathers. He saw large, lumpy swellings on their heads and separated them from the rest.

Next day, the guard handed him a package, without comment. It was from his brother. Marc had sent it with a covering letter to the warden. The package contained more than a dozen bird remedies in liquid, powder and capsule form. Some had their ingredients listed, some did not. They included citro-carbonate, potassium chlorate and hydrogen peroxide. There was also a book from England on canary breeding.

Stroud now knew that others were aware of the disease among his birds. Even the warden must have known, to allow this extraordinary privilege, this package. Potassium chlorate was an explosive chemical, and the prisoner could see that the bird remedies had been unopened. He breathed thanks for the trust exhibited in him.

Nervously, he snapped his fingers as he tried to assemble some plan of attack. There was a fluttering above, and Runt came down. Stroud had forgotten about the bird. The sparrow's flight was erratic. He missed Stroud's wrist and had to hop up to it from the bed.

Stroud watched his pet sparrow with sinking heart. Runt was very, very old. The game-legged, tough little bird was panting, his feathers fluffed out. Gently Stroud placed Runt on his favourite low perch, a stick tied to a pipe underneath his wash-bowl. Later in the day he heard a small sound. The old sparrow had fallen from his perch. He stood swaying and panting. Suddenly Runt pushed out one wing and fluttered in a small merry-go-round of convulsive death. When he stopped, lifeless, there was the fatal green sign on the floor.

In all probability, the only factor which saved the prisoner's mind then was responsibility. Sick or not, his remaining birds had to be fed, watered, cleaned.

Gaunt-eyed and desperate, he leafed through the English book, which described as "septic fever" an entirely different disease. But Stroud saw one sentence which clung to his attention. A brief mention was made of potassium permanganate as a swift cure for lesions and sores.

During the next weeks his birds sickened and died at the rate of three to five a day. His imported birds died before their young could hatch.

Convicts and guards in Isolation became aware of Stroud's tragic battle as it deepened. Gomez grew profane about "the joint".

Prisoners offered food and the guard ran out of rules to stretch for Stroud. The convicts hid their feelings. "How come they let him have them in the first place?" exclaimed a prisoner wrathfully. "The joint is stinking with them lousy birds. Now they're dying. Anything would die in this hole."

The prisoner's grotesque situation became more complicated with another development. His birds began to mate, nest and sit. He did not have space or equipment to control them. New life and lingering death lived side by side in his crowded cell.

A peculiar change came over Stroud. He described it later in his monumental *Digest of Bird Diseases*:

> Years of work, of study, of careful observation; the lives of literally thousands of birds, the disappointments and heartbreaks of hundreds of blasted hopes have gone into these pages; almost every line is spattered with sweat and blood. For every truth I have outlined to you, I have blundered my way through a hundred errors. I have killed birds when it was almost as hard as killing one's children. Birds died in my hand when their death brought me greater sadness than that I have ever felt over the passing of a member of my own species. And I have dedicated my book to the proposition that fewer birds shall suffer and die because their diseases are not understood.

The weeks of suspense and torment nearly broke his heart. When he saw the agony through which his birds were driven by the disease, he killed them, using the most humane method he knew: quick pressure on the back of the skull with the thumbnail.

Then Stroud changed. The fierce observer in him rose over his anguish and moved beyond love or pity. Instead of killing his dying birds, he used them in an effort to save the rest. "No bacteriologist or doctor would ever have tried the things I tried. . . ."

Out of the fire which consumed the prisoner, phoenix-like, a scientist was born. . . .

He began a series of experiments. He fed his birds concentrated salt solutions and killed them. He cut the solution in half, and killed them.

He broke up match-heads, made a sulphur solution, fed it to the birds, and killed them.

He packed their sores in serial progression with every chemical he had. And they shuddered and died.

Jacky had weathered the omnipresent disease, but suddenly she also developed bumps and lesions on her head, and the ochre-coloured droppings began to show in her cage. Stroud cut open the bumps and packed them with potassium permanganate.

At the same time, he remembered that a certain solution of potassium chlorate had reduced the bounding temperature of a sick bird. The bird had died, but he had noted the change. Dissection revealed less disease damage in the liver and spleen.

When Jacky showed a slight improvement after the permanganate application, Stroud administered a more dilute solution of potassium chlorate into her watering cup. In the afternoon of the same day he added one grain of citrocarbonate.

She had reached the stage of the disease where convulsions and death were imminent. Stroud marvelled at the strength of Jacky's resistance. Tensely, he watched as her fever dropped. He dared not let emotion enter the portals of his experiment.

Next day, when she should have been dead, Jacky was hopping about her cage merrily. Still not daring to hope, he continued the treatment and began it on three other birds.

Thirty-six hours later two remained alive. Jacky had lost all symptoms of the disease.

Stroud concluded that certain chemicals, known as oxidizing salts, when buffered by effervescing acids in the stomach of the bird, somehow killed the disease. The age-old problem was posed: how to kill the disease without killing its victim.

He found that birds had difficulty ingesting the potassium chlorate. He now tried another oxidizing salt found in one of the bird remedies his brother had sent—sodium perborate.

And with the use of this chemical, internally injurious to man, but not to hot-blooded birds, Stroud discovered the long-sought-for internal avian antiseptic.

All strength and emotion drained from him, he fell upon his bed and slept. The birds went unfed, unwatered, untreated.

The following day Stroud was awakened by pounding on his door. The warden, his deputy and the guard stood outside his cell door.

"What's wrong, Stroud?" the warden said. "Are you sick? If so, why don't you say so? The guard tells me you've passed up five trays now."

The prisoner kept shaking his head, still not fully awake.

"No, sir—just tired out . . . but I feel all right."

"Good . . . Stroud, we've been keeping close tab on this bird operation. I haven't said anything and, if you recall, I bent a rule or two for you. But this disease trouble is dangerous. Getting out of hand. There have been dead birds, pieces of birds, all kinds of waste coming out of here for weeks. We don't like it." He shook his head. "I know what you're going through."

Stroud opened his mouth, but the warden went on, "Or maybe I don't—but in any case this is a prison, not a bird hospital. I'm afraid we may have to make some changes."

His words brought Stroud wide awake. But there was serenity on his stubbled face.

"It was very bad," Stroud said.

"What do you mean *was*, Stroud? I'm talking about right now."

"It's over, sir. I found a cure. It worked. A dozen birds have already recovered and if—if"—he hesitated, then plunged on—"if there is a single sick bird in here after four days, I will go back to painting. But it's whatever you say, sir . . ."

The warden studied the blinking, smiling birdman, turned to his deputy and conferred. Then he took a long look at the tiers of cages. After all, he had inherited this operation from two former wardens. If he now removed his birds, what would happen in Isolation? The prisoners had done their part. Stroud in particular had performed prodigies of work. It wasn't his fault if a disease struck his birds. Maybe he *had* found a cure.

"All right, Stroud. We will forget it, not for four days, but for four weeks." He looked at the deputy warden, who nodded.

Stroud held his breath until they were gone. He was glad they had not come sooner.

SEVENTEEN

SEVERAL MORE BIRDS had fallen ill. He placed all the birds which showed the slightest symptoms in one cage and treated them, watching until he was certain they were taking the medicine, perborate in the morning and the "citro" in the afternoon. He then cleaned, disinfected and reorganized his entire cell. He freed Jacky from her cage and petted her fondly.

Over a period of many months, he outlined a series of experiments and studies. He had discovered the cure, but not the cause, of the mysterious disease. His researches ultimately led the prisoner, who had no microscope, into bacteriology. Using wood glue and liver scraps from the guard's lunch, he made scores of cultures from his birds.

Through his mother, he ordered pure sodium perborate, citrocarbonate and other effervescent salines. Eventually he discovered that by treating the external lesions of his diseased birds with permanganate, watering them with the oxidizing solution in the morning and flushing them with his laxative salts in the afternoon, he could cure most birds within thirty-six hours.

"We won't have many new birds for a while," he told his mother, "but we can catch up later."

He was astonished at the persistence of the disease. He could cure the birds, but he seemed unable to stamp out the sources of infection. He washed all his equipment daily in strong solutions; buried all bird droppings in a box containing chloride of lime; and scrubbed his cell from top to bottom with disinfectant, covering every square inch where a bird had so much as rubbed its head.

One morning Stroud found he himself could scarcely breathe. He was taken to the prison doctor, who informed him that he had inhaled so much disinfectant that he had an infusion in both lungs. This forced the prisoner back to soap and water. He discovered that two vigorous scrubbings provided the answer.

The informal connections which Stroud had achieved with the prison laboratory proved helpful. Politely sceptical of the prisoner's claim of a cure, the technicians believed that the disease had simply run its course, but they studied slides of his cultures under the microscope.

His pursuit of the disease germ over the following two years, despite other events, was to result in a spectacular identification of the cause of "septic fever".

"Septic fever," Stroud discovered, "was a name to cover ignorance. The disease was caused by a filterable virus, invisible to the microscope. This dreadful poison so weakened the bird that other bacteria, secondary invaders, finished him off." He showed that the disease was identical with avian diphtheria in other birds and poultry. He staked out three distinct types of this bird scourge, the bronchial form, pox form and external diphtheric form, and described the symptoms, course, and method of treatment for each. This line of research was later to produce a second brilliant discovery. Stroud knew he was camping on the trail of "the hydra-headed chameleon of all bird diseases".

Now Stroud, who had been driven to distraction locked in a cell with dying birds, astounded the warden with a request for permission to buy diseased birds. He wanted "culls"—discarded canaries sold by jobbers for a quarter apiece. He wished to isolate and control bird diseases. The warden granted permission. Stroud set up a rigid rule of three weeks' quarantine for every new bird. The incubation period of the fever was fourteen days. Stroud knew that any recurrence of an uncontrolled "epizootic", as he termed a bird epidemic, might well end his career as an imprisoned bird scientist. But he had never hesitated to take a chance. Stroud, the lifer, had found his life's work. He was thirty-eight years old. He had spent nineteen years in prison and twelve years in solitary.

Stroud now worked eighteen hours a day. He would douse himself with cold water while the prison slept, and perform the morning chores of a farm-hand in an area of seventy-two square feet. After feeding and watering 300 birds, he would clean their cages, examine each canary with meticulous care for mites, fever, swellings, feather problems, egg trouble and diet deficiency. He would carefully dissect birds which died, and draw what he saw. He made detailed notes.

Using the morning bucket of hot water from the cell-tender, he would bathe some birds by hand, lathering them with a shaving brush and swathing them in handkerchiefs.

At exercise time on sunny days, he would transfer every cage of his twittering songsters to the bull pen, where he would arrange them along the wall for the noonday sun. Then he would cultivate greens growing in flat boxes.

In the afternoon he would hand-print laborious answers to his growing correspondence with bird-breeders. His correspondence privileges were increased and he received new bird journals. Absorbing bird lore, physical sciences, pathology and dietetics, he behaved like a celled monk pursuing some hidden alchemy. Without any social obligations, required to do a minimum of dressing and undressing, eating alone from a tray and shaving once a week, he became the only man in the world who spent twenty-four hours a day with his birds. Pleased officials allowed him to have extension cords and brighter lights.

Throughout the evenings and on into the night, guards going off shift grew accustomed to the tiny square of yellow light which shone in the north end of the Isolation Building.

"We don't know when he sleeps," exclaimed a watch-tower guard, going off shift. While other prisoners sank into a sea of stupor, the lean Stroud could not find enough time for his activities. He was approaching his prime of life, making a future of a futureless existence.

Stroud secured permission to write articles for bird journals. An informal but binding agreement was religiously observed between the warden and the prisoner. Stroud was allowed to write and to conduct his affairs, provided he conceal his identity as a prisoner. He was not to draw sympathy to himself, nor attempt to exploit his privileges by agitating for his freedom. The humane pact was observed for years. Under the noncommittal address of Post Office Box 7, Leavenworth, Kansas, the prisoner gradually became known to hundreds of bird-lovers throughout the country.

One day, the mail clerk came to his cell.

"Stroud, these letters are terrible. We can't read 'em. Your writing gets worse all the time. Can't you print any more? We're going crazy in there making out what you put down."

Stroud looked at his tired fingers, cramped by laborious handwriting in answer to scores of letters.

"I write a lot, answering all these letters. If I had a typewriter, you'd have a cinch out there. It would save hours. A man can go blind reading such stuff. I know. I nearly went blind myself."

"But you haven't got a typewriter, so why bring that up?"

"I was just thinking. If you explain the difficulty to the warden after I tell him, maybe he'll let me do something."

A month later Stroud was asking the library for a book on typing. In his cell was a battered Remington. In two months he was typing answers, and keeping well ahead of his increasing correspondence.

Stroud's articles about canary care and treatment were accepted and printed. They increased his correspondence and all inquiries received quick answers. Whether the request came from a casual bird-lover or a master breeder whose aviary held thousands of birds, Stroud answered them all. He rarely asked any return favour except further information when he saw a chance to learn.

As time went on hundreds of bird breeders reported their success with Stroud's advice to their local bird clubs. Thus many clubs became aware of a strange "bird doctor" whom no one had ever seen or visited. Bird showings, conventions and bird fairs were held, but the man so many of them knew by correspondence was never present.

Stroud was not unaffected by his new outlook. Each letter he wrote forged a tiny link in a new kinship. The cement which held together the "Grey Brotherhood" was hatred—hatred of the world which immured them. But Stroud's second loyalty was held together by love—the love of birds. Curiously, Stroud was to retain this twin loyalty throughout his life.

In 1928, convinced he had found a way to benefit his fellowmen and pay his debt to society, Stroud pounded out his first petition for Executive Clemency, and addressed it to President Calvin Coolidge. Incapable of the repentance customary in such pleas, Stroud based his appeal on the question: "Would or would not your petitioner make a useful and honourable citizen if restored to society?"

He then outlined his life and his triumph over obstacles in a solitary cell, and climaxed it by relating his discovery of a cure for septic fever in birds.

"The force of desperation worked ideas that any medical man would have pronounced absurd," he wrote. "They were tried without hope, or probably more correctly with the hope of the hopeless, akin to that of the shipwrecked swimmer in mid-ocean with no help in sight."

He stated that his mother was "near seventy and still forced to earn her living as a factory hand", and that this was due not to his incompetence, but to the limitation of his environment. "The prison officials with unfailing kindness have tried to make those limitations as small as possible, but they, too, have restrictions to face . . . what I want is a chance to develop my business interests, follow up my scientific interests and discharge my natural obligations in life. If I get that, I shall not resent any restrictions thought necessary."

The prisoner had little reason to expect Presidential notice, and there is no indication that he was shocked when President Coolidge did not choose to comply.

Another incident gave a glimmer of hope to both Stroud and his fellow bird-lover, Gomez. During the Presidential campaign of 1928, several officials from the Department of Justice visited them, remarked upon their changed deportment for eight years, and marvelled at their birds. According to Stroud, one of the officials, a woman, expressed a hope that when the new President was elected, she might be placed in a position to recognize their merit and reward it. But when the campaign was over and the election proved successful, the official did not receive the post.

One day Stroud eagerly uncovered the cage of a new arrival he had long awaited—his first trained, pure-bred roller canary. Sent him by a grateful California bird breeder, the bird was described as "a perfect tutor of direct St. Andreasburg stock".

Stroud peered at the canary and was disappointed. The thin, mottled little male was a plain specimen, far removed from the bright warblers Stroud knew. No sound was forthcoming, although it hopped about and seemed healthy enough.

Stroud hung up the cage and leafed through bird books for information. The late afternoon sun was fading when Stroud listened to a song he had never heard before. It lifted over the warbling of his canaries with a long melodious roll like the rippling of unseen waters, on and on—until the prisoner's skin tightened with suspense. Then the tone broke into a shower of what the breeders called "bells"—the tolling intervals of the roller's music pattern. The bird began anew and sustained its song through four musical phrases. Even Stroud's birds seemed abashed before the concert of the scrubby little roller, which echoed with a tiny resonance through the corridors of the Isolation cell block. A plaintive, nostalgic quality in its evening song brought a catch to the throats of hardened inmates. It was an enthralling experience for Stroud. This was a night-singing roller, trained to pour out its heart at sundown.

"What in hell you got in there, Stroud?" called out Feto with a reverence his words did not conceal.

"I got a roller canary, Feto, a real one."

"How could a bird learn all them sounds?"

"Two centuries of breeding and careful training."

"No bird could be that old," Gomez scoffed.

"I mean he comes from a long line of birds that sing, from Germany. This canary has been trained to sing from the time he wobbled out of his egg. Now he's going to breed me some and teach them too."

"Whadda you mean, teach 'em?"

Stroud explained that the roller canary with a good song is actually placed in a tiny cage by himself, surrounded by his pupils, young birds who imprint upon their vocal patterns the musical "tours" of the master. On the cell block, the little singer became known as "Prof".

Soon Stroud was raising rollers. A newspaperman from the St. Louis *Post-Dispatch* visited Stroud's cell.

"There were a half-dozen canaries in separate cages grouped around the singing teacher, who was alone in another cage. This veteran was teaching the young birds to sing." Prof taught his sons, and the sons of his sons, for several years.

Stroud now advertised regularly in the *Roller Canary Journal*, where most of his articles appeared. A two-inch, one-column insertion appeared on the inside front cover.

REAL BARGAINS
in
Pedigreed Glucke Rollers, Fancy Crested and
Crest-bred Warblers, and the very best of recleaned bird
seed at prices less than usually charged for inferior seed.
Write me your needs! Tell me your troubles!
I can save you money! I can save your birds!
Robert Stroud, 1345 E. 10th St.
Kansas City, Mo.

This was the address of his mother.

Disappointed in repeated attempts to rival Stroud with birds, a change came over Feto Gomez. His half-dozen birds all became ill, and Stroud saved four of them with his medicine. Feto was too moody to submit to the discipline and exacting routine of bird breeding under prison conditions.

Feto's melancholy increased when the hopeful words of the Department of Justice officials failed to materialize after the election of 1928. He lost interest in birds. He sold them and his forlorn equipment to Stroud. He turned to religion and was allowed to mingle with other prisoners. But, after several incidents, the authorities returned him to a solitary cell, where he resumed his old work on hand-illuminated mottoes, which now contained pious homilies. He grew hostile to the dedicated Stroud, who reacted by keeping his plans and information to himself. Stroud had seen such changes before. The silence of Feto troubled him, but he could not help his once-attentive friend.

EIGHTEEN

AT ABOUT THIS time, and unknown to Stroud, a lonely widow in Shelbyville, Indiana, named Della May Jones, inspected her bird sanctum and covered her cages for the night. She had a pleasant face with heavy-lidded eyes and a generous mouth. It was a warm spring evening. Della turned on her tasselled bridge lamp and settled comfortably into her wicker rocker to her favourite reading—the *Roller Canary Journal*.

Her interest was soon drawn to a thought-provoking article about "Haemorrhagic Septicaemia in Canaries", written with many technical terms by one Robert F. Stroud. She read part of it, wishing she could understand it better. Then her attention wandered to another article which announced the prize-winners in a canary contest. She was thrilled to see that she had won second place. First place—and a prize, had gone to the same Robert F. Stroud.

The contest had been for the best "character sketch" of a mother canary under the title, "My Best Mother Bird". First prize was a small 20k gold heart.

Della read the prize-winning letter which had bested hers. It told how the same Mr. Stroud's canary hen had adopted a sparrow found in his yard. The feeling in the letter was warm and gentle. What kind of man, Della wondered, could write so understandingly about a canary hen, and still write so impressively about an obscure canary disease? He must be some university professor or, perhaps, a retired scholar whiling away his time with birds.

He had a yard, she reasoned. Such an expert must be living in a large house. She made a mental note to look for more of his writings.

Several months later, two of Della's canaries fell sick. She cured them, following the advice in Stroud's article.

The canary contest had proved popular, and soon another was announced. This time Della Jones offered one of her young warblers, "Green Sally", as second prize.

Two months later the magazine announced that the same Robert F. Stroud had captured second prize this time. And that meant her Green Sally. There was something almost fateful about her canary going to this Mr. Stroud.

When Della prepared to ship her bird, she discovered that the only address the magazine gave for Robert F. Stroud was P.O. Box 7, Leavenworth, Kansas.

Della looked at her prize canary. "Sally," she told the pretty warbler, "how can I send you to a P.O. box? You'll have to wait for your trip to your new owner."

She wrote that same evening to P.O. Box 7. Would Robert Stroud, she asked, identify himself further? And would he give her a better address?

Della naturally concluded that P.O. Box 7 was the mailing address of some imposing institution. She soon discovered how imposing it was. The replying letter dropped from her fingers.

P.O. Box 7 was Leavenworth Penitentiary, where the writer had lived for many years. He was permitted to inform her that he was a life convict. And he looked forward to receiving his prize, Green Sally.

Della was intrigued. The unusual had flown into her life on the wings of a bird. It was challenging. She decided to meet the challenge, and a correspondence started. Shy letters, definite only on the subject of canaries and their problems, passed between them. She hesitated to ask about Mr. Stroud's past life. But eventually she inquired of the prison authorities.

Della's second and third shocks came then. Her bird's new owner had completed only three years at school. He had killed two men.

His age, however, was reassuring. He was not too much younger than herself. Her reaction was entirely feminine and she became fascinated. How could he have educated himself to write such articles? Della tried to picture a prison cell occupied by a man and living birds. . . .

In time their letters warmed and her sympathy deepened. There must be, she felt, much good in a person so gentle, so persistent in his love for canaries.

They began to discuss a canary business together. She grew more amazed at his acumen and his uncanny grasp of canary diseases and their cures. She felt she could bring this knowledge to the world outside with profit to them both.

She tested his specific for septic fever and found it worked. In order to market it, money was needed. Della had some.

Soon, she decided, she would look up Elizabeth Stroud in Kansas City, and then arrange to visit, for the first time, the man who held her interest.

Meanwhile, as the absorbed Stroud toiled with his birds, history was shaping the forces which were to cut athwart his strange career at its prime, provoking the most curious conflict in American prison history.

In 1929, citizens adjusted their earphones and listened to the inauguration of President Herbert Hoover. On March 2, the Jones Law took effect, making bootlegging a Federal felony. The St. Valentine's Day massacre served a bloody greeting card upon the country, announcing the arrival of gang power. The Attorney-General's office was beset by twin clamours for legal crackdowns and for Federal prison reform.

President Hoover appointed a new Superintendent of Prisons, Sanford Bates. An experienced penologist and adept politician, Bates later recorded in his memoirs an astonishing conversation during which he convinced the President of a sweeping policy change. The President had before him detailed information about Federal prisons, which now housed 90,000 inmates.

"If you were provided with the utmost in the way of buildings, equipment and help, how many of these 90,000 could be reformed?" the President asked.

A possible two-thirds, Mr. Bates told him.

"Which is the more important," pursued Mr. Hoover, "to reform the 60,000 or to teach 122,000,000 citizens that crime does not pay? To which effort should we give most attention?"

"Why not do both, Mr. President?" answered his new chief. "Why not so contrive the punishment of the 90,000 that it will be both deterrent and constructive?" And Mr. Bates went on to explain. "The answer must have satisfied him," concluded Mr. Bates. His new policy and programme received the President's approval.

It was another attempt to bridge the chasm in penology most cogently outlined by George Bernard Shaw. Speaking of the aims of jail commissioners that imprisonment must be retributory, deterrent and reformative at the same time, Shaw commented, "If you are to punish a man retributively, you must injure him. If you are to reform him, you must improve him. And men are not improved by injuries."

During the summer of 1929, while prison riots were sweeping

the country, Sanford Bates and his determined protégés drafted a far-reaching series of laws. Congress passed them, and a new Washington bureau of enormous power was born. Its planks were security, standardization, uniformity and centralized control. "There is strength in uniformity," reiterated Director Bates.

One effect of this uniformity was to transfer the power of prison wardens to that of the bureau. Their policies and methods became subject to scrutiny from Washington. This included the warden of Leavenworth and his policies.

Multiplying Federal laws were sending new thousands of prisoners to swell Leavenworth's bursting bastions. The big prison, with a capacity of 1,640 inmates, had reached an all-time high of 3,770. Convicted bankers, politicians, police officials, bootleggers and former congressmen rubbed elbows with the robbers, counterfeiters and killers of the formal underworld. Prisoners were quartered in basements, halls and improvised dormitories behind the great wall.

The vermin problem grew so acute in Leavenworth that blow-lamp committees worked night and day to burn from the cracks billions of prison-hardened bed-bugs, roaches, beetles and lice. The enormous dining-hall served food continuously and irregularly. Underpaid guards were spread dangerously thin, with 163 watching 3,700 inmates.

The prisoners, including Stroud, remembered the blistering summer of 1929, when the huge concrete pile of overcrowded Leavenworth sucked in heat like a rock stove. The prison cooks, sprinting in a rat race to feed the prisoner army, seemed unable to serve anything except Spanish rice. In August the prison reared up like a whale and shook itself against the intolerable heat, food and housing. The riot began in the dining-hall, and fighting went on for hours. Prisoners tore up shop machinery and pulled iron railings from the cat-walks. One prisoner was shot to death and a score injured. Crammed with new prisoners for solitary, the Isolation cell block received eyewitness reports of the riot. Stroud noted the details, and later included them in the huge manuscript he put together about prisons. He was interested in caged men as well as in caged birds.

A bacteriologist without microscope, Stroud steadily added to his rude laboratory equipment. He acquired test-tube racks,

Erlenmeyer flasks and a wood-alcohol Bunsen burner. His bottles of reagents multiplied. He utilized every square inch of his tiny cell, hanging his cages overhead. He became expert in making smears and slides, and his informal connections with the prison hospital brought occasional help in naming his germ cultures, which he now grew on standard agar matrix. He even acquired a small icebox and permission to receive ice from guards. This increased his control over temperatures. By now Stroud had become an experienced practitioner of science's greatest weapon—the controlled experiment.

Still dissatisfied with his research into apoplectiform septicaemia, which he had shown to be identical with the poultry scourge, Stroud began a series of experiments which were to last for years.

Early in his investigation, he isolated the germ and grew it in cultures. The prison hospital confirmed his finding. This strengthened the bird prisoner's hunch that the canary ailment was identical with the poultry disease.

The onset of symptoms in the sick bird was spectacular. He later described it in his *Digest on the Diseases of Birds.*

> A bird, apparently in the best of health . . . suddenly, usually upon hearing a loud noise or receiving some sudden fright, goes into a violent fit, a paroxysm of wild, aimless flight, battering itself against the wires of the cage or the walls of the room. Then it falls to the floor, unconscious. Sometimes the bird is dead when it hits the floor, but in many cases it is only stunned. . . .

His dissections revealed a massive haemorrhage somewhere in the body of every bird felled by these fits. He also found a characteristic enlargement of the spleen.

This made him suspicious of the usual explanations for the deaths of canaries from "malnutrition", when stale egg-food was around. To prove a theory, Stroud now produced symptoms of the disease in healthy birds by injecting a sterilized toxin from the bacterial growth. He later concluded that apoplectiform septicaemia and egg-food poisoning were caused by the same thing—toxin from the streptococcus germ. He was unable, however, to proceed further with the toxin for lack of laboratory facilities.

Despite this obstacle, Stroud's accomplishments by the close of 1929 read like the brochure of some avian foundation:

1929. Discovered all bird infections of the haemorrhagic septicaemia group could be controlled and cured by the same methods proven effective in avian diphtheria.

1929. Discovered and described a typhoid-like disease of canaries and discovered that it could be cured almost instantly by a modification of the treatment used in avian diphtheria and fowl cholera, but not by treatment as used in those diseases.

1929. Discovered that apoplectiform septicaemia as described by Norgaard and Mohler as a disease of poultry is also a disease of canaries; that it exists in two forms; that the source of infection is usually food containing egg material.

The birdman's desire for a microscope became overwhelming. He felt handcuffed because of the lack of laboratory facilities. His increasing bird sales enabled him to set by some money; he had managed to save $70. Stroud was still a distance from his goal of $120 when a letter arrived from an old friend—Mrs. Grace Miriams, the widow who had helped him with painting lessons by correspondence years before. She was now seventy, and the stock-market crash had wiped out her slender investments. Mrs. Miriams needed money to get to her relatives in Texas. When Stroud learned of her troubles, he immediately sent her the $70.

"What is a microscope when a friend is in need?" Stroud told his mother.

Despite the depression, their little business grew. Elizabeth Stroud acted as his agent in her spare time away from the casket factory. She devoted Saturday evenings and Sundays to the bird work, as well as an occasional noon hour. She became a familiar sight in the streets of the town, a dignified and stiffly well-dressed woman in black, trundling to some pet shop a covered cage-full of chippering warblers.

She was inordinately proud of her son's lively products, and she found that her enthusiasm for his birds was contagious. Birds hatched in prison, moreover, excited the fancy of buyers.

It was not until 1930 that the prisoner realized the wish closest to his heart. Elizabeth Stroud gave up her job in the casket firm. The margin was close, but with help from her younger son Marcus, she was free at last to live upon money earned by a son in solitary confinement for life.

One night Elizabeth Stroud opened her door to a gentle

knock. A middle-aged, neatly dressed woman smiled at her and introduced herself. Her face held the remnants of an appealing charm. Her mouth was wide and generous and her eyes were warm and friendly.

"I am Della Jones," she said.

Elizabeth had heard her son speak of a widow from Shelbyville, Indiana, who had corresponded with him frequently. She was impressed with her visitor's modest ways and she soon learned that behind the pleasant face was a devoted love for birds.

"You seem to know my son well," said Elizabeth Stroud warily, after a while.

"Only by correspondence," said Della. She noted the relief on Elizabeth's face. "I just came to offer my help. In any way that will aid your son's bird business," she added quickly.

Mrs. Stroud thanked her warmly and proudly pointed to her son's paintings on the wall.

"He seems to be able to do almost anything," Della murmured. "Perhaps if he can market that wonderful cure he discovered," she went on, "it will bring him closer to freedom."

"Things like that take money."

"I know," said the widow. "It seems to me that it would make a good investment."

This unexpected turn surprised Elizabeth. She noted Mrs. Jones's appearance with more care. This woman was business-minded. Before Della Jones left, the two women had reached common ground of mutual respect and interest. But Elizabeth still preferred that the widow should not see her Robbie.

Della returned to Shelbyville without attempting to see Robert. As a woman, she immediately sensed Elizabeth's total absorption in her son and the wordless relief in the mother's face when Della informed her she had never seen him.

More intrigued than ever, Della decided to apply for a visitor's pass. Prison authorities had allowed their correspondence and had been friendly. She wrote for permission to visit, and was surprised when it was refused. Informing Stroud of this, she waited impatiently.

The resourceful Stroud wrote to a Federal judge. Shortly thereafter Della Jones received permission to visit. She wondered whether Elizabeth Stroud, who was cordially respected by prison officials, might have intervened.

On April 13, 1931, Della saw Robert Stroud for the first time. She watched the tall, thin prisoner stalk in. He was blinking and adjusting his metal-rimmed glasses. They looked at each other for a long moment—and both smiled with mutual relief. Middle-aged, with sex a remote memory, they soon found themselves talking excitedly about their common interest—the canaries which had drawn them together.

Della left the prison determined to befriend Robert Stroud. In a matter of weeks she had let her home in Shelbyville and moved to Kansas City. She took an apartment in the same building as the prisoner's mother, the address of Stroud's canary business. Then she proceeded to invest in a partnership with Stroud to sell his bird cures. Through her bird-club connections, she eased some of the load from Elizabeth's shoulders in marketing her son's birds.

There were many technical difficulties involved. They discovered that "Stroud's Specific" could not be sold in one bottle, because the chemicals deteriorated too rapidly. Other problems centred around Stroud's insistence on fresh sodium perborate, a volatile, oxidizing chemical. The remedy began to be used with benefit despite difficulties, and soon achieved notice in slow but growing word-of-mouth commendation from satisfied users.

Stroud now answered his mail on printed note-paper, and wondered about the money troubles of his correspondents on the outside.

The year 1931 saw the country tumbling into an economic abyss. Economic pumps sucked up only the confident promises of the sunshine prophets of the day; prosperity lurked around none of the corners of those years. Under the political winds blowing up from the miseries of mass unemployment and breadlines, the nation set sail for the left. Rugged individualism became less attractive.

Stroud's curious little boat, however, was tacking rapidly into the changing winds. His articles, appearing now as features in the *Roller Canary Journal*, were attracting interest from Canada and England as well as the United States.

A leading English fancier, J. Tomlinson, wrote to E. J. Powell, the editor of the *Roller Canary Journal*, requesting permission to reprint two of Stroud's articles for the benefit of English canary lovers.

"I do not recollect ever seeing canary ailments so ably discussed, and beg to offer my congratulations," he stated.

This notice naturally gave great pleasure to the ego-starved prisoner. Letters began to arrive, asking advice, from bird-lovers throughout the English-speaking world. He made a card index of correspondents, and kept a record of the results of his recommendations. He was receiving an average of a dozen letters a day and his card index contained 2,000 names.

He was delighted by a letter from a California poultry raiser, who told him that a mixture of Stroud's Salts had curbed a deadly fowl flu in his 156 pullets. Stroud estimated he had already saved the lives of thousands of birds. Moreover, the efficacy of his "Specific" with chickens caused him to eye the vaster poultry field with interest. An incorrect diagnosis of a bird disease might spell a $500 loss in a day. Stroud began to feel that, even under restrictions and despite the depression, he would prosper if set free.

Unknown to Stroud, however, a vast plan for expanded prison industries was taking shape in the Bureau of Prisons in Washington. Federal penologists had placated organized labour and businessmen.

Leavenworth was still a powder keg. Warden White sat upon it, encouraging hobbies and handicrafts where he could. With the example set by Stroud, after a decade of good behaviour in the tough Isolation Department, hundreds of prisoners in Leavenworth devoted their idle hours to handicrafts. Some prisoners had made such progress with their hobbies that, with the aid of an outside contact, they earned as much as a thousand dollars a year, although the average was much smaller. The activities developed in many prisoners the small businessman's love of independent effort.

"They were learning the secrets and pride of honest industry," Stroud later wrote, "and the men who learned those lessons did not return to prison."

Unfortunately, there was a parallel growth of ugly little rackets among some prisoners. It was in the name of abolishing the rackets that severe restrictions on all activities were ordered.

Many kinds of food and materials were requisitioned by prisoners from local merchants. Officials claimed these merchants were mulcting the convicts with double prices and poor products.

In June, 1931, a commissary was opened in Leavenworth, government-owned and operated, and supplied through large companies who outbid local merchants. Hotly opposed, they protested that the Government was doing them out of a million dollars a year.

These seeming irrelevancies to the story of Robert Stroud were shortly to become pointed and germane. On July 29, 1931, Warden White received orders from the Federal Bureau of Prisons instructing him to order Number 17431, Robert Stroud, to discontinue his bird business forthwith, and to dispose of his birds.

The astonished warden telephoned his superiors. Many wardens had assisted in Stroud's efforts to rehabilitate himself, and none had known the convict to take advantage of leniency or to violate his word. Stroud had become the prison's most picturesque exhibit of Dangerous Prisoner Reforming. His birds had brought a shine to the eyes of many visitors. Even the Director of the Bureau had visited his cell.

Warden White was unable to get his instructions altered. Failing to move those over him, the warden reluctantly prepared to break the news to the prisoner under him.

Stroud was watering his birds on the hot afternoon of Friday, August 18, 1931, when a guard opened his cell door.

"The warden wants you," he said.

Stroud threw off his white visor and combed his hair. A call to the warden's office meant something where the warden wanted to be on his own ground.

"Stroud," the warden began, "I'm afraid this is bad news for you. First off, I want you to know I've done my best to help."

After this portentous beginning, the prisoner tensed, waiting.

"I have here," the warden went on, reaching into a drawer and producing a telegram, "a wire from the Federal Bureau of Prisons in Washington. It is two weeks old. My efforts to alter it were fruitless. I am, therefore, ordering you to cease any further activity with birds and to take immediate steps to get rid of them. I will give you sixty days to do it and I think that's generous."

Stroud's hands gripped the table. After a stunned silence he looked up at the warden.

"Why?" he asked. "Why?"

The warden hesitated. A fair man, he searched for words.

"You must have known," the warden resumed, "that something was coming when your last request for bird supplies and note-paper was turned down."

"No, sir, I did not. I thought that was because of the new commissary and new methods of ordering."

"In any case," pursued the warden, "that is the situation. Call it policy and policy is obviously changing. Let it go at that."

"But . . ."

"If you're going to plead for your birds on your behaviour, I already know that and agree with you. You have a perfect record over many years. But—there have been complaints, despite the record."

Stroud looked at him, stunned. "But, sir, this is my life. Without birds . . ." He stared at the warden. "I kept my word and my record."

"I *know*, Stroud. But this is an order."

Stroud's face grew cold and a hard light crept into his blue eyes.

"All right, Warden," he said with a tight, one-sided grin. "I see how it is. There is nothing you can do." The grin vanished. "So far as I am concerned, all bets are off."

The warden's eyes glinted.

"Are you threatening me? What do you mean by that?"

"I don't know—yet."

"Our discussion is at an end. I'm warden here. This is a prison, not a bird hospital." His tone changed as he rose to terminate the interview. "I will help you in any *other* way I can."

Stroud said nothing. He seemed already removed from the room. The warden fitted on his glasses and looked at Stroud carefully.

"Watch yourself," he said.

The guard escorted Stroud back to his cell. His birds set up an agitated twittering. Stroud stood inside his cell, motionless, looking at his birds.

He began to pace, ducking his head away from the hanging cages. His birds were threatened again, not by a disease, but by an order from a bureau a thousand miles away.

Suddenly he picked up his hand glass and hurled it across his cell. It shattered against the wall. Ten years of work wiped out by a four-line telegram.

"Whatsamatter, Stroud?" yelled a prisoner. "Big doin's, huh?"

"Nothing," Stroud returned in a strangled voice.

His mistake had been in trying to be a person, instead of a number. The thought of more decades alone, a marked guard-killer, moving through a tunnel of time down which he would pursue a bagful of oats in the form of a parole, sickened him. One slip, one impulsive act, and the oat bag would dance out of reach farther down the tunnel. He wondered whether Guard Turner's blood, crimson-wet upon the stone floor of Leavenworth's dining-hall fifteen years ago, would ever dry.

Stroud went to his window and stared out. The hot red ball of sun was being sliced in two by the north-west wall. "Prof" his roller, opened his evening concert. Stroud straightened slowly at the sound. His eyes were tearless, his lips tight.

A sudden surge of energy welled in him as he came to a decision. His mind raced ahead as it had done during the great sickness of his birds. He suddenly knew what to do and how to do it. Striding to the small wooden table which held up his battered Remington, he whipped out a ream of onion-skin paper and began to type. Using many carbons, he wrote every kind of appeal he could think of, marshalling his facts and drawing upon his photographic memory. He wrote a detailed news release and copied it on onion-skin paper until his fingers were numb. He addressed radio stations. He wrote letters to congressmen, appeals to the bird journals, and letters to bird clubs.

When he finished, his carton of cigarettes had vanished into a mound of stubs. He had typed for more than thirty hours. One of his letters was an urgent plea to Della Jones to see him as soon as possible.

He was taking an irrevocable step, and he knew it. Once begun, there was no turning back. In prison, it was a die cast by the hardy or the foolhardy, never forgiven, nor forgotten. But Stroud was resolute. He could not envisage living without his birds. . . .

When Della Jones left the prison after their visit two days later, her capacious skirts rustled like autumn leaves. To the rustle of satin was added that of a large amount of onion-skin paper.

NINETEEN

DURING THE NEXT thirty days bird-lovers throughout the country were amazed and appalled. Their birds, they read, had been cured by a convict. The man who had found the cure for septic fever, and whose articles they had read and consulted, was a sentenced killer living in solitary confinement in Leavenworth. A jailbird had learned to save their canaries by curing his own canaries behind the largest prison wall in the country.

Now, a Washington bureau proposed to take his birds away from him. He was crying for help.

The story carried from coast to coast, and citizens greeted it with anger and dismay.

A prisoner in solitary had made a job, only to see it removed. Millions were unemployed outside and the right to work was the slogan of the time. It was a day for underdogs.

Pressure through letters and telegrams began to build in Congress. Kansas congressmen had already been nettled by Leavenworth and Kansas City businessmen who were complaining about the loss of their lucrative business with prisoners.

Della Jones carried on the appeal to bird breeders. "At every turn he was hedged in and handicapped by a mass of red tape never before known within the prison. . . ." read her letter. "Think of it! Two months to sell $1,000 worth of fancy stock in the depressed market that now exists."

Little businessmen understood this language, and so did the congressmen. They had heard it before.

"He has proved himself by years of honest, faithful effort. He is carrying on a work of inestimable value. He has not waited for a future freedom to make himself useful but is being most highly useful right now, and has been for years. But see what it gets him."

"Is it wise," continued the letter, "to encourage prisoners to put forth their best efforts to aid themselves and others and then wreck all their hopes? . . . And forgetting Stroud, what of the interests of those hundreds of bird fanciers everywhere who rely on his aid when disease and death stalk their birds? If this man has grown too big for a solitary cell, is the only solution to step on him, regardless of who else is hurt?"

Lowell Thomas, John B. Hughes and other national commentators aired the story over national networks. They stressed the ageing mother and the problem of a lonely prisoner and his birds. The convict's notorious record before 1920 made a telling contrast with his faultless record for the eleven years that followed. The story made good copy.

Bird clubs circulated petitions. Thousands of names appeared upon them, especially from Kansas and Missouri. When the petitions were finally mailed to the President, they contained more than 50,000 signatures.

The little group of hardworking penologists who were nursing the unfledged Bureau of Prisons in Washington must have felt like men who pulled a mouse's tail only to encounter an elephant. Over a hundred congressmen descended upon their heads with wads of letters. Some favoured Stroud's immediate release.

According to Stroud's later petition, a ranking Democratic member of the subcommittee that studied appropriations for the Department of Justice warned the Director that the broad powers granted the new bureau were not intended to deprive any man of the fruits of good conduct.

The penologists were stunned. Telephone bills mounted between Washington and Leavenworth, and lights burned late. But the Bureau's men were resolute, with a system to build and a programme to follow. The public knew next to nothing of problems faced by prison executives.

By October, the Bureau had revealed that a regulation had been passed on July 28 which provided that, "The conduct of outside business affairs by inmates, except in the extent specifically approved by the warden, is prohibited."

This strange declaration threw the ball to the warden of Leavenworth, who was himself precluded from making statements without clearing through Washington.

A Washington-released news story of October 3, 1931, was carried in the St. Louis *Post-Dispatch* and the Kansas City *Star* stating that "The prison officials have given no order for Stroud to destroy or get rid of his stock of canaries while looking for a solution of the problem. The authorities are desirous of encouraging prisoners . . . the prison board has not yet reached a solution of the perplexing question. . . ."

Meanwhile, the editor of a country weekly in Sabetha,

Kansas, where one of Stroud's paintings had found a home, was refused an interview with Warden White of Leavenworth. The editor wrote to his friend, A. B. Mcdonald, of the Kansas City *Star*. Mcdonald, one of the leading feature writers in the country, journeyed to Leavenworth. Warden White would neither see him nor allow an interview with the bird convict. Mcdonald then sought out Elizabeth Stroud.

An illustrated feature article appeared in the *Star*'s Sunday edition, October 4, 1931. It was an affecting story. Much of it was told within the quotes of an aged, white-haired woman who prayed to God that the Government would not take the canaries from her son's prison cell. Around a photo of Elizabeth Stroud seated, gazing down at her son's first bird cage, Mcdonald told the story of the convict up to that time.

He had interviewed the owner-editor of the *Roller Canary Journal*, Edward J. Powell.

"Stroud has been writing my chief articles right along," Powell was quoted. "They are so finely written, so authoritative, that I print them as leaders in my magazine. The following articles were all written by Stroud in the last year:

SPECIFIC TREATMENT FOR SEPTIC FEVER
HAEMORRHAGIC SEPTICAEMIA IN CANARIES
ASPERGILLOSIS IN CANARIES
SEPTIC FEVER DISCOVERIES
FEEDING—SOME RESEARCHES"

The *Star* article concluded in the words of Mrs. Stroud:

"A man in prison who has the heart to do such things, who loves his mother as Robbie does, cannot be a bad man. . . . What is a prison for, anyway, to punish a man or to try to reform him? If for reformation could there be better proof of reformation than for a man to raise himself above his own suffering and devote himself to a life of service to others? That is what my son has done, and the least reward that the prison authorities can give to him is to let him keep his birds."

The article was picked up by many newspapers and, ultimately, reverberated in Washington.

It contained a statement that Stroud had been ordered to get rid of his canaries and equipment by October 14, 1931. On the same day and in fact in a box on the same page, the Bureau had denied that it had ordered the convict to get rid of his birds.

"In letters being sent by the Department of Justice in response to persons who object to Stroud's being deprived of the privilege of continuing in the canary business," wrote the Washington correspondents of the *Star* and the *Post-Dispatch* in identical phrasing, "it is stated the Prison Bureau desires him to raise canaries. The Bureau asserts also that Stroud is satisfied to remain in solitary confinement and does not desire to be moved to other quarters. . . ."

The Prison Bureau now made a decision unprecedented in prison history. It was couched in elaborate face-saving terms, faithfully reported in the Press. There were restrictions as well.

"Robert Stroud . . . may continue to raise canaries under a plan worked out by the Prison Bureau of the Department of Justice," stated the *Star*'s Washington Bureau. "Profits from the sale of canaries will be turned over to the prison fund for the benefit of the convicts. Stroud will be permitted to draw a salary in the form of a share of the profits. What percentage will be permitted Stroud was not revealed." It was ten dollars per month.

"The salary," stated the St. Louis *Post-Dispatch*, "will be for extra duties performed. In that way the prison officials will not violate the rule adopted July 28 by the Board."

A more astonishing reaction by a prisoner to a more flattering compromise can scarcely be imagined.

Stroud was furious. The convict claimed that the Director of the Bureau was trying to socialize his business. He requested permission to see an attorney and his request, he said, was refused. He felt that his initiative was being destroyed, his constitutional rights abrogated. His reaction was like that of a businessman convinced of the virtues of private enterprise. Had Henry Ford been forced to share his business with the Federal Government through expropriation, his reaction would have resembled that of Stroud, whose political views were similar.

Stroud secured an extract of Rule 60 of the Federal Bureau of Prisons Manual which read in part:

> An inmate cannot be permitted to direct his business, no matter how legitimate it may be, while he is in prison.

How, Stroud inquired, can a prisoner be prevented from directing his business, and yet Government be empowered to do it, in partnership with him, under the Constitution of the United States?

The implications of this legal question were profound enough to worry the Bureau. They feared possible legislative damage to the largest work programme for prisoners ever devised by a prison system. The Director of the Bureau now sent his trusted assistant to the prison to make a counter-proposal.

No truer index to the all-out character of Stroud was ever shown. He played his hand to the limit of the stakes.

For hours the strangest conference in American penal annals raged in the solitary cell against a background of twittering birds. The convict later wrote that he was warned by the official that public memory is short. But Stroud stood his ground. The official was forced to return to Washington empty-handed. Stroud claims that this official never forgot it. The Director then assigned an older penologist to deal with the situation. But before he had so much as purchased transportation, an appalling event placed Stroud's non-violent battle against a bloody background.

Warden White, deep in the vortex of the Stroud controversy, was sitting on more dangerous unrest in Leavenworth. Still bulging with twice its capacity of inmates, the big prison had remained "tight" most of the time since the riot of 1929. The warden and the Bureau warned Congress and the public of the dangers of insufficient personnel and overcrowding. In 1930, three prisoners dug under the wall of the "Little Top"—the annex prison—and escaped. A year before, the warden had received an anonymous note that an escape effort was pending by dynamiting the front gate. Around that time, sticks of dynamite and loaded revolvers had been discovered hidden in a stove-pipe inside the wall.

In December, 1931, a prisoner in one of the main cell blocks received a telegram informing him that his Aunt Emma was ill. Later, a barrel of shoe paste arrived and was checked through to the shoe factory.

It contained four revolvers, a sawn-off shotgun and a 30-30 Army rifle.

Two days later six convicts moved with forged passes as far as the administrative offices. There they took Warden White hostage with drawn guns and left via the front gate in the most dramatic break from Leavenworth since 1910. They jammed the front gate locks, commandeered an automobile, ran it into a ditch, and had stopped another when Warden White saw an opening and grappled with one of the convicts for the shotgun. The warden was severely wounded in the left arm and chest. The arm was eventually amputated. In a matter of hours three escapees were killed. Later the rest were captured.

Warden White, crippled but unbroken, was transferred. His place was taken by the deputy warden, Fred Zerbst, warden of the annex prison and now a man of thirty-six years' experience. He had known Stroud before the killing of Guard Turner in 1916.

The tragedy diverted public attention from Stroud and his birds, but centred it deeper upon Leavenworth, the "Big Top".

Early in January, the seasoned penologist dispatched by the Bureau to handle the Stroud problem reached an accord with Stroud.

Stroud was placed under direct jurisdiction of the head of the Bureau. He would be allowed to keep his canaries. He would be given a special corner cell to house them. A doorway would be hewn through the wall of his Isolation cell to make the canaries' cell accessible to him. The Prison Bureau, it now developed, wanted him to raise canaries.

He would be provided with laboratory equipment, including a microscope and chemicals, in order to continue his experiments. And his eyes would be checked by a government eye specialist to prevent any deterioration in his vision. There was also guarded mention of a possible parole for the convict when eligible, which would be in 1937.

One lone prisoner, locked with his birds, had battled one of the most powerful bureaux in the country and won. He had enlisted the one force greater than any Government bureau. He had appealed to the people and the people had responded.

For the first time in Leavenworth's history, a legal hole was made through a solitary cell wall. To Stroud the sounds of pneumatic drills were music. He had never listened as pleasurably to the clamour of razing since he had heard the shriek of the planks when his gallows was dismantled.

A full-sized open doorway was cut between the two cells of Stroud's new home. The cells were wired with thirteen electric outlets. For the first time in fifteen years, it was moving day for Stroud.

The better cell of the two was the corner one. He immediately designated this for his birds. Two guards joked about it while the cell tender helped the convict move birds, books and paraphernalia into what the newspapers called a "prison suite".

Stroud shared his new hope by sending a long letter to a twenty-two-year-old girl in Alexandria, Louisiana. The girl had had five surgical operations, including the amputation of her leg. She had attempted suicide in her despair, was rescued and, during convalescence, she had read about the prisoner's fight for his birds. "When I read about you," she had written to him, "I felt a new duty to make the best of things."

She was fortunate, he wrote her, to be able to wheel her chair as far as her strength would take her, to move about freely in the sunshine and outdoors.

"Neither of us can afford to know the meaning of the little word c-a-n-t," he wrote. "I am sending you a canary who will tell you that over and over himself.

Shortly after Stroud was moved, Feto Gomez was also rearranging his effects after a visit to the warden's office. The convict had achieved another transfer from solitary to join his fellows as a first-class prisoner.

"Hey, Gomez," Stroud called to him.

"The hell with you, Stroud," rumbled Gomez.

"Can't blame you for trying," Stroud rejoined. Feto did not answer.

Stroud resumed his work. He had spent his savings in the expenses of the campaign. It would be difficult to raise birds on the ten dollars a month allowed him from their sale. His business, in so far as profit was concerned, had been effectively hobbled.

This drove him to concentrate even more on the problems of research; and he planned a programme of extensive writing.

Several weeks passed before Stroud actually became aware of a change in the official attitude toward him.

His article writing for bird journals was stopped. His letters were cut to two per week. He was unable to answer bird-lovers and bird breeders. Urgent pleas and descriptions of sick and dying birds saddened his heart. Each week he selected the two most in need.

Sitting in his "prison suite" with more space but less latitude, the prisoner began to feel the chill from the distant Bureau. The walls of the prison had never seemed more formidable.

Had he really won a victory, after all? Or was winning intolerable in prison?

New difficulties arose in obtaining supplies through the prison commissary. There were material delays, omissions, red tape.

Heartsick, Stroud realized after a few months that he had overplayed his hand. He must have wondered what had happened to the intense concern for his "desires".

The memory of this discovery, when as an old man he wrote about it seventeen years later, is an outcry filled with frustration.

> Never in any single instance was any favour or privilege granted me freely as a recognition of good conduct or the good and useful work I was doing. If just once they had treated me with the same faith and confidence I had been treated with before the establishment of the Bureau, I would have reacted in the very same way. I would have walked through fire rather than have violated that confidence. . . .

Another development which bothered him at this time was the growing coolness of his mother. Mrs. Stroud had not been consulted when the canary prisoner decided to fight for his birds. She had always been his mentor and always at his side. With a will and an ego as overweening as his own, she had always insisted that Mother Knows Best.

The campaign, however, had thrown her into prominence. Sympathy for her had been unbounded. One feature writer had even stated, "It is she who is serving the sentence rather than her son." But Elizabeth remained uneasy about the campaign.

When her livelihood was cut off by the decision of the Bureau, she took the blow without visible rancour.

"We will miss the money we used to get from selling the canaries Bob used to send us, but it is a comfort to know that he will not be alone in that cell without any living thing near him.

"We haven't very much to live on now," she continued, "I guess I'm like everyone else who is seventy-one years old. When you get that old you can't drive yourself as hard as you once could. Sometimes I get a little sewing or quilting to do, but there isn't much of that to be done now.

"I think the Government officials are trying to be fair," she added, "but naturally we are sorry to hear that the Government couldn't see its way clear to let him continue his canary business, as it was a great help to us."

Some of the letters received during the campaign contained money from sympathetic readers. A Kansas City banker accompanied a ten-dollar bill with a note. "Anyone whose heart is normal can define in that good woman's countenance," his words intoned, "the noblest of motherly virtues . . . forgoing the loss of her son makes for her indeed a burden which we must help her carry with her sorrow and broken heart. I conscientiously consider the status of this good woman exceptional and most worthy." The note seemed sententious for such a sum, but in 1931 ten dollars had a considerable stretch.

The actual campaign, however, had been handled by the tireless widow, Della Jones. It was she who had spent money and endless time copying the letters and releases so hospitably received by Press, bird clubs and bird journals. Now Della struggled to keep afloat the tiny canary remedy business.

Since Della had been designated by Stroud as his agent, a coolness developed between the widow and the mother which grew more marked as time went on. Mrs. Stroud regarded the widow as an interloper, not good for her son, and this was reflected by her younger son Marc. Marc was a successful businessman. After corresponding with his mother, Marc took up his mother's problem with his prisoner-brother, who was requesting money to continue his campaign.

"Marc wrote he would not give me a cent unless I broke with Dell. That if I would, he would give generously. I told him no. We did not correspond for nine years."

The distinguished old mother was always received with courtesy and respect by prison officials. They appeared less cordial to the widow.

Stroud grimly noted the developments and took refuge among his birds.

Deeply shaken by the ruling that he could no longer openly send out advice and articles to the bird journals, he increased his articles output. They found their way to the journals *sub rosa*. He manœuvred, worked, researched and wrote with indomitable energy. He was a dedicated man and would not turn back. It was work and study and fight, or succumb to prison stupor in the midst of his chirping birds.

The man he might have been began to fade out before the aggressions of the continual solitary struggle. He struck out in every way he could think of, short of the violence he had put behind him.

Prohibited to express himself, he wrote an entire book on canary diseases in sixty days. It was based upon his articles. Canary fanciers supported his claim that it was the first "scientific" treatise ever written specifically classifying diseases of canaries. He was encouraged by the bird journal publisher whose magazine had increased its value and circulation because of the prisoner's articles.

The manuscript, of some 60,000 words, was smuggled from the prison and published, with a considerable outlay of funds, by the editor-publisher of the *Roller Canary Journal*, E. J. Powell. A university professor was so impressed with the work that he undertook to edit it free of charge.

The book was launched through the bird magazines in 1933. The announcement advertisements ran:

> MY BIRD IS DEAD
> WHY DID HE DIE?
> ROBERT STROUD CAN TELL YOU WHY
> Nearly ready for the press is the most complete and thorough work on the diseases of canaries that has ever been written. Price $2.00. Reserve your copy by writing at once!

The book, shoddily published, nevertheless proved of value to bird-lovers and began to sell readily even during the depression. It was some time, however, before book sales offset the printing investment.

Stroud complained that he was receiving no royalties, and contended that the agreement called for his receiving a dollar per book. He also claimed that the assignment of copyright was his, duly filed with the Library of Congress.

The publisher realized that Stroud, a felon, was precluded from bringing a civil suit for damages, and was angered by what he considered Stroud's ingratitude. Powell stood his ground and the prisoner received nothing. Stroud's effort to recoup his finances proved fruitless.

The irate convict now smuggled out articles to a rival magazine and traded them for advertising space, which he used to complain about his treatment by his publisher.

Powell, whose magazine goodwill was hurt, now came to the prison authorities and complained that Stroud had "kited" magazine material from prison. Since the book manuscript had left the prison in similar fashion, Powell's complaint had authority.

This irritated the warden and the Bureau. Stroud was questioned. He stared at them, coldly polite against the background of his churring birds. They could prove nothing. Their irritation deepened.

It was in the hot summer of 1933 that the seasoned, grapevine-informed Stroud first felt the cold breath of what then was only a name: *Alcatraz*.

TWENTY

As THE COUNTRY jolted through the hard bottom of the depression, grinding through bank closures and farm foreclosures, the people's anger began to centre upon the Government and its policies.

In criminology, this was reflected in a growing criticism and demand for action against the multiplying kidnappings and gang homicides. The two-year-old baby of Charles Lindbergh, kidnapped in March, 1932, was found dead two months later. In Kansas City, under the shadow of Leavenworth, gangsters machine-gunned four officers to death in a futile attempt to rescue one of their number. In Lansing, Kansas, eleven prisoners broke over the reformatory wall, taking the warden with them as a hostage. John Dillinger masterminded the escape of ten convicts who shot their way out of Indiana State Prison.

Riots, escapes and scandals multiplied. Congress passed new laws. The Department of Justice tightened its organization and struck out at the rampant underworld with the fist of the F.B.I.

The Attorney-General, Homer Cummings, began to think that no existing American prison was tough enough to punish, or secure enough to hold the crooked, politically connected, well-heeled public enemies who ran wild among the nation's bankrupt citizenry. He began to dream of a super-tough punitive prison, a dead-end bastille where the enemies of society could be quartered as examples of the dictum that Crime Does Not Pay.

Months before the Attorney-General's announcement that a maximum security prison would shortly be established in California, the prison grapevine hummed with rumours of an American Devil's Island.

Seasoned older convicts like Stroud were used to interpreting the penal decisions of state in terms of their fates and futures. Matching information from chance remarks of prison officials and Washington correspondence somehow perused by prison eyes, these older convicts had no trouble reading between the lines of the announcement a second policy later to be revealed.

They knew that the harassed wardens of every Federal "big

house" in the country would strive to include on their list for transfer the prisoners who caused them trouble. It was human nature to brush off annoyance. Their constant justification was "improving prison morale".

Stroud was no longer an acclaimed prisoner-scientist suddenly deprived of his birds. He had his birds, and an extra cell for them. His mounting difficulties inside the silent walls-within-walls of the Isolation cell block would not capture the imagination of a fickle public again. His attempts to fight back merely gained him notice as a contentious gadfly who lived with birds.

When the grapevine was confirmed in the announcement of the prison island of Alcatraz and some of the plans were revealed, Stroud felt a small chill tickle his taut nerves. He had tasted power for a brief time; now he felt more than ever helpless and utterly trapped. He turned to his canaries and comforted himself with their song.

Della would be visiting him in a day or so. Stroud was glad she could not see his birds. His entire aviary was a sorry-looking exhibit, with the canaries going through their annual moult. Their hot vitality was absorbed in the curious process of dropping their feathers and growing new ones. A rare cold spell had forced them to moult early. It was September, 1933.

As he fretted over his birds, Stroud smiled grimly at the memory of how hard Della had worked, speeding him to his empty victory, forcing the mighty Bureau to bend before public opinion. But public opinion had changed and its fleeting interest had shifted elsewhere. Stroud's apprehension about a sudden transfer to Alcatraz, now nearing completion, gnawed at him. A sudden decision would take him away quickly. Away from his birds. It would be a *fait accompli*, impossible to alter if placed in effect.

Through his connections and the grapevine, Stroud felt confident he could get forewarning of an impending decision. But what could he do? It was the idea of helplessness, even with foreknowledge, which sent his thoughts skimming desperately for an answer. Perhaps Della could do something for him—but what? Or his mother? Stroud worried about her, too. In her last visit Elizabeth had reproached him. When she mentioned Della her manner turned cold. She bitterly resented the widow's role as his agent, even while conceding her competence. He remembered the worn news clip given him by a friendly guard. The story had stated it was really his mother who was serving his sentence.

For many years, Stroud's habit when at a loss was to turn to books. Now from sheer boredom, he selected an old text of historical law.

The book had been donated by some barrister long deceased to the 10,000-volume Leavenworth library. Even the librarian had forgotten about it. He picked up the dirty volume. Its brown leather binding cracked as he opened it.

Idly, he perused a discussion of the legal background of the Louisiana Purchase in 1803. He read about the legal rights of the people living in the French territory which later became the United States. This included Kansas ground. The rights of the settlers had been protected by the Treaty of Paris. The book discussed a contention that the rights of the inhabitants carried over from the Treaty of Paris, to be honoured by the purchasing country. The Treaty, for example, recognized as legal in this territory a signed declaration of a man and woman that they were husband and wife.

Stroud started as he read the faded print on the yellowed page. He read it over again. The point reminded him of the Federal jurisdiction which had nearly stretched his neck at a rope's end. Leavenworth was Federal property immune from the Kansas state law which had prohibited capital punishment.

Stroud pondered over the page. If Federal property could ignore state law, could an old treaty law antedate Federal law? It was a strange thought.

He closed the book with a sharp slap as an idea swiftly shaped in his mind.

Why not get married under the Treaty of Paris? Although he was a life convict in the keeping of the warden, he was living on Federal property. Why couldn't he ignore state laws, citing the Treaty, and marry without state licence, or ceremony, with a simple sworn contract?

The eerie thought made him grin. He knew the warden would as soon ascend in a smoke balloon from the bull pen as allow Robert Stroud to get married. The crusty and troubled old warden would not only turn him down, but conclude that the rumours were true that he was "all-out bugs".

But—why not get married *without* the warden's consent?

An unaccustomed sound stirred the inmates of the Isolation cell block. Stroud was laughing. When a con got "laughing-bugs", that was the worst kind. Bug-eyed—in the midst of those screeching, moulting birds.

A guard came to his cell door.

"What's the big laugh?"

"Something struck me funny."

"You must be sousing up on your bird dope," the guard said.

"No," Stroud said. He came to the cell door. "I've decided to get married," he whispered.

The guard's jaw dropped and he stared in at Stroud. He doubled up in laughter.

"You know what I thought you said? You were gonna get *married*!" The guard laughed again.

Stroud cut him short. "That's what I did say. I *am*," he told him, his face straight.

The guard gaped at him. "Never thought it would get you," he said. "The con that says that is *gone*." He pointed to his head and walked away.

"We'll see," Stroud muttered, eyeing his book.

Soon the rapid clack of his typewriter rose over the whirring and twittering of his birds.

Della Jones visited at two o'clock on her appointed day. The guards had long sensed the warmth between the convict and the widow, and had grown used to her visits. They intruded reluctantly on what seemed a shyly private rendezvous. The pair hardly seemed a romantic couple, however. Robert was forty-three and Della approaching forty-nine. Their conversation was low and at one stage of it Della blushed.

". . . So I have prepared it ahead of time, dated as of today," Stroud said in a quick, low tone. He looked at her with an odd warmth in his narrow blue eyes. "It'll take guts for you to do this," he said.

"I know, Bob," Della said. She lifted her chin and in her candid brown eyes glowed a bright devotion. "I'm not worried. Nobody worries when they do what they want to." She casually watched the guard, who was posted to one side facing the prisoner's back. "This will show the world we're still trying. But"—her eyes met his—"don't talk about courage. What about you, living in here? And your mother, she won't like this."

"I know, Della. We can't risk telling her."

"She's acted strange lately."

"If they transfer me, she'll hate that more."

Della shook her head slowly. "No, Bob," she said. "I think she'd stand anything so long as you were—well, all hers. She feels you are hers"—she smiled into his eyes—"exclusively."

Stroud's face darkened.

"I can't help that. Not any more. I'm cemented into this stone lavatory. They can put me in a worse one and take the birds away, unless people stop it."

Della was looking past him, at the guard. He had turned the other way to glance at the clock.

"Quick," she whispered. "Give me the paper."

The strange contract, tightly folded, passed into her hands and disappeared into her bodice. She smiled nervously.

"Don't release it until I tell you," he cautioned. "Now about the autumn bird season . . ." They passed into a discussion of avian affairs.

Two weeks went by. Though they corresponded, Stroud mentioned nothing further about the contract. Word meanwhile passed around the Isolation Building that Stroud was growing crazier than ever and now talked about getting married. "Can't keep a con alone without he goes bugs," whispered the prisoner across the corridor to the cell tender. "Stroud was a square con, always for his side. But he ain't got them marbles no more."

A month went by and Della was with Stroud again. "There's a lot in the paper about that new place in California," she said nervously. "How long do we wait?"

"We have to wait," said Stroud. "I've got a pipeline right out of the throne. Nothing on me so far. They won't like this story if it takes hold."

Three weeks later the widow saw him by special permission in answer to an urgent letter. Della looked pale. Stroud's face was a mask.

"Is it too late?" Della asked.

"No. Release it right away. They've made up half a list of one hundred cons to be shipped."

"You're—on it?"

"At the top."

Della's eyes flashed and her breath quickened. "I knew it

before you said it." She watched him tenderly. "I—I wish we—wish you could be with me, Bob."

"So do I, Dell."

"The papers will get it tomorrow. Goodbye."

When Stroud returned to his cell, the big guard was smiling. He was whistling, "There's a Long, Long Trail," as he paced up and down the corridor.

"You aren't whistling 'California' any more," said Stroud.

"Nope. Got tired of it."

"*You know* I'm on the list," Stroud said softly, as the Isolation guard walked by.

"Nothing fazes you, does it? You're a hard-shell con." The guard took another tack.

"Maybe . . . Should I sing 'Here Comes the Bride', eh? You pulled my leg on that. Better hurry, old con." The big guard peered close to Stroud's face. "You ain't what you used to be," he laughed.

A gleam crept into the prisoner's eye as he watched the fun-loving guard. Then he put his head to one side like an old bird and regarded his teaser with sardonic amusement.

"I'm already married," he said.

"Sure," the guard said, straight-faced.

"It's true," Stroud said. "I'm married *now*. Watch for the announcement."

"Where?"

"In the newspapers."

"When?"

"Soon," Stroud said carefully.

"You sound like you mean it. Everybody's crazy in here."

Eyeing the puzzled guard, Stroud looked like the father of all jailbirds.

That week, Della Jones put on her best dress, took a deep breath, and set out for the Kansas City *Star*.

When she appeared there, she was wearing a small gold heart pinned to her lapel and she held a folded paper in her hand.

The reporters did not pause to fathom the curious legal quirk behind the marriage contract. The Treaty of Paris meant nothing to them. Nor was the matter very clear to Della. It was Romance that caused the flurry around the city desk as the assignment was made and a reporter hurried from the library with the Stroud file. He saw his lead before the widow had half-finished her story.

DISCLOSES ROMANCE WITH LIFE TERMER, ran the St. Louis *Post-Dispatch* headline. "Woman 'Wed' to Him Through Contract—Met as Result of Canary Contest."

LOVE ON A BIZARRE TRAIL, said the *Star*. "Life Term Convict Reveals Strange Wedding Pact. 'Contract of Marriage', according to Robert F. Stroud, Binds Him to Mrs. Della May Jones, a Widow."

The amazing career of Robert F. Stroud, serving a life sentence for murder and held in solitary confinement in the Federal prison at Leavenworth, has turned to a romance as strange as the chapters of his own life story.

The man for whom a gallows once was built . . . has taken a wife within the meaning of the law. Stroud, the convict who has built from illiteracy and handicaps of solitary confinement a reputation nation-wide as an authority on canaries and is a skilled mathematician . . . became acquainted in a canary contest . . .

The Associated Press put the story on the wires and it ran throughout the country on Saturday and Sunday, October 21 and 22, 1933.

A week later there was a follow-up, when the widow appeared at the office of the Recorder of Deeds to file the contract.

Stroud's pact titillated the fancy of a million readers:

CONTRACT OF MARRIAGE
BETWEEN ROBERT STROUD AND
DELLA MAY JONES

In the State of Kansas, County of Leavenworth, upon the territory of the Leavenworth Military Reservation and under the exclusive jurisdiction of the government of the United States, on the fifteenth day of August in the year of our Lord nineteen hundred and thirty-three.

It is agreed:

By Robert Stroud of postoffice box 7, Leavenworth, Kansas, and Della May Jones of 1345 East Tenth Street, Kansas City, Missouri, that they are and henceforth shall be, for so long as they two shall live,

MAN AND WIFE

And the said Robert Stroud states that he is a citizen of the United States, of legal age, of sound mind and unmarried; that the above mentioned Della May Jones has been to him everything that a true, loving and faithful wife could possibly be, and he hereby promises before the world to love and cherish her above all others so long as his life shall last;

And the said Della May Jones states that she is a citizen of the United States, of legal age, of sound mind and unmarried; that the above mentioned Robert Stroud has been to her everything that a true, loving and faithful husband could possibly be, and that she hereby promises before the world to love and honour him above all others so long as her life shall last.

The import of the contract was lost upon many who read the story. How the widow could be "everything that a true, loving and faithful wife could possibly be", with the greatest prison wall in the country keeping them apart, ironically ignored the marriage bed. And yet, they "were to each other" all that circumstances would allow. It was the flavour of one man's incredible defiance of prison walls and bars which captured the imagination. Casual readers and eager bird-lovers alike exclaimed over the story, and not a few shed a quiet tear or two.

It was a *fait accompli* in Stroud's manner . . . another misapplication of the genius which, outside the prison system, might have lifted him to the top of society.

Few readers on the outside, however, sensed the cold and fearful backdrop of Alcatraz behind this sentimental tale adorning the feature sections of the Sunday Press.

The first news prison officials had of the matter greeted them over breakfast in the pages of the morning paper. There is little evidence that they were moved to tears by the story. A prisoner had got "married" without their knowledge or consent.

"That crazy, bird-happy s.o.b.," snarled the lieutenant as he stared incredulously at the one-column headline.

"So now he's a Romeo," said a deputy. "We got him on the shelf, been there for years and he gets more in the papers than an ad. man."

"Stroud's on the list for the Rock. This cinches it."

"I wonder," grumbled the lieutenant. "Them bird bugs will start writing again. So they got to kick it around in Washington. Don't forget, he's *their* con."

In Washington, the story was read by eyes that were quieter and cooler. There, too, feeling was not of romance. It may well have been rage.

Prison officials opened piles of letters from bird fanciers asking consideration anew for the sequestered canary doctor. Stroud evidently was not carried in the public mind as a gangster or supercriminal, but as a possibly dangerous lifer who raised wonderful canary birds, cured their diseases, and had now "married" despite prison walls. The Stroud matter was treated with care.

News reports had the Attorney-General himself disclosing that Stroud's original sentence called for solitary confinement until hanged, and that this interpretation would be carried out. It was readily admitted that Stroud was on the list for Alcatraz. Late in October Washington agents of the Department of Justice appeared at the prison.

A national radio commentator, however, discovered that the convict was afraid of losing his birds through a prison transfer. He wrote to one of the Presidential aides. As a result, word came through that Stroud need not be moved, and should be allowed his birds.

When the One Hundred Worst Convicts from Leavenworth were chained and entrained to join the Fifty Worst from Atlanta in Alcatraz, Robert Stroud was nowhere among them. He remained with his birds.

For thirteen years officials had stated publicly that Stroud was "too dangerous to associate with other prisoners". His sentence had been interpreted as demanding solitary confinement for life. Now the unprecedented publicity and the White House nod which was accorded to the birdman of Leavenworth produced an astonishing offer.

Officials would consent, the Press reported, to restore Stroud to the class of a first-grade prisoner with the right to associate with his fellows. They required but one detail. They wanted his word that he would be a model prisoner. It appeared to be a word they respected.

But Stroud had become a stir-wary recluse, a cautious jailbird who thought he sensed a trap. He reasoned, rightly or wrongly, that if he were turned into the prison population, the next step would be removal from Isolation. Would this deprive him of the extra cell now provided for his birds?

Stroud promised nothing. "I don't want any liberties within this prison," he said. "I just want to get out of here."

Stroud believed that he had warded off a punitive transfer on the one hand, and refused an offer to rejoin his fellows on the other hand, as successful decisions to retain his birds. In any case, he kept his avian ark afloat.

What the egocentric convict did not foresee was a third and catastrophic result of his prison romance. The dove of his "marriage" to Della flew back to roost as a raven.

Stroud lost the support of his mother.

TWENTY-ONE

THE AUTUMN ROMANCE of her strange son with the Indiana widow was something Elizabeth Stroud had tried to ignore. She clung to the business aspect of the three-way relationship and tried to help where she could. The "back seat" which awaited most mothers was now a vacant chair ready to receive even her. But the indomitable seventy-three-year-old son-protector would not sit in it.

The announcement of her son's "marriage" was something handed to her shyly by Della Jones as a news article on the front page of the Kansas City *Star*.

The old lady took one look and slowly crushed the paper in her bony hand.

"This—this will help Bob keep his birds . . ." Della pleaded.

Elizabeth Stroud glared at her. "I wish you—would just—*go*. Leave me alone—leave—leave . . ."

Something in her face hastened Della's departure without a word.

Mrs. Stroud smoothed out the crumpled newspaper. She wiped the mist from her glasses and read it again. It was unbelievable, mad. This was the first time since 1909 that another woman had received the limelight as a contender for the attentions of her son. The wording of the article twisted an iron stake of jealousy into her mother's heart. She stared at the subheading before her: "Contract of marriage binds him to Mrs. Della May Jones, a widow."

Binds him . . .

Elizabeth Stroud had lost her Robbie to another woman. After all she had done. Since his infancy Robbie had been her first love. Robbie had been her own little man. A strange man-father—paternal even to his brother. When he needed her in Alaska in the first fight for his life, she had uprooted herself without a second thought and rushed to her son's side. She had abandoned a lucrative business there, to hasten to him when he killed Guard Turner. On Robbie's defence she had lavished an inheritance which would have comforted her old age. She had saved her son from a gallows rope; always she had remained near him, sewing miles of casket-satin for twelve dollars a week.

She had held off every rival, from the girls of his childhood to the Alaskan dance-hall woman. Now he had forsaken her.

Elizabeth Stroud's mind tottered a little under the blow.

On visiting day, Elizabeth Stroud went to the prison and had a little chat with some of the officials. Their respect for her was genuine; they were always cordial. She seemed a bit dazed. Her hat was askew and her hands were trembling.

Then her Robbie appeared. Her tall, round-shouldered, middle-aged son, blinking and squinting in the unaccustomed light. He held his perforated, white-topped eyeshade in his hand. They looked at each other and said nothing. For the first time in a thousand meetings, they did not kiss. Elizabeth's old eyes were dry and bright behind her glasses, and her son's were unaccountably seeking corners.

Her tone, when she finally spoke, was trancelike and there was distance and condescension in it.

"I never thought you would do a thing like this to your old mother, son." She did not use "Robbie" this time. "You have taken up with that—that woman—publicly. She's no good for you. The officials are angry. They think you are crazy, son. You must be a very sick boy to do this to your old mother."

The son's voice was placating, gentle. "You are not using your head, Mom," he said mildly. "They had me on the list for a transfer."

The old lady shook her head. "Robbie, do you think Mother would ever let them take your birds away?"

"I know they'll try to break anybody who defies them. I live here, Mother. I know."

"No, Robbie, you're wrong. They've been trying to help you. If you were not sick you would understand. I've talked with them. Don't you realize how you've hurt them?"

Very slowly her stoop-shouldered son straightened and his eyes focused on hers. "Mother," he exclaimed, "since when are you worried about them? Their job is to *hold* me. To them I am already dead. Dead since 1916."

"They know you are sick, son," she interrupted. "You're here for your protection. I thought you were getting well, but now . . . Taking up with that woman, after all I did for you. Only a sick person would do that."

Stroud looked at his mother, aghast.

"I'm not sick, Mother. Don't keep telling me I'm sick. It's because of Dell that you feel this way." In a shocked voice, he added, "You sound like you are on the other side."

She shook her head pityingly. "No, Robbie. I'm on your side. Give up this woman and this silly publicity. . . ."

Stroud's gentle tone vanished. "Dell and I are the same as one person," he said. The old lady flinched and her mouth closed like a steel trap. "Mother, I know what this is all about . . . Me, and you, and why I did what I did . . ." The prisoner stalked from the room, his face working strangely.

The guards exchanged glances. One of them helped the old lady to her feet. Her eyes were glazed. She stopped again at the warden's office.

When Della tried to see her later, Mrs. Stroud refused. When Della tried to visit Robert Stroud, she was turned away. Then the widow's correspondence was cut off and her letters returned.

Late in January, 1934, a reporter with a hunch knocked on the door of Elizabeth Stroud's apartment.

"A petition has been circulating for your son's parole, Mrs. Stroud. Are you leading a new fight for his parole? How is Robert, Mrs. Stroud?"

She glanced distractedly at the reporter.

"I have nothing to say," she murmured. "Nothing."

"Mrs. Stroud," persisted the reporter, "is Della Jones heading the fight this time? Do you think she'll get him out?"

The old lady suddenly swung her door wide and motioned the reporter in. "My boy is where he belongs and I shall do nothing to obtain his release from the penitentiary." Her words seemed torn from her.

The reporter waited.

"I know he is safe where he is."

The reporter wrote rapidly. Then he looked at the paintings on the wall. He was silent as his eyes took in the canvases—the weird nasturtiums painted by a man who had forgotten how they looked; the bright pictures of dimly remembered Alaskan streams; the portrait of a deputy warden of fifteen years before.

The reporter wanted to be sure. "Mrs. Stroud, you mean you would rather have your son in there than free? You now oppose his parole?"

"It's for his own good." The old lady stood immovable.

The reporter thanked her and left.

Next day, the Kansas City *Star* carried a copyrighted story which became a wire-service dispatch printed throughout the country. The news angle was no less irresistible than the prisoner's romance.

MOTHER FIGHTS LIFER'S ATTEMPT TO GET PAROLE, ran the one-column head.

> Her son has been in solitary confinement for 17 years, the longest time any inmate of a Federal prison has ever spent in isolation from his fellow men. But she would rather have him there than free. She opposes his parole. . . .

Prison officials made no comment.

Back in the recesses of his stone womb, Stroud sat with his birds. A small mound of ashes lay at his feet—the remains of the clippings he had saved about his mother.

"A parole is the only thing that Mrs. Elizabeth Stroud lives for," M. W. Childs had stated in the St. Louis *Post-Dispatch* in November, 1931. "The last 14 years of her life she has spent in an effort to secure the freedom of her son. Her story is an amazing instance of the persistency of the human will."

"They should parole him," Mrs. Stroud had stated to A. B. Mcdonald of the *Star* in 1931, "and let him carry on his business outside; surely he has proved himself worthy of it."

"Are you going to deny the regenerating power of the human heart?" she had exclaimed to the feature writer. "My son's whole life, his mind, his heart, his soul, have been transformed by his contact with those birds."

The silver cord—in this case, one forged of wrought iron—had broken at last, severing this indomitable mother from her unbending son. It broke late, with disastrous results to all the principals—son, mother and intruding widow.

Mrs. Stroud's statement was given wide notice. It took the heart out of the campaign for Stroud's parole. Who would go against nature? Who would support the release of a son whose mother deemed him better off in prison?

The implacable old woman lived in a daze behind locked doors. Her *raison d'être* had dissolved in the hot lead of the linotype machines which slugged out her statement.

Bitter and broken, Elizabeth Stroud removed herself from the arena. Fleeing from her son, from the widow, from the great stone wall which held her hopes, her prayers and her great mother's heart, Elizabeth limped home to the hearthstone of her noted family in Metropolis, Illinois. There she endured, hoping against hope for some development which might alter the Aeschylean pattern. Her son's first parole hearing was scheduled for 1937. After begging a long-time friend to carry on a struggle for her son's pardon, she died several months later at the age of seventy-eight.

If Robert Stroud was aware of the mighty blow dealt his future by his mother, he said little about it. He moved ahead on the course he had set. He still hoped for parole in 1937. There is little evidence that the loss of his mother's support altered his course. He later wrote about it in a letter to a friend:

> It was not a case of grudge. There are some things that burn so deeply into one's being that they can never be forgotten. Some day, if we both live long enough, you may read the whole story.

Elizabeth had always been faithful to him, and no other person had so claimed her heart. In middle age, he had broken through the maternal net, and he may have considered her reaction a predestined thing. He may have sensed that the central character in this obscure drama had never been named, the character who played all roles, the Bride, the Groom, the Mother, a force which slowly crushed them all. It was the Prison.

Della Jones was permitted neither to see nor write to her figurative groom. Stroud made repeated requests. Their business, impeded and clogged, fell to lower and lower levels. Della lost her investment. But Stroud and the widow both clung to their curious compact and lived on what were, at best, tenuous memories.

A close friend of Elizabeth Stroud's offered the convict a sum of money he needed desperately in his bird business. The price of the gift was that Stroud "break with Della"—a woman he now could never see nor write to.

Stroud flatly refused. He would not compromise, and for years he was to persist in efforts to reach her. Prison records reveal, for example, that on April 22, 1937, Stroud requested of a new warden permission to write to his "wife".

"You are advised that I do not care to make any change in the mail restriction with reference to Mrs. Jones," the warden replied.

Two years later, on October 17, 1939, Stroud again requested permission, based on his need for some business documents.

"Correspondence between you and Mrs. Jones cannot be permitted," was the official reply.

Della Jones fought for her man month after month and year after year. She was unable to change the iron-fisted decision of Stroud's keepers.

After many years, the widow, who had become an old woman herself, grew weary and dropped from view, closing the door on their strange attachment.

Some observers familiar with Stroud's life have contended that the bird convict's relation with Della Jones was merely a business one. If so, it was singularly tenacious. It seemed impervious to time, or money, or prison walls. The widow remained in Stroud's mind for years. She may have been the symbol of Stroud's effort to free himself from his mother. The real meaning of their attachment lies hidden in a strange mind and heart.

TWENTY-TWO

BEHIND THE Leavenworth wall in 1934, Stroud was able to greet February with a small success. He secured a supply of paint from the prison commissary. He set to work on his new quarters, where it looked as though he might remain a while.

"I am still working on my bird house," he wrote to a bird breeder. "I have been painting steadily for weeks. I am painting every thing, cages, rooms, furniture, yes, even the floors, with enamel. Everything is in white, blue and a reddish brown. The floors will be black. To show you what a thorough job I have been doing, I have used thirty pounds of putty. I have not left a crack where a roach or a mite could live."

The bird convict was proud of his refurbished quarters. He was unaware that he soon would have a distinguished visitor: the Attorney-General himself.

In July, 1934, Attorney-General Homer S. Cummings embarked upon a tour of Federal prisons. His dream, Alcatraz, had been made real.

One hot day he appeared in the Isolation Building with warden and entourage. He heard the faint chirp of many birds, and looked inquiringly at the warden.

"That's the birdman's cell down there. You *know*—Stroud."

As the Cabinet official listened to rollers lilting in song, he saw a thin, sallow face under an eyeshade pressed against the wire-netting.

"Mr. Cummings, could I have a word with you?" asked a respectful, careful voice.

The officials waited, eyes on the Attorney-General.

"Why, yes," he decided. "I'll talk with you."

A guard stepped forward and unlocked the cell door. The official took a deep breath and looked at the guards and officials behind him. They waited for word from the Chief. It was an old problem. Would he ask for a guard? Risk losing face?

The top official stepped quickly through the open door of Stroud's cell. The singing and fluttering grew louder.

"Mr. Cummings," began Stroud, "don't you think I've spent

long enough in this place? I've been here eighteen years and it gets a little—well, monotonous."

His listener made no response.

Stroud moved back into the recesses of his cell. The official followed, peering at the birds in the cages. They chippered and scolded excitedly.

"This place looks neat and well-painted," said Cummings. He took in the typewriter. He squinted at another object which had a handle.

"You're well-equipped, for a prisoner. What's that?"

"Oh, that's a feed-grinder."

The official examined some objects gleaming in the half-opened desk drawer. "What do you have in here?"

"Oh, dissecting instruments—scalpel and so forth. A screw-driver. Scissors."

"Hmmm," said the Attorney-General.

"I have some trouble getting research stuff. But most of all I am worried about correspondence."

The official nodded. "I'll check it." He looked Stroud in the eye. "You've caused a lot of trouble, Stroud," he said in a low voice. "That marriage of yours, especially. You sought publicity. Is that how you expect to get along?"

Stroud was taken aback. Talking turkey here, alone. What an opportunity! He blinked at the official. "Sir," he said, talking low and fast, "I want to explain that. It was raw from your view. But did you know I was slated for Alcatraz? It was act, or lose these birds."

"You could have complained. Written."

"I wasn't supposed to know about it. If I had written, it would be denied—and then going over the administration here would have got me in bad, too."

"Well. So it was more than just a headline hunt. I am glad you had a reason. I see it now, here, in these birds. . . ."

Stroud said nothing.

The official gestured at the teeming cages of canaries. "This must keep you working harder than the men do in the shops."

"There is a lot to do," answered the prisoner as the official walked toward the door.

"Sir, will you help me?" asked Stroud. There was an unaccustomed tone in his voice.

"I will investigate it," said the official gruffly.

The key turned in Stroud's lock. He saw the expressions of relief on the faces of the group as their chief rejoined them.

"Well, he saw me anyway," Stroud told his birds.

He could not join cause and effect, but noted that shortly thereafter his correspondence privileges were increased by one letter a week, and when he requested permission to buy some chemical reagents, the order went through. The convict's avian researches increased.

Some time during the twenties, a new disease found its way into American aviaries. It was first reported in the eastern United States. The ailment seemed to strike weanlings, and the first noticeable symptom was a peculiar twisting of the neck, always to the right.

Stroud first noticed the odd symptom in one of his fledglings in 1929. He had amassed a considerable ornithology by this time, but his research failed to uncover any mention of it. The disease was not, apparently, contagious. Neither old birds nor nestlings seemed much affected by it.

The young birds which were affected, however, were pathetic. The little bird's neck would twist so far to the right that it could not take food.

Stroud was baffled. He remembered that a cinnamon-coloured canary he had purchased had slept with its head between its legs. Since none of the babies he had bred or fed became ill, Stroud had checked it off as an anomaly.

He recalled that every young bird which had contracted the disease had been fed greens from the little plot he had planted in the bull pen. Unable to get soil, he had used cage refuse, vegetables and sand, which he had "sweetened" with a pailful of lime. He had washed the greens carefully before feeding.

The puzzled convict-scientist made blood cultures from the affected birds. They remained negative. He fed only the tops of the greens to healthy birds. The birds stayed well.

Then he fed them the roots of the greens only. The old and very young birds remained well, but fledglings developed the disease.

Next, he isolated some healthy young birds and fed them drinking water containing dissolved droppings from diseased birds. They drank it and remained well.

As grimly determined as a detective on a homicide case, he

now secured five gallons of clean sand and somehow persuaded either a trusty or guard to have the sand roasted to a red heat and placed in a box.

He contaminated the sterile box with diseased droppings, sowed it with rape seed and fed the sprouted plant, roots included, to susceptible young birds. They developed the disease.

These experiments went on for four years. He could not locate the cause. He could not arrest the disease. But in dissecting the birds which died, he noted an enlarged liver and evidence of digestive disorders.

In 1931 he had read the first description of a similar condition. It had developed into a formidable disease in young poultry and was called "fowl paralysis". The article was written by a university veterinarian and was entitled, "Fowl Paralysis, Its Cause and Remedy".

The prisoner subsequently acknowledged his debt to the article for the information on the disease in poultry, but he was irritated by the article's misleading title. It promised a "remedy". But the article ended: "There is no cure for fowl paralysis and not knowing the cause of the disease, control methods should be based on general sanitary measures."

Stroud's scientific passion for exactitude and facts caused him to criticize this type of veterinary science. His frankness made him enemies. A psychiatrist commented that the embattled prisoner was sublimating his aggressions in the field of science. It was not a new phenomenon.

Stroud later secured some diseased droppings from infected poultry. He fed susceptible baby canaries on greens raised in ground infected with the chicken droppings. His young canaries contracted the disease. In chickens, the malady paralysed wings and legs. In canaries, it twisted their necks to the right. But it was the same disease—he had proved it.

Stroud had not received the microscope he had hoped to get. He had never again been able to save up the money he had sent to the aged woman who had helped him.

But he drew ingenious inferences from his limited facilities for observation and experiment.

The singular tenacity of the scientist growing to fulfilment in the brain of a prisoner was never better shown. He refused to give up.

He wrote out a detailed experiment and begged other bird

scientists to use their superior facilities to demonstrate and to improve his findings. The cure could not be found.

It was seven years later, in 1941, when Stroud finally discovered an absolute specific for the disease in canaries, which cured the infection with a single dose: one-tenth of a grain of the new drug sulfanilamide introduced into the canary's crop.

On a hot summer day in 1935, Stroud received a cage containing six canaries. They were all dead on arrival. They were sent by a desperate Missouri woman in the hope that Stroud might save their lives, and prescribe for her remaining birds. She had lost more than 100 birds of a flock of 160.

She also sent a letter describing symptoms. The bird would sit with feathers fluffed out, eyes closed. At intervals they would cry out as in pain, seemingly in their heads, which they threw back. Rapid breathing followed and death came in a convulsion.

The express man who delivered the birds had carefully noted the time each bird died. It varied from three to twelve hours before arrival.

Stroud dissected the birds at once. He found curious changes in the spleens of the birds—which were greatly enlarged and had turned a deep cobalt blue.

Besides being without a microscope, Stroud had run out of culture media to grow and test the germ. The bird convict tentatively diagnosed the ailment as B-Paratyphosis B, and prescribed a "slightly alkaline, effervescent saline" in a dosage he had found effective. The treatment arrested the disease in the flock and saved all but one bird of the score taken sick.

It was only several months after the outbreak had been stopped that Stroud learned that his diagnosis had been confirmed by a doctor of veterinary pathology in one of the Iowa colleges. The professor had found bacteria in the organs and placed them under his microscope. The germ was *Salmonella Eartrycke*, also known as *B-Paratyphosis B*. Stroud had diagnosed from symptoms and dissection alone.

One day Stroud received a letter from an eminent doctor and professor from the college of medicine of a leading university. The doctor had found a rare illness in one of his favourite canaries, and had written to a fellow professor in the South, the man who had edited Stroud's first book. He sent the worried physician a copy of the book, and the physician found the condition and treatment accurately described by the prisoner. In gratitude, the physician sent Stroud a letter and offered a copy of one of his own books, a scientific study of fungi. Stroud applied to the new special school officer of the prison, a Ph.D. who happened to know the physician and had read the book. The school officer himself was unable to get official permission for the book to be sent to the bird prisoner.

Stroud's vexation increased. "I have done time under all kinds of conditions," he wrote. "I was in prison when they had the silence system. I know what hard time is. But never in all the years I have been in prison did I ever know the prisoners to be more bitter and less subject to reformation than is the case right now, and it is all due to the college punk reformers sitting on top of everybody in that Bureau."

Such terms from a lifer did not endear him as a parole risk.

The convict was slowly torn within by survival problems. He could not understand the vast prison transformation occupying the minds in the Bureau he had angered. But one Bureau official was to aid in realizing one of the convict's fondest hopes a year later—after the official had left the Bureau.

He was a good lecturer who had accomplished many reforms. When he spoke at Wesleyan University, he mentioned a prisoner at Leavenworth who was interested in canaries. The prisoner's fondest desire, he told his audience, was not for better food or even association with other convicts. It was for a microscope to enable him to learn more about the diseases of birds.

A professor of biology who was listening remembered a battered Spencer microscope no longer used in the laboratory. He had it overhauled and the university sent it to the warden of Leavenworth for Stroud. The auspices of the gift were overwhelming. On April 15, 1936, the deputy warden brought an oblong wooden box to the cell of Convict No. 17431-L.

The birdman was expecting his breakfast tray and was not surprised when he heard the sound of his cell door opening. He saw the deputy warden with a box instead of the guard with a tray.

"You'll like this better than breakfast," said the official. "Sign here." The bewildered convict took the proffered indelible pencil suspiciously. Then he read:

RECEIVED OF DEPUTY WARDEN'S OFFICE, THIS INSTITUTION, ONE MICROSCOPE, COMPLETE WITH CASE AND EXTRA PARTS.

Stroud's hand shook as he hastened to comply.

"Some time ago," he later wrote in thanks to the university, "I read a newspaper account of a man, blind since birth, whose sight had been suddenly restored. At the time, I wondered how this man must have felt as he gazed for the first time upon the world in which he lived, a mystery shrouded in darkness. I know now."

Stroud was an excited man with his new "eye". He trained its glassy magnification on all manner of objects: feathers, cells, blood, bacteria, muscle, gland and bone. Half-suspected, dimly visualized structural matter was thrown up in earthquake eruptions of sudden size before his astonished gaze.

He had already developed an excellent technique for developing cultures and making bacteriological smears. He had studied bacteriology. All but the actual mechanics of the 'scope, and practice, were his. Now he could see what he wished.

One of the hospital lab men, hearing of Stroud's new acquisition, came over to give him pointers. He made his suggestions through the bars.

"Don't squint your other eye," he told the bird convict. "Just relax it and leave it open. After a while it won't see a thing unless you want it to."

"Thanks," murmured Stroud. "By the way, you can't see much of the tissue unless you can see right through it—get a lot of light. Doesn't this require thin slices of tissue?"

"Very thin. Down to thousandths of an inch. What you need is a microtome."

"A what?"

"A microtome," said the technician. "It's a little machine that cuts tissue very thin—down to 1/12,000 of an inch."

"Can you get me a picture and description of one?"

"Yes, there's one in a lab manual. I think they will let you look it over."

"I'd appreciate it."

"Remember, you've got enough with just plain smears—slides of bird blood, disease germs—to keep you going for life."

"I'll *start* on that. I've already started."

Stroud studied the manual with great care, copied off the description of the microtome and directions for its use. Then he made a careful copy of the drawing.

For many months, between his intricate forays into bacteriology and haemotology, the idea of a microtome slept in his mind. He would idly muse about it. His first thought for a cutting edge was the object for which he had probably found more use than anyone else in the country—a safety-razor blade.

It took him two years in between other activities, but he built a microtome.

The following letter probably contains a description of the most ingenious do-it-yourself accomplishment, by a prisoner, of the many that have come to light in world history. It was written late in 1939.

I am typing this letter with rather sore fingers. Whenever I do any mechanical work I always tear my hands. Friday I finished a new microtome, and I am rather proud of the job . . . the cheapest one made costs from $150 to $280. . . . For material I had a few pieces of hard wood, some glass, a piece of ½″ rod with threads on it, a tin can, and a few scraps of sheet copper, and some black enamel and wood screws. Not a promising collection, but from it I built a machine that will give me cuts down to two microns, and the best made will not cut thinner than that. The big problem was to get smooth, uniform motion. I accomplished that by binding all the moving and bearing surfaces with tin and copper and polishing them. The screw presses a thin copper wedge under a tin-covered block that is forced up between two glass guides upon which the razor blade, held in a plane-like oak block, slides and does the cutting. The tissue is imbedded in wax and fastened to the top of the block that comes up between the glass surfaces. Since two microns are equal to 1/12,000 of an inch, you can see that any lost motion would upset the whole operation. An irregularity of 1/1,000 of an inch would give sections you could not see through.

I have already made a good rough study of the anatomy and histology of canaries and mice, but now I am going in for the finer details. And, because I want to get back to it, I am going to make this short.

Even in his letters, he seemed pressed for time. . . .

During the years following 1934, the big prison settled down a little. The depression ended slowly. Bank robberies, which ran nearly two a day for an all-time high in 1932, began to fall off. John Dillinger, symbol of an era, was shot to death in 1934.

Alcatraz was in business, and the F.B.I. agent became a national hero. But while spectacular gangsters were broken, the larger gangs found substitutes for illegal liquor traffic, and deepened their merger with political machines.

Prisoners' descriptions of Leavenworth at this time are consistent. There were liquor and dope traffic, privately cooked steaks on private stoves for those who could afford them; and for anyone ambitious to learn, excellent company—college professors, brokers, lawyers, judges, governors, congressmen, heads of companies, hijackers—all members of the prison fraternity.

Money was made on the stock market by brokers while in prison. For local gambling, there was a completely organized betting set-up for prison baseball. There was some counterfeiting.

The prisoners themselves, though, clung to their hobbies and handicraft work wherever possible.

For some men, the prison was not a complete loss. In fact, men survived in prison at this time who might have fared more miserably on the depression-ridden outside.

The Director of the Bureau was well aware of this when in a letter to a woman who inquired about Stroud in 1932, he informed her that Stroud had three square meals and a place to sleep, which was more than many enjoyed on the outside.

There was, in the writings of prisoners, considerable variance with the picture given by Stroud in his letter. The difference may have been in their objectives.

The unforgivable sin, from the point of view of "getting in bad", was to incur publicity. Any prison publicity whatever, good or bad, was regarded as bad. Those who tried to bring conditions to light, or call attention to themselves, received a hard fist of reprisal. Leavenworth had been in the glare of national attention in 1929, 1930, 1933, and Stroud had not made it any easier with his amazing campaigns.

The bird convict had committed himself to a battle against overwhelming odds. He could not turn back from his course. His facilities, as well as the red-tape restrictions which smothered him, were the measure of the notice he had received and the formidable scare he had thrown into the growing Bureau.

Stroud was trying to achieve release through appeal to the public on the basis of his accomplishments and service to the public. A self-made scientist, he dreamed of raising money to establish a large bird farm.

Year by year, Stroud toiled to perfect himself in his field. He developed complete facilities for staining bacteria and even for making blood counts. He had blood counting chambers, gram stains and buffer solutions ready to hand.

With his cell wired for many outlets, he kept his birds warm with 100-watt light bulbs in their cages. He promoted a complex bargain which eventuated in the sudden disappearance of the electric motor from a Hoover vacuum machine in a distant part of the prison, and he now used it to power his feed-grinder.

The quality of his birds improved. He developed, through careful breeding, scores of pure white Yorkshire canaries—stately and beautiful creatures which also had a melodious warble. These birds he sold for $25.00 each.

He had long since developed the spectacular crested warblers—the "mopheads" which appear grotesque to the average citizen and are prized among canary fanciers.

He dyed his white birds a pale pink by feeding them red pepper preparations, and then experimented with anthroquinone dyes sent to him by the du Pont Company.

Through these dyes, he produced the only pink and lavender canaries then in existence. He discovered, however, that these colours faded when the birds were exposed to sunlight. But sunlight also turned yellow canaries a ruddy hue, returned red to the faded breasts of captive robins, and brown to sparrows grown white indoors.

Stroud had a convict's love for the sun, and he grew absorbed in the question of its effect upon skin pigment. He hoped to produce permanent colour changes in birds by the use of ultra-violet light.

"Not having my handicaps," he wrote to a friendly bird breeder, "you could try this without much difficulty. All you need is one of those new mercury vapour bulbs or a naked carbon arc. Expose naked areas of the bird's skin to this light, in doses not quite sufficient to cause sunburn. If this worked you would be doing something never before accomplished by man—forcing recessive qualities of tissue cells to become dominant under the influence of external stimulation."

Unable to follow this line, Stroud continued his work with dyes. It was during these experiments that Stroud discovered therapeutic properties in anthroquinone violet.

He found that it cured birds infected with aspergillosis, a

"pathogenic fungus". The disease was known to affect all varieties of birds. "It has been observed in young ostriches, and in canaries and sparrows—which about covers the field so far as size is concerned."

Stroud, remembering that sulphanilamide had been used in dyeing for forty years before its therapeutic properties were discovered, believed he might have come upon another drug in anthroquinone. Its properties as a bird medicine were unknown to the du Pont laboratories. Several years later, the convict was visited by a professor of bacteriology from Iowa University. This doctor agreed to experiment on guinea-pigs and white rats to explore the chemical as a possible weapon against tuberculosis. The professor spent a sum of money on thirty experiments, but was unable to achieve conclusive results. But he respected the convict's observations, and commented:

> "He was doing an admirable piece of work under restricted conditions. His earnestness impressed me. In fairness to the prison officials, I think they were encouraging as much as they could under the circumstances."

Now Stroud was reaching out beyond the confines of his solitary cell to widen scientific inquiry to serve his fellow men. He was recognized in his field.

The expected release on parole shone like a beckoning light.

He read about the release, in 1935, of one prisoner who had killed his mother, spent many years in jail, then suddenly fed a mixture of opium and prussic acid to two guards in their lemonade, killing one and seriously injuring the other in an attempted escape. After years in solitary confinement, this prisoner had finally been pardoned by the Governor of Michigan. He had "accomplished" nothing, yet he was freed. It gave Stroud hope for himself.

But his hopes, which had been predicated upon what he claimed was the word of the Director of the Federal Bureau of Prisons at that time, a word assertedly given during the settlement following his 1931 campaign, received a serious setback.

The Director of the Bureau, Sanford Bates, resigned in February, 1937, after giving notice in 1936. He denied that he had indicated a parole for Stroud.

During these years it again became *comme il faut* to include the birdman of Leavenworth in tours of the institution. This was especially true among Government officials, many of whom visited Stroud and purchased his birds.

In late summer, 1936, Stroud was honoured by a call from the head of the G-Men himself, J. Edgar Hoover.

Mr. Hoover was drawn by a large cage containing snow-white canaries. He purchased one of the younger birds for ten dollars. It was boxed at once and addressed to Hoover's mother, Anne M. Hoover, in Washington, D.C.

Since the bird was young and untried, Stroud guaranteed that if the G-Man's purchase did not sing by October, Stroud would replace it at his own expense. With characteristic thoroughness, he typed a long letter to Mrs. Hoover which was virtually an article on the care of a canary.

Dear Madam:

I have just had the pleasure of meeting your remarkable and illustrious son, and of selling him one of my fine white canaries.

The bird . . . should reach you almost as soon as this letter does, if not before. He will be in tip-top condition at the time shipped.

If for any reason he should not arrive in good condition, please make the man delivering him place a "bad order" notation upon your receipt and return it to me. I will then ship another bird at once. . . .

Despite his efforts, Stroud heard that his bird had not performed, displeasing Mr. Hoover. Stroud replaced the ten-dollar bird with a twenty-five dollar one.

Years later, however, Stroud was nettled by gossip which he claimed prison officials were circulating "nation-wide" from Washington: that he, the Birdman, had sold J. Edgar Hoover a painted sparrow for ten dollars. Stroud was more offended by this than by graver accusations. A painted *sparrow*! The convict never forgot the matter. Many years later he answered the "libel and discredit" to his avian reputation by inserting his reply as "Exhibit A" in a sworn court document.

When Stroud learned of the resignation of Sanford Bates who had built and launched the mighty Federal Bureau of Prisons, he felt a severe blow to his hope for parole.

When he received further information that the new Director was James V. Bennett, Stroud's hope for parole dimmed. For the new Director was the man originating from the Bureau of Efficiency, the same man who made a fruitless effort to settle

Stroud's dispute with the Bureau, at the height of his victorious campaign in 1931.

Stroud was familiar with the operation of the Board of Parole. Rightly or wrongly, he took the view of most prisoners that Federal parole decisions did not operate in a vacuum; and that politics, internal and external, entered into its scales.

His course had been charted: to achieve freedom through public recognition of services performed. But he was no longer the Robert Stroud whose fight for his birds reached Congress and brought national notice. He was now Number 17431-L, Leavenworth.

On February 11, 1937, Stroud's application for parole was denied. No reasons were given by Ruby M. Carr, the Acting Parole Executive, in answer to scores of inquiries over the following months. No explanation was legally required. Whatever the factors, they were deemed by the three eminent members of the Parole Board and the Parole Executive to be good and sufficient. The matter ended there.

For lack of anything else, Stroud still clung to his forlorn hope despite the prison-wise voice of experience. The bird doctor had neither committed nor attempted violence since a President had handed him his life—seventeen years without a blemish on his record. He had endured solitary confinement for a longer period than any Federal prisoner. He had triumphed over prison torpor and educated himself. He had supported his mother from a solitary cell. He had gone forward through a series of mind-cracking crises to become a bird scientist whose contributions to bird pathology and therapy had saved thousands of dollars, an estimated 50,000 birds and uncounted human heartaches in the lives of bird-lovers throughout the world.

He was unable, reflecting on his record, to see wherein at any stage of his avian pursuits he could have done other than he did without losing his birds. He was convinced that his course had saved him from Alcatraz; that he should have been paroled; that a high official had pledged his word to it; and that this cell-filled wonder of hot and vital, beautiful white and yellow birds which now were lilting in a mating song, would not be here, had he not done what he had done.

He was forty-eight years old. The average "stretch" for prisoners sentenced to life in United States prisons at this time was between eight and eleven years. He had now served twenty-nine years.

Stroud concocted a strong glassful of ethyl alcohol, citric acid and water. After feeding his birds, he went on a silent, solitary drunk. He could not get the powerful "choc beer" which was brewed across the alley from the commissary by a royal clique of prisoners and served ice-cold to the anointed. It was too far away, and considered too good to sell. Next day, he was back to his microscope. There was much work to be done.

Stroud now had in mind an enormous project. He proposed to write and illustrate in one volume a complete system of pet bird pathology and avian therapeutics, in dictionary form, and in a language understandable to the average bird-lover. But he worried about his writing.

In March, 1937, he wrote to Fred Daw, president of the Chicago Cage Bird Club, a friend since 1928:

> You are right about one never knowing how little one knows until he starts to learn something. Wanting to write better on birds and bird diseases, I took a course in English syntax. . . . When I went over the stuff I had written before taking the course, I was actually ashamed of it. I had thought it good before. When I finish the course I probably will be ashamed of what I have written now and have to do it all over again.

Because his researches were incomplete, and his histological studies via microscope hardly begun, he knew it would take years. He started the writing about what he knew, prowled through avian literature for what he did not know, and embarked upon personal research in quest of what nobody knew.

Sharply observant and literally living with birds, Stroud even speculated on psychosomatic bird behaviour. In his bird book he wrote:

> A bird fluffs out his feathers when he is cold, when he is tired, when he is angry, when his feelings have been hurt, when he is sleepy or when he feels bad for any reason.

He noted that birds are under nervous strain when they are being taught tricks, however patient and kind the teacher may be:

> Many birds of a nervous temperament cannot stand this. They go into a decline and die. It has always been my opinion that such birds were suffering from shock-induced diabetes.

As his studies extended deeper into the histology of the eliminative system in birds, Stroud marvelled at their hot, fast metabolism, and he thought he could understand why nature combined their two eliminative functions in one release. Again, it was their high temperature, added to the economy imposed by flight, which required a bird to excrete the waste products from its kidneys as a pasty solid. He understood why a sudden change of temperature might well affect a small, hot bird more than a human being.

Stroud knew from his own experience and collateral reading that prolonged chilling can induce kidney trouble in man. He had suffered his own worst siege of the ailment as a result of severe prolonged chilling.

It had occurred to him even before 1933 that what many veterinarians diagnosed as sporadic pneumonia in birds, might be due to uraemic poisoning, caused not by germs, but by chilling. Stroud noticed that bird chilling set into motion a train of symptoms with a fatal termination.

Stroud observed that sick canaries instinctively sought heat.

> If the [100-watt light] is hung so they can get under it, they lie down and spread their feathers and allow the heat to beat upon their backs, over their kidneys. Sometimes this starts the kidneys functioning, and birds apparently at the point of death may be eating and singing within the hour.

But what did cold air do to a bird's kidney which could cause such a swift accumulation of changes?

After reading his books, scores of bulletins from state and Government experimental stations and thousands of bird articles, he found none accounting for the condition he described.

It was when he trained his microscope upon the bird's kidney *in situ* that the canary doctor made his astonishing find. He saw large, jagged crystals rocked into the uriniferous tubes of the kidney, with the sharp points anchored there, plugging the tubes, which were distended in irritation.

Uraemic attacks, he speculated, were caused by air blowing on a bird's feet, lowering its temperature gradually, but not enough to awaken it. As the temperature fell, uric acid formed larger and larger crystals, plugging the kidney tubes.

Stroud developed an effective medicine for bird uraemia—diurol.

For general conditioning of both birds and men he paid homage in his writings to the basic effervescent mixtures of tartaric acid with sodium bicarbonate, under their many trade names and added ingredients. As a diuretic as well as laxative, he had found them good for himself as well as his hot-blooded canaries.

The strange blood of birds now began to fascinate Stroud. He discovered that it is more difficult to make a microscopic "smear" from bird blood than from human blood. He first practised upon his only source of blood with a larger supply—himself. After perfecting his technique, he went back to his canaries.

Only a bird doctor can describe with what difficulty blood can be secured from a feathered bundle of energy whose temperature is normal at 107° F. Stroud's method rarely left the bird with so much as a sore claw. He discovered that the simplest method of securing a drop of blood from a canary, which can ill spare much, is to snip off one claw, pinch out a tiny droplet on a smearing slide, touch the claw lightly with the brightly burning end of a cigarette, and return to cage. He saved three sick birds in 1937 by locating lead poisoning through blood tests.

After locating the most up-to-date texts of his day on human blood and the blood of birds, he began to search for the various cells described.

What had appeared a simple chore developed into a challenging complexity. He soon was convinced that most observers "have simply applied what they have been taught concerning blood, ignored what they did not understand, and let the subject [of bird blood] go at that".

After testing sixty-five original staining techniques and spending thousands of hours at his microscope, and after carefully drawing what he observed five times, he made twenty-six illustrations to scale of bird blood cells. He described carefully what he had observed and later incorporated his findings into his major bird book.

"I probably do not know what I am talking about," he wrote, "and have grave doubts about whether anyone else knows anything about the subject, either; but . . . after 3,000 hours at the microscope, I pass that nothing on to you."

Such wry comment, after years of eye-straining discipline, typifies a dedicated scientist.

TWENTY-THREE

ONE DAY EARLY in 1938 a new deputy warden's assistant was detailed to interview Stroud. The classification department had discovered no "Admission Summary" in Stroud's file, although he had been in prison since 1909 and in Leavenworth since 1912.

The story, whether true or false, of Stroud's fixed "assaultive character", was preserved among prison personnel. It conferred importance on older guards and assistants to dramatize the danger of their convicts.

After telling the story of Stroud's violent crimes, the senior warden's assistant handed the new junior warden's assistant some papers, summoned a guard and ordered the new man to Stroud's cell.

To Benjamin Levy, social worker, it was better to risk a knife thrust from a convict than to lose face with shrewd older officials. Levy tried to remember his boxing lessons, and set out for Stroud's cell.

At the cell door, he turned to the guard.

"You can take off. I won't need you." The guard shrugged and locked the door upon the young official. He introduced himself to Stroud, who seated the assistant and stood against the wall, waiting. Stroud remained cold and aloof throughout the long Admission Summary questions. When the subject turned to birds, however, Stroud's eyes warmed and he unbent, outlining with eloquence that amazed his listener, the qualities of pedigree in canaries.

Then Stroud, warming to his listener, changed the subject.

"I suppose you are going to climb the Civil Service ladder like the rest," said Stroud.

"It's the way to get more money," said the assistant, wondering what was coming.

"Better dig into your books," Stroud said with an enigmatic gleam in his eye. "You're bucking a Phi Beta Kappa college con."

"What do you mean?"

Stroud would not elaborate. "It's not my affair," he said.

The young official remained in the convict's cell for three hours, punctuated only by occasional check-ups by the "shelf screw".

He had spent a longer time with Stroud in his cell than any man in twenty years. It put a "feather in his cap" among associates.

Later, Levy discovered the meaning of Stroud's remark about "bucking a Phi Beta Kappa con". Working in the warehouse was a bright young prisoner who had been head of his college year. Guards taking correspondence courses for promotion soon discovered that the young prisoner could answer test questions.

Later in 1938 Stroud was notified of the death of his mother. To the isolated man, the news came as a mournful shock. Had he expected his mother to be exempt from death?

Stroud felt a profound sadness and regret. The morbid music of his youth had long since changed its rhythm. The old discords and the tragic conduct which followed had lost their bright colours. He himself was nearing fifty and felt more alone than ever.

After the denial of parole, the death of his mother and increasing restrictions upon his activities and efforts, his former sardonic humour reverted to a more bitter, aggressive tone.

His mother's total absorption in him, the notoriety of his trials and marriage, had combined alternately to deprive, then inflate his ego.

Day in, day out and year in and year out, his main contacts were confined to the pedestrian minds of his underpaid keepers. He ricocheted like a spinning stone from repeated contact with himself, himself, himself—always himself and the walls and back to himself. When he fought for his birds, he was also fighting the phantom of prison psychosis.

Now the sheer weight of days, the same cell, the same cages, the same food, the same lavatory, the same bed—ate into his temper and disturbed his equilibrium. He had been behind walls for thirty years. There was no Grand Canyon of the Colorado to yawn before him on a vacation to cut him to size; no metropolis, no mountains, no sea. And few people whose contact might wear down his ego-growth.

The slow rot of prisoners under their rocks and roosts of steel, especially those living alone, produces a phenomenon known as "con's ego"—an egregious egocentricity, nourished by their feeling of being token victims, who carry not only their own, but the million-numbered guilt of the unconvicted, the uncaught, the unpunished.

This swelled mountainously in Stroud. He was utterly the master of his tiny kingdom of birds—yet powerless to open the door of his cell. In addition, there was the further prestige and power of the doctor. For Stroud was now a canary doctor, so recognized and consulted by as many anxious bird-lovers as he was permitted to answer.

The only egos which towered into the stratosphere of Stroud's were those of persons subjected to some of the same influences.

Stroud appeared capable neither of bending nor breaking. But now his body began to erode. He became snappish, on edge. His glands seemed to respond with electric force to irritation. He drove himself through his chores.

These activities, in addition to the breeding and selling of canaries, still did not satisfy him. In the recesses of his mind another project was taking shape.

He was not only interested in caged birds. He had become fascinated by the problems of caged men. Before he had known of birds at all, during the mad and suspenseful period when he had watched the construction of his gallows, he had meditated on his personal problem. He had coursed through books of psychology. He had journeyed with the smoking torch of Freud through the caves of his own fearsome personality.

First and always, he identified himself with the Grey Brotherhood—prisoners who had transgressed laws and were set apart. He was fascinated by penological theories. He had observed from the inside the operation, from 1912, of the attempted prison reforms.

Stroud's observations had been coloured by his own conflicts, but his passion for facts had improved over years of scientific observation.

There was practically no prison scandal, no horrible and hushed-up brutality, or conversely, no shining success in prison work, which escaped his notice. He had on call the 10,000-volume library, extensive contacts, and the services of one of the most amazing news systems in existence—the prison grapevine.

Dishonest wardens, homosexual guards, dank and scandalous

prison crimes, had come within the narrow but deep perspective of Stroud. He exploited his situation where he could, in the relentless politics of the prison. He also knew precisely in what sense it is true that prisoners actually do run a prison.

His observation had been powered by hatred and a determination to survive. His prison-starved ego abhorred the penal system which had held him since his fateful trip to Alaska in 1909.

Stroud now began to turn his trained mind and incisive pen upon the prison system itself. He set down information gathered from prison history and followed with observations from his penitentiary life.

His bird projects, however, came first. Ironically, he lacked time to do more than make notes about prison. It was to be years before radical changes in his living caused him to write in detail about jailed men rather than caged birds.

As Stroud rounded into the finishing touches of his bird book, he wrote:

> I will have the finest set of pathological and histological slides on birds in existence. Right now I am working on an embryo—a chick dead in the shell—and have made one thousand sections. I have between four and five thousand from a sparrow. In both cases the bodies are decalcified and sectioned, bones and all. In the embryo I have been able to identify every object found in the field so far.

In the spring of 1939 he blazed through the balance of his exacting bird book, and by the summer of that year he had completed approximately 200,000 words and 240 drawings in a work which contained everything he knew about birds, salted in his typical mordant style with an occasional observation about life.

There were two problems, both connected with his writing in his field, which brought him into contact with the Bureau.

The first was the bird book which he had just finished. Instead of trying to smuggle the book from prison, he applied for permission of the Bureau of Prisons to submit the work for publication, and offered to turn it over for scrutiny.

The Bureau, responding in like manner, gave him permission to negotiate for publication of the book. A Chicago businessman, after showing the manuscript to leading bird authorities, agreed to undertake the venture. But he was unable to finance it. The manuscript, after nearly a year of delay, was finally returned to the Bureau in Washington.

Stroud watched the months drag on as he chafed and waited. His language grew sharper.

In April, 1940, the warden's assistant handling Stroud's case received a letter from L. G. Marcus.

> I am the brother of Robert Stroud, 17431, and I am writing you relative to his manuscript pertaining to birds and their diseases. . . .
>
> I feel that I am in a position to get this manuscript published and placed in the proper hands for distribution, but naturally I have my own business to attend to, and it is not convenient for me to travel often. I have made arrangements to visit my brother in the near future which will be the first visit in about nine years, for the purpose of discussing in detail the publication of his book as well as seeing him.

After nine years of coolness because of Stroud's stubborn loyalty to Della Jones, the brothers were getting together again.

Marc, a successful businessman, spent an hour with Warden Hudspeth. "He was the fairest warden I think Leavenworth ever had, although Mr. White was a very fine man also," Marc wrote. "We discussed Bob and he told me that during his time of about twelve years Bob had not caused him any trouble and was an unusual man but always fair in his demands. He had not received a black mark during all of his régime."

When the warden asked Marc if he would like to see Bob's birds, the brother was surprised. The warden told a guard to take Marc to the cell instead of the visiting room.

Stroud was more surprised than Marc. "You must be some salesman to get in here. You're the only person aside from officials that has been in here." He was delighted and encouraged to see Marc. They were allowed a long visit, and Marc agreed to act as his brother's agent.

Stroud's health was poor and the distortions of his long confinement were shocking to Marc, even as he marvelled at his brother's birds. Marc left, carrying the good wishes of the warden in the effort to help the bird convict and to see his book in print.

Late in June, 1940, Stroud received word from the Bureau that it had sent his manuscript to one publisher and had received it back as of insufficient value to merit publication.

Stroud was advised that the Bureau was discontinuing further effort. The manuscript was kept in Washington.

Stroud was crushed by the news, but he kept on working. He was deep in a microscopic study of the anatomy of birds.

The enthusiastic reports of Chicago bird experts on the value of his brother's manuscript prompted Stroud's brother to request permission to receive the manuscript and to submit it himself.

Meanwhile, Stroud, tortured by increasing restrictions, delays and frustrations, lost weight and in the autumn of 1940 fell seriously ill of lobar pneumonia. He was taken to the prison hospital while the guards, orderlies and cell-tender joined in caring for his canaries.

In the hospital, Stroud later wrote, he nearly lost his life because of a conflict in prison regulations. "One set of regulations provided that certain medicines cannot be given to a man in his cell. Another set provided that any man sent to the hospital from Isolation must be placed in a locked room." The convict insisted that he was placed in a locked room without toilet facilities or running water for twenty-four hours without a drink of water, "almost at the point of death from lack of oxygen, when there was an oxygen tank standing outside the door." Stroud after that refused to go to the hospital unless assured the treatment of a first-grade prisoner. Since this was refused, he endured illness alone.

Several bird breeder friends offered to care for his birds. He was sent birthday gifts and food packages, which were returned, although money sent was placed to his account.

He was able to raise only twenty canaries in 1940.

Despite his increasing disturbance, the convict remained cooperative. He received help from the guards and continued his research work. He respected the new warden, an experienced penologist who had operated state prisons.

But in 1941 new regulations shut down on the convict even tighter. In July, he requested purchase of chemicals from the hospital after one of the physicians had encouraged the request. It was refused by the warden because of regulations prohibiting purchase through the hospital.

A week later Stroud's request for purchase of dyes for bird experiments was refused, whereupon the canary doctor wrote a long letter to the warden:

There was nothing on [the last order] the least bit out of the ordinary or not ordered before; in fact, there was nothing on it that I do not have on hand now. It was put in simply because the supplies on hand are running low. . . .

You have always been extremely kind and considerate in granting my requests for reagents, though I have little doubt that at times my desires have seemed to you insatiable and beyond reason. But this has only been because the problems involved in the study of bird diseases are no less complex than those in human diseases . . . of a nature to tax human ingenuity to the limit, even under the best of circumstances. I have felt you realized this and that it was a prompting motive behind your many kindnesses. In appreciation I have been meticulous and diligent in applying these reagents to the sole purpose for which they were granted me . . . since these items were not of an objectionable nature, the presumption is created that maybe my own conduct has been in some manner objectionable. . . . If this is the case, I would like to know it and to correct the matter.

Stroud then asked whether outside forces might have impelled discouragement of the researches.

I hope you did not feel that I had in any way let you down or been deficient in my gratitude or appreciation. For, holding you in the esteem that I always have, such a thought would be very discomforting.

The warden replied by informing the convict of a new and recent order prohibiting drugs and chemicals.

"This in no way reflects against your conduct," the warden assured him.

Later in 1941 the Isolation guard who had tried to help Stroud was transferred. Stroud was no longer able to get ice. He begged again for assistance.

As you know, for the last five years I have devoted time to study of avian pathology and have cut thousands of sections from canary tissue. I am sure some of my pathological drawings will perform a service long after we are both dead. But under the best conditions such work is not easy, warden. It is so difficult that they do not attempt it in the hospital laboratory but send all such work to the Hygienic Laboratory in Washington. All of the doctors here have expressed amazement that I have done such good work under the conditions.

One great difficulty is the fact that the cutting can only be done at the correct temperature. On the outside it is done in air-conditioned

> rooms where the temperature is thermostatically controlled. I overcome this difficulty by putting my microtome in the icebox until the wax has chilled, and then making the cuts during the few moments when it was just right. But to do this I have had to have ice.
>
> I have had an order for ice first issued by Warden White. During the last few years I have been able to get it simply by explaining the need to the guards who understood my work and were sympathetic. Under a change in detail here these conditions no longer exist.

The convict's request was of no avail. He worked on, however, studying, writing and hoping as he tended his diminishing supply of birds. He now had sixteen birds left.

He continued to help bird breeders to the limit of his correspondence rights. He helped a Tennessee breeder save her flock in a letter written a week before the nation was plunged into war by Japanese bombs on Pearl Harbor.

TWENTY-FOUR

In world war ii, Leavenworth inmates exhibited the proverbial patriotism of convicts. Prison industries rose to new levels of production. Prisoners produced five million dollars' worth of shoes, brushes and clothing during the first year of war. They donated their blood to the Red Cross and made no complaint when their work hours were increased. The prison population fell off 9 per cent., for the first time in decades. Prisoners purchased war bonds—$64,000 worth.

In the Isolation building, life went on as usual. Prisoners listened to war programmes through their radio headphones and tried to occupy their time.

A new blow now struck Stroud. When Warden Hudspeth resigned, the convict moved rapidly into a darkening cycle of his life.

The vast prison was taken over by a former Army Colonel, Walter A. Hunter. Within two months Stroud's situation grew worse. Stroud incurred Warden Hunter's ire, and his only recreation was taken from him, his radio. Stroud contended, in his irritating fashion, that the radio facilities had been installed through the prisoners' fund, paid for by themselves, and were therefore not subject to disciplinary measures.

Sick with prostate and kidney disease, Stroud wrote three copies of a long article about himself and somehow placed them in the hands of three prisoners due for release. One prisoner was the son of a famous political boss. Another was under extradition to another penitentiary.

The manuscript was intercepted by prison authorities on two of the prisoners. They did not anticipate the third copy, which was later posted to his brother with a scrawled note from Kansas City. "Bob said to send you this."

Stroud, incapable of breaking, had exposed himself. His writing termed the prison officials a swarm of petty, tax-eating bureaucrats; and in the same paragraph, pleaded for his freedom. He called the warden "Herr Heydrick", and described an October meeting of the Classification Committee which had met to consider, he said, ways and means of separating him from his birds.

He said the meeting was divided about whether to declare him incorrigible and ship him to Alcatraz, or insane and send him to Springfield. He demanded the right to be present and defend himself.

Then he retained an attorney in order to file a writ against the warden for unwarranted persecution. He claimed his business had been hampered to the point of extinction and that he might not be able to feed his flock through the winter.

During November, the convict had been too ill to exercise, or even to read the bird journals. In December, he walked slowly around the bull pen. He was used to giving his spare scraps to the wild birds. Stroud lingered, shivering and watching the birds until they soared away.

On Tuesday, December 15, 1942, at 5 a.m., the door of his cell was unlocked and the old prisoner was shaken awake by an unknown guard. Another guard played a flashlight into his eyes, as the birds churred sleepily under their covered cages in the next cell.

"Sorry, Buster—but let's get going."

The convict kept blinking and shaking his head. "Go? Go where?"

"Places. Here, put these on."

Stroud was handed fresh prison clothes. He put them on.

"Can I wash my face?" he said hoarsely.

The guard nodded, and Stroud washed his face. The icy water stung the stubble on his chin. Now he was wide awake. "Why this hour? What's the big secret?"

"Orders. Hurry it up, will you?"

"What about—this?" he gestured around his cell, his laboratory, his books, his microscope, his slides, his microtome.

"Our instructions are that you walk out of here with nothing, Buster—just the clothes we brought you."

Stroud said nothing. He stood there, stony-faced.

"Let's get these on now," said the guard quietly. He lifted the convict's arms and slipped handcuffs on his wrists. "Let's go."

Despite the confusion, Stroud remembered something. "There's a sick bird back there. Can I fix it?"

One guard stared at the other. It was not covered in the instructions.

"And get that light out of my eyes," added Stroud.

"All right. Fix the bird."

The handcuffed bird doctor quickly moved into his adjoining cell, followed by the guard. He lifted the cover of a small "quarantine" cage. The bird's feathers were fluffed into a ball. It was shivering. Stroud returned to his cell with the watering cup and filled it. He dropped the cage cover. Then he lifted the cover of his large cage and stood still, looking at his birds. One of the guards coughed. Stroud made a curious gesture toward the cage and slowly backed away from it. Then he turned on his heel and faced the guards.

"Merry Christmas, boys," he said. "I can use a rest." His face was rock-hard as he left the cell. He did not look back at the block of steel and concrete where he had lived for twenty-six years.

Handcuffed, chained in leg-irons and accompanied by three guards, the canary convict was hurried into a Pullman compartment and sped across the country. Robert Stroud had begun his journey to the Rock.

BOOK THREE

TWENTY-FIVE

IN HANDCUFFS and leg-irons, accompanied by three guards, Stroud was sped westward in a compartment. It was a week before Christmas, in the depths of World War II. Glued to the train window, he looked out on a country he had not seen since 1905, and slaked a thirst for travel which had accumulated for thirty-three years. He saw for the first time the geranium glow of neon and the silver glitter of cities decorated for the Christmas season; he gaped at strangely dressed people and helmeted riveters hurrying into defence plants at night. Automobiles he had seen only in pictures sped along the highway with the speed of the train.

San Francisco was a blacked-out city where Jap bombs were expected, and he heard the guards discussing the candle shortage. Soon he found himself seated in the Alcatraz prison launch, on his first boat ride since another craft had wallowed from McNeil Island to Steilacoom in 1912.

As the launch pointed through the mist to the looming Rock, Stroud watched hundreds of gulls wing up from the shore. A feeling of unease came over him, as if he had forgotten something. It was time to feed his canaries, a habit of twenty-one years.

At the dock his leg-irons and handcuffs were unlocked and he was searched by the electronic eye of the "mechanical snitch-box". His ankles were swollen. He was taken up the island hill to the prison. By the time he had been stripped, examined, checked, outfitted and showered, he was exhausted.

A spectacled guard was studying his commitment papers. The old convict watched him.

"I'm not used to people," Stroud said. "All these young prisoners. They must be pretty tough."

The guard looked up. "Don't worry about it. You won't be among 'em."

"How come?"

"You're tagged for Dog Block. Orders from Washington."

Stroud's jaw dropped open. "You mean they're putting me in solitary here on the Rock?"

"It's not solitary. It's segregation."

Stroud's jaw clamped shut and he asked no more questions. A silent guard took him through still, spotless halls, past electrically-locked, tooled-steel doors, into the three-tiered network of cells which was D Block. Through two rows of windows with incurving bars he could catch a glimpse of San Francisco Bay as he climbed the iron stairs. On the ground floor he had noticed flats, what looked like a wall of solid steel about thirty feet long. Then, focusing, his eyes made out faint vertical lines marking doors. Stroud had heard about the Rock's new "Hole Cells". Behind one of them he heard a faint pounding. The rest was a shining silence.

His cell was three feet shorter than the barred room of his Leavenworth quarters. There was a toilet, wash-basin and drinking fountain. He kept staring at one wall, where his Leavenworth cell had held a doorway to birds. He made his bunk, fell upon it and slept.

News of his brother's transfer to an undesignated prison greeted L. G. Marcus in a Minneapolis newspaper. By the time he had wired Leavenworth and Washington and received answers, his brother had spent December 25 on the Rock, where it is a calendar date. Worried about his brother Bob and angered by what he considered to be vague reasons in the Bureau Director's reply, Marcus wrote a high-handed letter to James V. Bennett, Director.

Your wire received relative to the destination and reason for the transfer of my brother, Robert Stroud. However, you say in your wire that recent actions of his indicated that he should be transferred to Alcatraz. . . . Are you referring to the fact that possibly he resented having his letter-writing privileges and radio removed for no infraction of the rules, or was it merely that the new warden and yourself . . . felt that his activities in corresponding with breeders have been curtailed to the point that he could safely be removed to another prison without causing any public reaction?

Your predecessor, Mr. Bates, found that the voices of 100,000 bird-lovers could create quite a protest. . . . Is he to be accorded the same privileges as any other first-class prisoner at Alcatraz, and is he to be allowed to continue with his bird experiments?

You have not always taken the trouble to answer my correspondence in the past, a fact which I have overlooked, but I can assure you that you will find it to your advantage to answer the above questions. I told you and Warden Hudspeth, both, that I would do nothing to create any sympathy in behalf of my brother as long as he was allowed to publish his book and continue with his experiments. . . .

The Prison Bureau has gone on record to the extent that Stroud was to be allowed to keep his birds. This was in answer to public protest in an attempt to deprive him of them in 1931. Is it your intention or desire to repudiate these statements at this time? . . .

Five days later, Marcus had heard from his brother on the Rock, but not from the Bureau. He wrote again.

I received your wire and I have also received two letters from my brother . . . and I'll admit I probably misjudged you. . . . I apologize . . . and wish to thank you for having my brother's interest at heart. He tells me he feels much better on the coast. . . .

I have been deluged with letters from his many friends and they are all filled with gratitude that he has been restored to the privileges of other first-class prisoners but many of them express concern regarding his experiments because they miss his articles . . . I have also had letters from several magazine publishers . . . They all wish to know if he is to be allowed to continue his experiments and how soon they can get additional articles for their publications. . . .

This letter received a reply on January 19 from the Director.

I presume by this time you have been advised by Warden Hunter that your brother's personal property and his birds have been ordered shipped to you for such disposition as you think proper. Whether and to what extent your brother will be permitted to prepare articles for publication in trade journals will depend upon his conduct and adjustment in Alcatraz. I am not in a position to make any commitments just at this time concerning this matter.

If, some time when you are in Washington, you care to drop in to see me, I will be glad to talk over his case with you in detail.

On February 12, 1943, Marcus paid $25.62 express collect charges for three large cages of canaries, fifteen living and six dead. He brought them to Bertha Hayden's Green Gipsy Pet Shop in Minneapolis. The prison shipping office had packed them with care, but they had been on the road for two weeks.

Stroud's personal property of 1,144 pounds filled two barrels and three boxes.

In addition to thirty empty bird cages, gathered over two decades, piece by piece, and used in a cell twelve feet long and six feet wide, it was a mute record of intellectual striving and the strangest property list of any lifer in prison history.

It included 158 bottles, cans, boxes and beakers of assorted chemicals and laboratory equipment. There were 236 single issues and four bound volumes of bird magazines. There were twenty-two volumes on chemistry and microscopes; fifty-nine Government publications and one nutritional chart. There were thirty-three miscellaneous catalogues, indices, medical books and such odd volumes as *The Life of Shakespeare*, Boccaccio and *The Island Within.*

There were other items, such as forty-four boxes of slides, one box of hydrion test paper, two rolls of cotton, twenty-four sheets of filter paper and 347 different articles used in the care and feeding of birds.

Then there were twenty-four packages of tobacco, a typewriter, a watch and a box of watch parts, three fountain pens, two radio headsets and various other personal effects.

And there were twenty-five pounds of sunflower seeds, twenty-five pounds of brown birdseed, thirty-five pounds of mixed birdseed and thirty-two pounds of cracked wheat, corn syrup, ground feed and egg-yolk powder which was fed to the birds.

And, finally, there were 118 bird-feeding dishes, thirty-three bird cages, twenty-five roosts, laying and feeding boxes—and twenty-two birds.

Not included here were hospital pans, scissors, dissecting instruments, scalpel, screwdrivers, ice pick, ice box, microtome, wood chisels and a claw hammer.

TWENTY-SIX

ALCATRAZ, THE Federal prison with a name like the blare of a trombone, opened under the Prison Bureau in 1934 as the realization of an awesome concept: a Maginot Line against crime.

The rock island, a United States fortification since 1853, once held captive Indian chiefs. The administration building and cell house were built in 1909. It was a military prison during the Roaring Twenties, holding nearly 400 soldier-inmates. They had visitors weekly, wrote two letters a month, and were allowed to read and subscribe to newspapers. A trained psychiatrist was in residence. In 1924 its net cost was $272,000. It had a larger library then than now. Religious services were held twice weekly.

When it became a civilian prison to hold, punish and break the intractable minority of Federal inmates, Alcatraz cost ten times as much, housed half as many and became, depending upon who viewed it, a national symbol of security and strictness, or a dire monument to a dead penal concept.

The silence system was brought back. Radios and newspapers were forbidden, correspondence and visiting restricted, handicrafts prohibited, recreation cut down, commissary abolished, tear-gas bombs suspended overhead in the dining-room, and electric eyes and automatic locks installed.

Super-security precautions were adopted: tooled-steel bars, sharp cyclone fences, barbed-wire entanglements, tall towers and numerous catwalks. The island waters were zoned to prohibit approach, lending doubt to the claim that the island tides made swimming away impossible. The year before Alcatraz became a Federal prison, two women swam from San Francisco to Alcatraz, bucked the tide, circled the island and landed at the South End Rowing Club.

A dungeon was hollowed out and recalcitrant convicts chained in it until the new solid steel "Hole Cells" were constructed.

By the time Stroud reached the Rock in 1942, prisoners had adopted the century plant as their college flower.

From its inception, Alcatraz and the penology it represented drew criticism. The majority of the public, however, appeared to consider Alcatraz as a necessary and expensive evil. It became a symbol and an emotional release for the citizenry throughout the country, with the exception of San Francisco. The Rock lay on the city's doorstep. With the Statue of Liberty gracing New York, Alcatraz at the other end of the country made anatomical comparison inevitable.

After five years, Former Attorney-General Cummings proclaimed in a magazine article that Alcatraz was a success. The new Attorney-General, Frank Murphy, termed the prison under his charge "a hell hole".

"It is a great injustice to both prisons and to San Francisco to have that place of horror on the doorstep of the city," Murphy said. "Conducive to a psychology that builds up a sinister and vicious attitude among prisoners . . . there is more evidence of prisoners going 'stir-crazy' there than any other place."

The most expensive prison *per capita* in the world, Alcatraz remained a black molar in the jawbone of the nation's prison system, a rooted symbol with a life of its own. The Federal Prison Bureau itself recommended its being closed, only to discover that an atavism is difficult to remove.

To the prisoners throughout the far-flung network of Federal institutions, the Rock was something else. The grapevine version of Alcatraz which had filtered back through Leavenworth on the lips of transferred prisoners was perhaps closer to reality than the lurid recitals of the Press and the distortions of the official apologists. It was recognized in convict circles as a low-morale prison. It stood for utter isolation within sight and sound of a large city: the sight of pleasure boats in the bay and the sound of airliners overhead, the impact of hatred of its inmates as dead-end products of society, the obsession to ensure against escape in an "escape-proof" prison, the load of ninety-nine-year sentences made consecutive with sentences to life, and the precise and relentless regimentation of the inmates. There was the attitude of the guards, who, despite their careful training, were worked upon by the same influences.

It was the scientific drip of minutes on the foreheads of the prisoners which made the Rock a dread abode. It had its share of the ugly physical events of prison life, although these did not surpass those of many prisons. These were duly carried back to the prison populations of other Federal jails. Fourteen prisoners went insane in a year. In 1937 a prisoner named Percival severed his hand with a meat cleaver and begged a fellow convict to chop off his remaining hand. A prisoner attempting escape, Boarman, was shot to death before he drowned. Two others vanished in the densest fog in Bay history and escaped to South America, or were drowned. Prisoner Ed Watke committed suicide; others tried and failed. Limerick was killed on a catwalk in 1938; Barker in 1939. Guard Cline was bludgeoned to death. Al Capone was stabbed with a pair of scissors. The prison was always tense and rarely saw a month elapse without some minor violent episode.

Resistance was not always violent. A neurologist who visited the Rock regularly was driven to resign by the distrustful inmates. When he stepped from the launch the entire prison began to shake with a rhythmic "Quack-Quack".

What effect did Alcatraz have on Stroud?

His letters to his brother during his first year indicate that he was more relaxed than he had been in years. He met Warden James "Saltwater" Johnston and developed a sound respect for the tough but wise old penologist, whose impartial dealing had become proverbial. The warden extended first-class privileges to him, including four hours per week exercise in the yard. He allowed subscription to bird journals, permitted a study of bird books, and allowed Stroud to answer the queries of scores of bird-lovers through the medium of his brother.

Warden Johnston was an exact man who made clean-cut business and penological decisions within the area allowed by his Washington superiors. To Stroud, who had always inveighed against theory-ridden and sentimental authorities as the hardest types under which to "do time", it was encouraging to know exactly where he stood.

His letters also indicate that Stroud felt his solitary seclusion on the Rock to be such manifest injustice that it might aid in a campaign for release. The deadliest public enemies of recent vintage were allowed to associate with each other on the Rock; yet Stroud's last crime was in 1916. The sense of being a persecuted victim is not wholly without comfort.

Stroud was experiencing a change of climate, of scene. For a man who had lived in prison since 1909, he was relatively unaffected by the mental-prison aspect of Alcatraz. Psychologically, he was still with his birds.

Stroud had finished the thousand-odd typewritten pages of his bird-book manuscript in 1939. For three years his project had been gathering dust because of difficulties and delays. In 1942, the Bureau had given permission for its publication and had placed the manuscript in the hands of L. G. Marcus.

"Your brother's status as an inmate must not be publicized or exploited," a Leavenworth official had stated. A sharper caution was expressed by the Chief Parole Officer of Leavenworth in a subsequent letter:

> Please understand that publication of this book has been approved only with the understanding that there are to be no reprints of the book in newspapers and magazines. It has been brought to our attention that excerpts from the manuscript have appeared in magazines in the past and if this practice has not already been discontinued, it must be done at once.

The indefatigable Marcus had discovered a way to get the book published. In the January, 1943, issue of the *American Canary* magazine appeared an article by Robert Stroud. The title was "I Wonder". After outlining the contents of his bird disease *Digest*, Stroud wondered: were there enough bird-lovers whom he had helped and who wished to buy his book to subscribe five dollars in advance for its publication?

Orders began to pour in to Marcus from bird breeders, several university professors familiar with Stroud's work, and the keepers of several large zoos.

The February issue of the same magazine contained another article, "I Wonder Too", by Bertha Hayden, the Minneapolis bird breeder long familiar with the prisoner's research:

> A disease can wipe out an entire stud of birds. Five dollars, the price of Stroud's new book, is the price of one hen. Facing life imprisonment in a solitary cell, Mr. Stroud has not sat idly in his cell and whined his life away. . . .
>
> Robert Stroud is worth to the poultry industry hundreds of thousands of dollars in food and money saved. Yet he is prevented from doing his great work by a prison bureau which is supposed to be humanitarian. We Americans who are paying the taxes, who support the prisons . . . have long ago ceased to be a government

characterized by a spirit of revenge and hate toward those who have been sentenced to prison. . . .

Stroud was encouraged by the orders that poured in. Soon he was toiling over page proofs and technical problems concerning publication of his self-illustrated bird book. It was his labour of love.

Warden Johnston handled intricate correspondence problems with meticulous care. An author himself, the warden understood the work entailed in Stroud's project. Marcus wrote:

I wish to thank you for your fair attitude regarding the inquiries I receive from breeders who are in distress. . . .

I can appreciate your position but I want you to know that I am grateful for the favours shown within your province. . . .

I am enclosing herewith some sheets just received from the printer of my brother's book. I want my brother to correct them also. Thank you for giving him the others so promptly.

The warden answered:

When I received your letter containing pages of printing of Robert Stroud's book, I gave it to the Associate Warden who passed the proof sheets to your brother for his inspection and corrections. I understand that your brother has made his corrections and now is returning the sheets to you.

The crisp and pleasant correspondence, sometimes as often as twice a week, went on for a year. The warden, throughout, acknowledged and answered every letter, and the complex business was handled without breaking a rule.

Late in 1943 *Stroud's Digest of the Diseases of Birds* was brought out by the Webb Publishing Company under the auspices of L. G. Marcus. Handsomely bound and thoroughly indexed, the 500-page volume contained eighty-seven plates, most of them hand-drawn by the author.

The *Digest* caused a sensation in the bird fanciers' world. It was favourably reviewed in the avian journals. Two of the reviews were written by college professors.

The Kansas City *Star* reviewed the book in February, 1944:

Stroud makes unnecessary apologies for his literary style, for the book is written in clear-cut, pertinent sentences, well-suited to the subject matter, though it might have been less vituperative in places. . . . Stroud's book is a digest of bird diseases that is singularly complete and detailed. . . . It is easy to picture the man as an aggressive, self-confident person, tireless and patient in his work; one who has the scientific attitude of experimentation and originality rather than respect for accepted opinion and tradition.

Several syndicated columnists praised the book, and told garbled stories of Stroud's lurid life.

The *Digest*, however, was one of the highest-priced bird books in a market largely devoted to inexpensive booklets and bird journals. The Bureau had forbidden reprints of Stroud's work. As a result of this and the disadvantages of private printing, the *Digest* suffered the financial destiny of many technical books. It lost money.

Its purchasers, however, during the following years, included bird-lovers throughout the world. It has a lively circulation today in public libraries and it is still advertised in bird journals.

Those who read Stroud's book found an off-trail approach to many problems. He had put his heart, his starved ego and his haunted soul into it. Hungry for expression, he included his curious opinions about many things. There are frequent glimpses of an ironic humour—and a more frequent use of the perpendicular pronoun than appears anywhere except in the memoirs of other prisoners, or their keepers.

Stroud began to miss his birds, equipment and research activities. Turning more and more to books, he soon discovered what a Federal judge termed the Rock's Number One Indoor Sport.

The library of Alcatraz contained an excellent collection of law books. As Stroud scanned the library catalogue provided in his cell, he was astounded. He soon learned, from other prisoners and from guards, about the extensive self-taught legal training of the more intelligent inmates. Forty-five convicts, taking legal action on their own after study, had bettered their condition in one way or another. Twelve were set free by courts through writs of habeas corpus and motions to vacate sentence. Warden Johnson respected law. He put no obstacles in the way, and he noted that it gave hope to the hopeless, improved their knowledge and occupied their time.

Stroud soon immersed himself in law. After several months he petitioned the Federal District Court for a writ of habeas corpus.

He contended that the judgment and sentence upon him were uncertain and ambiguous in violation of the due process clause of the Fifth Amendment; that he had been and was being subjected to cruel and unusual punishment within the meaning of the Eighth Amendment; and that his transfer to Alcatraz had been effected under *ex post facto* law.

Stroud's petition was denied by the Court and the denial was sustained in the Circuit Court. The judges held that the Attorney-General's right to construe the original sentence of death as including solitary confinement for life was valid, and added that the prisoner was held in limited solitary in Leavenworth and not in solitary confinement in Alcatraz. The Court added that the Attorney-General's discretion in the transfer of prisoners was valid.

The prisoner commented on his first legal effort:

> It was very crudely drawn. An official said that had I raised my points properly, they would have had to give me my birds. I knew right then that my proper remedy was a petition for an injunction, but, being stubborn, I appealed. The issues raised could not be tried on habeas corpus.

Despite his failure, Stroud went on with his legal studies. He was fascinated by law and he had ample time to pursue it. Time began to yawn before him with empty space to fill. Despite his effort to crowd his solitude, he began to feel the mental chill of the Rock. Requests for diagnoses of sick birds dwindled. His restless mind, whetted by his study of law, veered back from caged birds to his old curiosity, caged men. While one laboratory had been taken from him, he had been provided with a larger one. Stroud, convict scientist, was seeing the Alcatraz method first-hand. Unable to leave his cell except for his weekly bath and exercise, he requisitioned and studied all available books on sociology and penology. He resumed an old project, a prison account from the prisoner's view.

TWENTY-SEVEN

THE END OF World War II and the blessings of peace had a reverse and ironic effect upon America's prisoners. Peace deepened their separation from the rest of the country. The common cause, the sense of striving together against a common danger had created a formidable work-production record inside the nation's prison walls.

Now the cohesive force was gone. There was no longer the incentive of winning the war to dissolve increasing tension over food, medical problems and futureless living which tightened and twisted the nervous systems of the inmates.

The ageing Stroud was no exception. Sitting in his cell, deprived of his birds, he watched the winking lights of San Francisco less than two miles away, yet as far as eternity. He saw moaning and shrieking prisoners snatched from the main prison body and quartered in sound-proofed cells on the flats below him, in what seemed to him an orgy of punishment. Stroud looked at his own body and believed the rumours which now pattered like rats through the faceless cells.

Inmates whispered that meat, in the midst of the meat shortage, was being carried away by guards for their own use. Some convicts in the shops revolted and were placed in segregation cells. The tense, near-crazed inmates of D Block compared their thinning shanks with the custodial figures. Calls for the doctor increased.

In 1945, after a visit to his brother, Marcus wrote a letter to the Bureau of Prisons in Washington:

> Recently I have learned of my brother's illness and condition through the lack of proper care. . . . He is suffering from malnutrition or slow starvation.
>
> Up to now I feel that I have kept my agreement with you in not seeking sympathy for my brother through his book. In writing this letter I am doing so with the hope that the present existing situation will be immediately changed. . . .

Families of other prisoners also complained. Whether it was pressure, or a country-wide improvement in food production, Stroud reported that the diet in D Block improved.

The inevitable danger signals increased, however. The guards reported more "rumbles" each week. They reacted by growing more nervous and snappish. No American prison could make the guards themselves feel more isolated and imprisoned than the Rock. Surrounded by routine, and physically separated from the mainland, wearing their lives away against the fearful sum of menace and hatred of three hundred suffering, desperate men, some guards grew no less savage and morose than their charges.

The situation erupted in the form of a revolt in D Block. What followed a week later opened a new chapter in American prison history.

On Sunday, April 28, 1946, the mind of one of the prisoners in D Block gave way and he began to yell in the hoarse, crackling screams of a man pushed beyond his breaking-point. Fuselike, the sounds set off other unstable inmates. Out of the clamour came a call for the doctor. Instantly, D Block shook with roars for medical attention. Guards hustled the screamer into Hole solitary and waited for the others to subside. Instead, the uproar increased. Up on the third tier of D Block, Stroud paced nervously in his cell as he heard sounds of pounding and tearing. Wrenching with hysterical strength, prisoners broke their toilet bowls, tore off wash-basins and hurled them against the tooled-steel cell bars. Others scrabbled at the floor linoleum until their fingers spurted blood, ripped up the tough covering and hurled it through the bars.

Fourteen of the twenty-six inmates of D Block, already isolated, were placed in solitary. All shoes were removed. Some of the prisoners had to be subdued. Cigarettes were taken away and a "restricted diet" was begun. Yard and exercise privileges were abolished.

One prisoner known to Stroud was Sam Shockley, a thirty-six-year-old man with an I.Q. of 54—the mind of an eight-year-old. Escaped from an Oklahoma reform school and later convicted of kidnapping and bank robbery, Shockley had been transferred to Alcatraz eight years before. On the Rock he had been placed in a hospital cage-cell for observation. Prison records listed him as hallucinated. Shockley believed he had stomach cancer caused by light rays flashing from a hidden machine. Radio voices whispered evil words to him. Put repeatedly in the Hole for the seventeen-day stretch allowed by law, Shockley was in solitary for stealing a steak from the kitchen. Shockley was to play a role in the events that followed.

In the late afternoon of May 1, an old Kentucky bank robber named Bernard Coy, who worked in the library, distributed magazines to various prisoners. Some received copies of *Travel*. Unknown to Stroud, this was the prearranged tip-off for a "crush-out".

Next day at 1.30 p.m. the lean, six-foot Coy was slowly sweeping "Broadway", the polished floor between the three-tiered cell banks of C Block. Coy edged up to William Miller, the only guard on the floor. Miller was unarmed.

Up on the third tier of C Block, tensely watching Coy, was Joe Cretzer. Cretzer had robbed nine banks and killed a United States Marshal. He had been held in segregation for eight years after an attempt to escape from the Rock, but he had recently been transferred to C Block. He was serving a ninety-nine-year sentence and had discovered that he was going blind.

While Coy was sweeping, a thirty-four-year-old Alabama convict named Hubbard finished his work in the kitchen, slid a butcher's knife into his sleeve and waited for a guard named Burch to leave his post in the caged gun gallery for a fifteen-minute inspection of D Block. At 1.40 p.m. Hubbard left the kitchen and tapped on the cell-house door. Guard Miller opened it and began a routine frisk of Hubbard. Coy dropped his broom and slugged Guard Miller. Coy and Hubbard took him into a cell where they beat him, tied him and seized his keys. Miller, during the fracas, had secreted the vital key to the recreation yard. Leaving Miller in Cell 403, the two convicts used the remaining keys to release Cretzer and two others, Miran Thompson and Joseph Carnes.

Next, Coy and Hubbard opened the door to the utility corridor and from threaded pipes, valve parts and pipe-pincers, they fashioned a bar-spreading contrivance in a matter of minutes.

Coy now climbed to the gun cage, spread apart the bars, squirmed through and crouched behind the steel door to wait for Guard Burch. Hubbard cat-called to distract Burch as Coy pushed the door open, grappled with the guard, tied him up with his necktie and key cord, grabbed the .45 pistol, threw it to Cretzer, and took the rifle.

Cretzer and Coy now had two guns and a total of seventy-one bullets. They were the only armed men inside the cell blocks of Alcatraz.

The older, unarmed Isolation guard in D Block saw the scuffle up in the gallery and turned grey. The convict orderly there told him to take it easy and left to tell the inmates on the second tier of D Block what was going on. The terrified guard did not telephone the alarm, although the phone was within reach. Had he phoned, events would have taken another course.

Up among inmates of the third tier, Stroud sensed the fateful moves and gripped his cell bars, staring down upon the small slice of flats within his view. He saw nothing and waited.

Now the steel door to D Block received a peremptory knock, and two eyes and the muzzle of a .45 looked in. The guard opened the door. Hubbard and Cretzer sprang through. They ordered the guard to open up the doors in D Block, but he shook his head. Hubbard lifted his knife. But the D Block orderly had returned. He stepped between them. "Now, you know the old man can't operate the doors on the flats," he whispered. "They're operated from the gun cage." Cretzer nodded and marched the guard from D Block into the cell with Guard Miller. Then Cretzer returned to D Block. Using keys, he operated the levers which racked open the second and third tiers of D Block cells. But he was unable to open the electrically controlled Hole cells. Part of the plot was to free Whitey Franklin, who had killed a guard in 1938 and was in solitary.

The released prisoners of D Block pushed out of their cells, tense with excitement and fear. Sam Shockley, his eight-year-old mind crazed by tension, ran bug-eyed through the open door of D Block and joined Cretzer, Coy and Hubbard, who now had with them Thompson and Carnes. At this point, Shockley was an incoherent madman.

Up in Cell 41 on the third tier of D Block, Stroud watched his prison door slide open after three and a half years on the Rock. He walked to the rail and looked down. The D Block cell door was open. He knew the convicts held in their hands keys, weapons and hostages. The siren had not sounded. Stroud did not know that the key to the yard was missing. He faced a cross-roads.

Here was a chance for violent escape, and his sympathies were with the snarling inmates of this sinister zoo. His own life seemed futureless. He had influence with prisoners and was certain of followers.

What course would Stroud take?

"Get back in your cells!" he shouted. "Take cover! There's going to be gun-fire!"

Shockley had disappeared. Several inmates yelled that the cons were taking over the joint. But most of the panicky inmates turned back to their cells or stood in front of them, waiting.

Then the siren started—a whining wail to freeze the nerves—a two-minute eternity which to a prisoner means danger and death.

Now Cretzer and Hubbard reappeared in D Block. Hubbard fired a shot from his rifle and ran out. Cretzer, his face working, yelled, "Everybody off the range!" and ran to the third tier to see a personal enemy, prisoner Henri Young. He levelled his pistol pointblank at Young in his cell, and grinned. Then he snapped on the safety catch and ran back into C Block where the guard hostages, taken one by one by Coy as they had walked into the "Broadway trap", now numbered nine.

Shortly afterward, the prisoners in D Block heard a series of pistol shots, then a pause, then more shots.

Now the crazed Shockley ran back into D Block and into a cell, where other prisoners grabbed him and forcibly held him down. He whispered that Cretzer had killed all of the hostages, and began to giggle hysterically. According to the testimony of the trial later, Shockley had frantically urged Cretzer to "Kill the bastards! Kill them all!" after the siren had sounded. Cretzer had fired pointblank at the helpless guards, turning the cell where they were prisoners into a bloody shambles. But only one guard, William Miller, died. Others were severely wounded and the living played dead and survived. They had been put through a horrible ordeal, beyond forgetting.

Warden Johnston received his first detailed news of the riot when Associate Warden Miller, his face a charred splotch and his eyes half-blinded, tore out of the main cell house, shouting that Coy, wearing an officer's coat, had shot at him with a rifle. Miller had thrown his tear-gas billy which struck a stanchion and bounced back in his face, exploding and burning him with tear gas.

Fearing for the security of his institution, Warden Johnston armed his guards with submachine-guns, rifles, pistols and sawn-off shotguns. He made sure the front gate was covered. Then he wired the Coast Guard, the San Francisco Police Department, the Army, the Federal Bureau of Prisons, the F.B.I., Press associations and San Francisco daily newspapers. Warden Johnston stated: "Serious trouble. Convict has machine-gun in cell house. . . ." This statement in an official telegram was accepted as gospel by reporters who covered the riot—with consequences later to occur.

The warden and his guards organized an attack to rescue the nine hostages. Two guards opened fire down the main corridor to draw attention from six guards, who rushed down the first level of the gun gallery. This was at about 7 p.m., May 2.

"One prisoner with the rifle fired on the officers from the upper tier of D Block," the warden later wrote. "Cretzer stood outside the floor between C and D Blocks and fired revolver shots. Guard Stites returned the fire but to do so he exposed his position. The other officers heard Stites cry out, 'They got me.' Oldham was disabled by a shot in his right arm; Richberger was shot through the calf of his right leg. Cochrane had a large gaping wound from a rifle bullet that tore through the triceps back of his left upper arm and furrowed across his back."

Stites was killed instantly. The account conveyed to readers an impression that Guard Stites was killed by the convicts. Most metropolitan dailies in San Francisco, however, carried on May 3, the day after the shooting, a strange detail about the tragedy.

"When Stites's body arrived at the morgue, attendants found that a row of machine-gun bullets had ripped up his back," the San Francisco *Examiner* stated. . . . No prison official explained how a felon got the machine-gun. It was a major mystery because no machine-gun is ever allowed in the cell house, even in possession of a guard.

A state of siege set in as darkness fell. Stroud and twenty-four others in D Block made breastworks of their mattresses and books, huddled behind them in their cells, and waited.

One guard lieutenant and several guards were in the gun cage overlooking the entire front of D Block, from four o'clock on Thursday afternoon until seven o'clock on Fridav evening, May 3. They shot out the D Block light.

About 10 p.m. on Thursday, May 3, a force of fourteen officers rescued the nine captured guards from the cell where they had been shot and abandoned. The rescue party was shot at from the top of C Block. Now a guard locked the door to D Block. The wounded officers were hospitalized, and the victims, shaking from their harrowing ordeal, told their story to the warden.

From then on the warden had the break under control. The guards had been rescued, the gates protected and the cell blocks locked.

The unarmed convicts who had played minor roles in the mutiny were all in their cells—Shockley, Thompson and Carnes. They had run there either during, or before, or shortly after, the shooting of the guards in "Bloody 403". The prison was secure against escape.

Somewhere in the smoke-filled, bullet-scarred Rock were three men—Cretzer, Hubbard and Coy—the original mutineers.

At this time, as was known to the warden and his men, and later sworn in court, the stir-maddened trio had between them a rifle, a pistol and a butcher's knife. If they had not shot their firearms at all, they would have had twenty-one pistol bullets and fifty rounds of rifle cartridges. But Cretzer had fired the pistol, and Coy the rifle. Their total supply was later estimated as forty bullets. They had shot and killed a guard. Their confederates had deserted them. Escape was impossible.

To handle this situation there were a capable warden and more than a hundred trained armed guards, with an arsenal of clubs, saps, pistols, tear gas, rifles and shotguns.

The Marines landed on the island with a force of eighty men in battle regalia. The Navy sent two destroyer escorts. The Coast Guard sent five patrol ships. The warden of San Quentin sent a squad of guards.

The San Francisco Police Department sent a boat and armed officers.

Generals "Vinegar Joe" Stilwell and Frank Merrill came over in an army boat and conferred with the warden. "This is strictly a Marine show, as far as the Army is concerned," General Stilwell was quoted in the press. He advised the warden not to use the block-busters now *en route* from Benecia Arsenal at the warden's request.

In Washington on May 3, the Director of the Federal Bureau of Prisons gave an order: "Take the remnant without loss of life." He then flew in from three other prisons twenty-eight trained sharpshooters, former Alcatraz guards and other experts.

As the sun dimmed and set in a hazy pall on the evening of May 2, prisoners of D Block peered over their up-ended mattresses and watched Navy boats coiling about the island. They heard rolling bursts from the guards' tommy-guns pouring fire into the buildings. They heard the zing of ricocheting bullets and watched the guards shoot out another light in the ceiling of D Block.

The door to D Block remained locked. The prisoners could hear the gunfire in the main cell house from one end and the answering single-shot fire of a rifle and pistol from the other.

The ribbons of tracer bullets began to arch in through the windows of D Block. One by one all of the windows were shot out. Wild cries were heard from the twenty-five terrified, smoke-blackened, bullet-dodging inmates locked in D Block. Someone believed that the armed Coy was there.

The guards were lobbing hand grenades through the broken windows from the lawn outside. A tear-gas bomb bounced back from the bars and set fire to the shrubbery. Smoke pouring from the windows and the blazing lawn startled the crowds collected on the mainland a mile away. "The Rock's on fire!" they exclaimed.

Heavier explosions now shook the prison. Water and steam pipes were punctured, and mattresses set afire. The cell galleries were soon covered with water.

The bombardment slacked off at midnight. Stroud called out to various prisoners to see whether anyone was hurt. But the Rock fortress which had been built so strong that no one could get out of it, proved equally strong against efforts to destroy its battlements. The damage to prisoners was small.

Stroud heard a moan from a cell three doors away on his tier. He tiptoed over to the cell and helped the prisoner back to his own cell. The prisoner had received several shrapnel scratches, but had been lying in cold water for several hours and was chilled. Stroud shared some dry clothes with him and gave him his shoes. Two other prisoners contributed an undershirt, blanket and a pair of prison trousers.

As one of them ducked into Stroud's cell, a bullet struck the bars inches from his face. But the smoke and darkness made targets difficult.

Stroud noticed that the wounded prisoner's body was covered with sores. The prisoner told him he had lost his teeth because of mouth sores that would not heal.

Grotesquely, Stroud forgot about the surrounding panic, riot and danger.

"Let me see those sores on your body again." He looked carefully at them in the dim light. "Those look like pellagroid blotches to me. You've got scurvy. Wait a minute." The birdman groped deep in his barricaded cell for some bottles. He crawled to the front of his cell. "Here." He gave the prisoner some ascorbic acid tablets and yeast tablets. "I've still got water. Swallow these." The bewildered inmate complied.

The prisoners listened to shuddering explosions which seemed to come from C Block. Guards had concluded that the armed prisoners had holed up in a shallow tunnel cut-off which was part of a utility corridor. These corridors contained the plumbing and wiring that serviced the cells. The guards were dropping tear-gas bombs and fragmentation grenades through the ventilators into the utility corridor. There was no response.

At dawn on May 3, the bombardment of D Block resumed. The six prisoners in solitary confinement on the ground tier were caged in cells which had not been opened since Thursday morning. They sat in darkness, protected by doors of solid steel —six impregnable pill-boxes.

But up on the third tier, where Stroud and other prisoners were barricaded behind mattresses and stacked-up books, the lethal barrage sharpened the danger. Through the grey dawn the prisoners watched a destroyer escort pull about and stand. Stroud and the sick prisoner ducked down behind mattresses, up-ended and rolled in front of the cell door. The cell rocked with explosions. Shells had struck the steel shelf above the cell door. The prisoners in solitary began to scream. "They're aiming at these three cells," muttered Stroud. "They're trying to kill us with direct hits."

Then a terrified voice came from the second tier. Stroud recognized it as that of "Stack" Butler, a Negro prisoner. He had made contact with two guards in the gun gallery during the night and had pleaded with them to stop the bombardment.

One guard said he was powerless to act. The other guard said the prisoners were going to get theirs.

"Bob," called Butler, "for Christ's sake, talk to these guys. Make them believe you."

"They can't hear me up here. We're being bombed."

Then Stroud whispered to his sick cell-mate—his first in thirty years—"I'm getting out. This cell will protect one man—stay behind the mattress and under the bed."

"If you go out that door, they'll kill you," said the sick prisoner.

"I'm going out fast. Maybe at the other end I can do something."

"They'll pot you from the gun cage."

"No, one of them is a square guard—he won't shoot me if he recognizes me. The other one is too excited to hit anything."

Stroud put a box of cigarettes under his arm, stuffed matches into his pocket and darted to the next cell. The cold water on the flooded catwalk wet his stockinged feet. Ducking from cell to cell, he reached the dangerous stairs between tiers. He waited until a bomb exploded and then quickly ducked into Cell 15, near the gallery.

"This is Stroud speaking," he yelled. "What I say is the truth and I will back every word with my life. There is no gun in D Block. What you are trying to do is pure murder."

"I know it's you, Stroud," said Guard Lieutenant Bergen, holed up in the gun gallery. "I wish I could believe you, but the evidence is against you."

"Shut up, you lying old ——," another guard yelled. "You cons had your fun and now you can't take it. We're going to blow the block down and I hope you go with it."

"What do I care," yelled back Stroud. "I'm an old man, spent my whole life in these outhouses. You're not beating me out of anything. If you have to kill somebody, I'll step out of here and give you the chance."

"Take it easy, Stroud," cautioned the Lieutenant. "You'll live to write some more books."

"There are twenty-five men in here innocent of any part in this nightmare."

"Take it easy," the guard answered. "Keep your heads down," he warned as more bombs hurtled in.

Suddenly the guard who had cursed him shouted: "If you're

so damned brave, why don't you go up there and make Coy throw that rifle down? You know he's up in 41."

"He's not here and you know it. There is no gun in D Block."

"You're just covering up for him."

"I just came from 41," yelled Stroud, still louder. "I was there all night. There are no guns in D Block."

Stroud waited, coolly thinking it over. Then he called out again. "Mr. Bergen!"

"Yes."

"You know the building better than I do. You say shots came from D Block last night. I say none were fired inside of D Block. Now where could they have been fired to appear to come from D Block, yet sound to me as if they were out in the cell house?"

There was a long silence.

"You mean the west-side ventilator?"

"Maybe that is your answer."

The Guard Lieutenant hurried away.

The shooting and bombardment continued. It concentrated on the four end cells of the second and third tiers. The youngest and best educated of the prisoners in D Block was "Crow" Phillips. Stroud shouted for him to leave his cell, before it was blown apart.

"And get shot?" called back Phillips. "I'm nice and warm in two inches of ice water, under a mattress with two solid feet of books in front of me. I'm O.K."

Later one of the prisoners cried, "Crow is hurt. He's bleeding."

"Bergen," Stroud called. "Will you take a message to the warden?"

"Yes, I will. I can phone him. What is it?"

"Tell the warden there is no gun in D Block. I back those words with my life. I will step out in front of any man he sends in here. He can use me for a shield. That's offering my life. I can't offer any more."

I ater Bergen returned.

"Stroud!"

"Here. What did the warden say?"

"The warden says tell the boys there will be no more firing through the windows and no more shells without warning. Tell them they can get up and walk around in their cells to keep warm. But no moving out of cell. If anything starts, duck for cover. And if you want to live—no wisecracks. We're going to try to take you out."

The bombardment stopped in the afternoon.

Stroud was spent. There was no drinking water in the cell. His feet were wet and his blanket was soaked. He still had cigarettes. No prisoners moved from their cells. The Guard Lieutenant returned every half-hour to reassure the prisoners.

At 5 p.m. on Friday, a single rifle shot was heard in the main cell house. A torrent of gun and grenade fire reverberated in answer. Then silence descended on the ringing ears of the prisoners.

"We're going to try to bring you out tonight," a guard told them.

Meanwhile, the cold on-shore wind from the Golden Gate whipped through the broken windows and chilled occupants and guards alike.

One prisoner had a bullet in his arm, another, in his hip, a third, a haemorrhaging superficial head injury, glass cuts and shock bruises.

The single shot at 5 p.m. had convinced the officials that one or more of the armed prisoners, Coy, Cretzer and Hubbard, were still alive, and that the C Block bombing had forced them to the east half of the utility tunnel. Guards half-opened the door and yelled, "Come out with your hands up." There was no answer. They fired blasts of shotgun bullets into the dark corridor, slammed the door shut and locked it. Then they dropped more bombs from the roof. This broke open more steam pipes, blasted electric cables and water mains and caused a torrent of running water, smoke and escaping steam to pour into the main cell house.

Incongruously, shooting at D Block now resumed, but on a smaller scale. It did not cease until 9 p.m. The Guard Lieutenant returned and told the prisoners there had been a hitch in plans, but to keep their chins up.

Shortly after ten o'clock, the guards were relieved. They had been on duty for twenty-two continuous hours in the D Block gun gallery.

The prisoners were left there all night. One prisoner in solitary had been without water since Thursday morning.

Stroud had assumed leadership of the prisoners capable of

following anyone. They realized they had come through without serious attack after the birdman's offer to expose himself to gunfire.

"I was thankful for two things," he said. "That box of cigarettes and the fact that some moron-type cons were too scared to be troublesome and did not peep."

At 7 a.m. on Saturday morning two officers unlocked the utility corridor, raked it again with rifle and shotgun fire, and crawled cautiously into the mucky black interior. They flashed a light with their .45's at the ready.

They found Cretzer dead from head wounds, close to his pistol. There were three live bullets left. He had fired a total of eighteen shots. They found Coy with half his head blown off. At a subsequent court proceeding, one guard testified that he found a clip of five live rifle cartridges and two loose ones. Another guard testified that he found fourteen live cartridges in Coy's breast pocket. According to this, the rifle had been fired twenty-nine times. Had a total of forty-seven shots been fired by two convicts in the "Battle of Alcatraz"? Hubbard was found dead, his body still warm. His knife lay beside him. They had all been killed by gunfire entering the upper parts of their heads.

The prisoners in D Block were left locked in the wet cell block without food, water, heat and clothing until late the following day. According to Stroud, the Guard Lieutenant had begged for permission to move them out. The mutineers were dead. Officials of the Prison Bureau from Washington were now on the island. The man in D Block with a bullet buried in his arm groaned in pain.

Stroud began to talk about the dangers of uraemic poisoning in cases of exposure without drinking water and of tetanus infection in gunshot wounds. His voice carried to the gun gallery.

About 4.30 p.m. on Saturday, May 4, the Associate Warden, followed by armed guards, marched into D Block. Visiting prison officials followed. "Everybody come to the front of your cell," barked a guard. "Grab the bars with both hands."

The shivering prisoners were ordered to step from their cells, walk to the rail, strip naked, and throw their clothing over the gallery to the floor, and stand with their hands over the rail. The floor was covered with water and broken glass. Several "dud" shells were lying about, and the guards warned the prisoners about them. "We know," whispered one.

The near-sighted "Crow" Phillips, youngest prisoner in D Block, was herded into another cell. His glasses perched precariously on his nose. Behind him a guard with a bullet burn on his unshaven face cautioned the prisoner with a kindly growl, "Keep your hands up. Watch that glass. Don't kick that bomb, it'll blow your leg off."

The prisoner grinned. "Don't fool yourself. Those things are a joke. I had twenty of them in bed with me last night. They only made a bad noise."

"Thought we'd be picking you up in a basket," the guard growled. Then he threw two dry blankets over Stroud's shoulders. The old prisoner was shaking from cold. Another guard shook a cigarette from his packet, pushed it between Stroud's lips, and lit it with his lighter.

"Believe it or not, I'm glad to see your ugly mug," Stroud quavered.

"Lot of you monkeys glad to see us today."

By 7 p.m. the prisoners were installed in dry cells. Some of Stroud's books and papers were destroyed. The unexploded shell duds were left alone. Sandwiches and milk, tobacco and matches, and dry blankets were distributed.

On Sunday the prisoners watched with savage grins while prison officials posed for news pictures below the bombed-out windows. They watched two guards enact a rescue scene arranged by cameramen.

Many of the prisoners saluted Guard Lieutenant Bergen and thanked him for keeping his head. They yelled up thanks to Stroud.

On that day, a uniformed man picked up the unexploded shells. According to testimony in the later trial, they were two-inch shells shot by the destroyer escort. Parts of the prison still smoked. It was the most spectacular mutiny in Federal prison annals.

TWENTY-EIGHT

AN EDITORIAL IN the San Francisco *Chronicle* described the bloody débâcle on the Rock thus:

It takes on the colour of classic drama, when man the dragooned protagonist of death is driven inexorably toward his goal . . . it was an epic drama of man bound upon a rock, and Aeschylus would have lifted it to the plane of universal tragedy and grandeur.

The mutiny was frightening, and the public reaction one of fear and demand for repressive punishment.

The Rock was shut tight under the angry scrutiny of trigger-conscious guards. The F.B.I. swept in to tie down criminal evidence for indictments of prisoners on conspiracy and first-degree murder. One by one, scores of convicts were racked out of their cells for grilling by Government agents.

The bombing of his cell in D Block and its harrowing aftermath drove Stroud into a cold fury. He wrote a document accusing the Prison Bureau of attempting to murder him. He claimed that the conditions in Alcatraz, the bombardment of D Block and the thirty-hour delay in rescue were as scandalous as Teapot Dome. He tried to get the matter before the courts and into the Press. From his accumulated book credits, he arranged to have $200 sent to the defence attorneys for Thompson, one of the three prisoners who had played minor roles in the mutiny.

The shock of the riot and his narrow escape when trying to save the prisoners of D Block revealed new layers of dedicated resistance in Stroud. He described D Block as "a private purgatory where a few carefully chosen victims can slowly be driven mad". Stroud felt responsible for his fellow-inmates. He had the paternal pattern and he was the oldest man on the Rock.

Other prisoners went to extraordinary lengths to support the defendants whose lives were at stake. Long-sought prison jobs, transfers and advantages were ignored.

The trial of Thompson, Shockley and Carnes opened on November 20, 1946. The prosecutor built his case around two charges: first-degree murder, and conspiracy to commit murder. The four defence attorneys constructed a picture of the mutiny as the product of prison conditions on the Rock and the negligence of the guards.

Federal Judge Goodman, however, repeatedly ruled that conditions at the prison, and the attitude and motivation of guards and prisoners alike, were irrelevant and immaterial. The prosecution established that all three defendants were involved in one way or another in the mutiny. The defendants were found guilty. Sam Shockley and Miran Thompson were executed in California's gas chamber, through arrangement with Federal authorities. They were the first Federal prisoners to meet their deaths in this fashion.

Miran Thompson gave his attorney a piece of paper for his fee. It contained a "system" for playing the dice tables in Reno. Attorney Ernest Spagnoli shrugged, tried it as a remembrance, and won $200. He tempted fate no further.

Clarence Carnes, the Choctaw Indian not yet twenty-one, received a more severe sentence. To his existing life sentence and ninety-nine years, he was returned to the Rock with another life sentence.

Through the 2,200-page transcript of the trial emerges a chill and inerasable picture of misery, terror and compounding revenge, the drama of the Rock. Little known and fast forgotten, the record lies gathering dust. The Alcatraz mutiny had cost the lives of seven and wounded seventeen. No prison in United States history had incurred this proportion of injury and death.

By 1948 Stroud had studied a sizeable portion of the sociology and law contained in the Alcatraz library. Its catalogue hung in his cell, well-thumbed. His prison writing began to take shape. With limited research facilities, he proposed to write nothing less than an analytic history of the Federal prison system from the convict's view. He studied Congressional enactments concerning prisons, from the First Crime Act of 1790 to the formation of the Federal Bureau of Prisons in 1930. He had apparently become familiar with the works of such penal authorities as Brant Whitlock, Thomas Osborne, Fremont Older, Donald Lowrie and Maud Ballington Booth. He had a phenomenal memory. Claiming that his work would become as significant in the realm of caged men as his *Digest of Bird Diseases* in the canary world, he toiled away his hours.

At the same time, Stroud tried to keep abreast of developments in bird pathology. Inquiries from bird breeders and bird journals concerning new research developments intrigued him. The use of penicillin and other antibiotics had now extended to sick birds. The warden had permitted him a reference library of ornithological books. Stroud anticipated the need for a revised edition of his bird book, and he collected notes and references. His first interest, however, had become his prison book. Birds now came second.

Having no typewriter, he laboriously printed his words. Books littered his cell as he toiled away amid his grim surroundings.

In May, 1948, the seventy-two-year-old Warden Johnston was retired. He recommended that the interior of the prison be painted in pastel shades for "mental therapy" and suggested that Alcatraz Island be landscaped to make it more beautiful. Warden Johnston had sat on the Rock for fifteen years, achieving what a penologist termed "a feat of administrative genius". He was moved up to the Federal Board of Parole.

The new warden of Alcatraz, E. B. Swope, proved different from his distinguished predecessor. A former New Mexico politician, he was assigned to Alcatraz at the age of sixty. His statement upon assuming the prison post was:

"Alcatraz gets all the rotten apples out of the barrel. If one can get a new seed to grow from those rotten apples, they're on the right track."

The warden's mixed metaphor was frank. The pose of rehabilitating prisoners on the Rock had been a standing joke among prison officials for years. Warden Swope installed four new gun ports, but he also ended the hated "silence system".

A new circumstance now made Stroud's work doubly difficult even as it drove him harder to perform it. His health broke and he suffered painful attacks of gall-bladder and kidney trouble.

The new warden discontinued the arrangement by which Stroud could keep indirectly in touch with other bird authorities. He also intervened in the matter of business letters written by the birdman to his agent concerning his avian interests.

Stroud filed an appeal in Federal court seeking to enjoin Warden Swope from interfering with his bird work and correspondence. Judge G. B. Harris dismissed the action with leave to amend.

"To deprive a man of the fruits of his industry," the judge said, "is to destroy that man."

"But, Your Honour," objected the U.S. Attorney, "a criminal is civilly dead."

"He may be civilly dead," countered the judge, "but he's not buried."

The added tension and irritation bore down upon Stroud. His illness continued, and he was transferred from the cell in D Block to a room in the prison hospital. There he was provided with drugs and medicaments to help him meet these attacks with less pain.

In the hospital, Stroud improved and resumed his writing labours. But now his bird library was taken away. His protest brought information that the warden had forbidden him the right to keep more than one book at a time. It made too much of a problem for the orderly, he was advised, to clean his room when it was cluttered with open books. This was a prison, not a research library.

Stroud reacted to his increased restrictions with more production. He continued to write.

In 1949 Mrs. Minnie King, Vice-President of the National Association of Canary Breeders, wrote to Stroud for advice on how to cure a sick bird. Her letter was returned unopened. She mailed the dead bird to prison officials to show her displeasure. "Stroud became the greatest authority on canary ailments," she told the Press. "We need his help."

Stroud had found a sympathetic and friendly guide in a prison chaplain. A pleasant and discerning man, the chaplain talked with and advised the bird convict twice a month. It helped to stabilize Stroud. This chaplain remained a good friend and welcome visitor for years.

Prison officials were nonplussed by the quality of persons attracted to the canary convict. At Leavenworth, several guards had been transferred because of their efforts to assist him with his birds. Stroud had maintained a relationship for years with a well-known bird breeder who was permitted to exchange letters with him. Former correspondents never forgot him. They seemed to sense the man Stroud might have been, lurking behind the ordeal-distorted ego so repellent to the authorities.

Now in Alcatraz hospital, the prisoner attracted the interest of an intelligent, well-educated male nurse. This man lightened

Stroud's physical pain, cut some corners to ease his darkening days and afforded him some intellectual discourse.

Day by day and month by lonely month, Stroud toiled on his prison history. He went ahead despite painful gall-bladder attacks.

While other prisoners were moving heaven and earth and guards to get anything—benzedrine, "goof balls", alcohol or even an extra ration of tobacco—for surcease from their discontent, Stroud's concern was to avoid taking morphine or atropine because the hangover from it interfered with his work. Concerning these attacks, he wrote:

> I can get treatments at once now, so that if a nurse is not handy, all I have to do is call a guard and he can hand me the things that have to be kept under lock and key. Milder drugs, I keep in reach at all times. If an attack hits slow, I take luminal and tresentin. If it hits faster, I take paregoric and elixir of nembutal; but if it hits very fast, I take codeine and atropine. That failing, morphine and atropine. The more powerful drugs mean a more powerful hangover, so I avoid them if possible, but the main idea is to control the attack, for the shorter it is the less it takes out of you.

Physical pain sharpened his temper and intensified his problems. The more duress he suffered the greater became his sense of persecution: and the more persecuted he felt the more his ego swelled in a dismal merry-go-round of grandiose torment. But his intellectual grip was tenacious.

In 1950 he appealed the 1948 petition for an injunction to the Circuit Court. Stroud had written his own legal pleadings, which he said "were not nicely drawn". A stinging gall-bladder attack had caused him to write both letters and pleadings in such an acidulous and mordant mood that readers outside of the prison were appalled by the bitter, grandiose, and scurrilous language with which he expressed himself.

His explanations and regrets alike were of no avail.

The Circuit Court was judging the contentions of a man pushed toward madness by thirty-two years in a solitary cell. But behind Stroud's apparently absurd suit to restrain the warden from interfering with his business correspondence were some profound legal questions. Much depended upon how the legal questions were put, and how far his legal approach would carry on appeal.

Stroud was determined to obtain a definition of the rights of a convict in matters of retention and control of property and property rights. He posed questions:

> Does a citizen of the United States, even though incarcerated in a penitentiary, retain property rights that his keepers are bound to respect? Are his rights to his property protected from official encroachment and conspiracy by sections 43 and 47 of Title 8 of the Constitution?

Stroud was aiming at the constitutionality of the same rules of the Prison Bureau which were invoked to cut off his bird enterprise in 1931.

The Circuit Court of Appeals threw out Stroud's brief with vigorous language. It sustained the lower court in denying the injunction and dismissing the petition.

TWENTY-NINE

BY THE TIME Stroud had decided to appeal his court action, he had written more than 100,000 words of his book about prisons in his meticulous hand. Word of the work began to spread. Writing about jailbirds in steel cages was less welcome in a prisoner than writing about pet birds in wire ones. But the male nurses, several guards and one of the chaplains read parts of it, as did several of the educated prisoners. Their interest spurred Stroud on.

The work did not concern itself with prisons after 1930: it contained matters little known except by inmates and officials. It was written with an irony, brutality and frankness which was appealing and repellent at the same time—like its tormented author. The chaplain cautioned Stroud to be more objective. Facts were facts, but why not tone them down?

Stroud paid little attention. He wanted to put matters down as he saw them. Then he proposed to make constructive recommendations for reforming prisoners. He felt he could add something to the literature of prisoners who had written about their confinement.

Prison officials looked with disfavour upon his enterprise. When he sent a chapter outline of his work to his brother, they sent the letter but withheld the outline, made a copy, placed it in his file and returned the outline to Stroud.

The prison-wise convict then realized that without some proof of the existence of his literary property, it would never get beyond the walls.

Since his book outline was an integral part of his writing activity, he hit upon the idea of including it as an Exhibit in his court pleading. When he appealed from the lower court, Stroud arranged to have the entire case printed for the eyes of the circuit court. By this means Stroud incorporated the outline of his book into an official document, and told the world outside of its existence. At this time the book was more than half-completed —one volume of a projected two-volume analytical study of the Federal Penal System from 1790 to 1930. Extracts of the exhibit disclosed the conception and scope of the work:

REHABILITATION

by Robert Stroud

VOL. I

An Analytic Study of the Federal Penal System from 1790 to 1930

TABLE OF CONTENTS

PART I. EARLY HISTORY

CHAPTER I. *The Purpose of Work*

A brief outline of the purposes of the work, beginning with a statement by Mr. Bennett admitting a 50 per cent. failure under present penological practices, and a statement of the enormous cost of the present system.

CHAPTER II. *The Right to Speak*

Biographical sketch of the writer's life and a statement of his qualifications for making the proposed analysis.

CHAPTER III. *Legal History of Federal Penal System*

This chapter lists and discusses all Congressional enactment pertaining to imprisonment from the First Crime Act, April 30, 1790, to 1929. The circumstances surrounding each development are briefly described, and in many instances court opinions are cited.

CHAPTER IV. *Conditions prior to 1910 General*

A discussion of prison conditions throughout the nation as they existed from earliest times until 1910.

CHAPTER V. *Conditions prior to 1910 Leavenworth*

Circumstances surrounding establishment of the penitentiaries at Leavenworth and Atlanta.

The Long March. A description of the marching of 400 convicts in chains from Moundsville, West Virginia, to Leavenworth, Kansas.

Conditions at Leavenworth during the building of the prison and the throwing up of the high wall.

Warden's Call. A discussion of administrative procedure of Robert McCloughry [first warden at Leavenworth] and a study of his penological philosophy expressed in his own words.

Medical Attention. A description of the medical attention given convicts at Leavenworth prior to 1910.

Spiritual Guidance. Biographic sketch and character study of first Leavenworth chaplain, 1901-1905, with description of church services.

Big Jim. A discussion of the first deputy warden at Leavenworth and the killing of an Indian boy which led to his indictment for manslaughter.

CHAPTER VI. *Early History Continued*

Atlanta. Brief sketch.

McNeil Island. Physical description.

The King and his Little Kingdom. Description of first warden and the prison he ruled.

O. P. Halligan, biographical and character study with stories from life.

Noblesse oblige. Illustrative stories of principles of penology and prison management.

CHAPTER VII. *Population*

Discussion of prison population as it existed around the turn of the century.

The Great American Bum. A discussion of the dominant criminal fraternity existing in this country from the time of the Civil War until the First World War, with discussion of mode of life, social relationships, training, and ethics, and their influences upon the prisons in which they were confined.

Changing Times. The influence of new legislation upon the character of the prison population.

PART 2. THE PRISON REFORM MOVEMENT

CHAPTER I. *General Discussion*

Early history of the movement and the men involved from the publication of "The Turn of the Balance" by Brant Whitlock, to the trial of Thomas Mott Osborne, with references to the work of Ben Lindsey, Fremont Older, Donald Lowrie, Maud Ballington Booth, and many others.

CHAPTER II. *Parole in Theory and Practice*

History of the enactment of the Federal Parole Law with description of man responsible contrasted to that of James Mann, author of the Mann Act, enacted on the same day.

Analysis of the theory of parole, from its origin by the Holy Office of the Inquisition in Rome to the present day.

An analysis of forty years of application of the Federal Parole Law and its influence upon population, prison management. This is the most powerful indictment of the theory and practice of parole ever written.

CHAPTER III. *The King's Capitulation*

The story of the adoption of the first reform measures at McNeil Island, with amusing side incidents.

CHAPTER IV. *The Liberalization of Leavenworth*

Morgan. A study of the first reform Warden of Leavenworth.

The Missing Link. A study of the first reform deputy warden and the principles upon which the greatest record as a disciplinarian ever made in an American prison was built, and the listing of the improvements made. Stories behind improvements.

Abolition of Stripes. The story of how this was brought about by men turning this badge of degradation into a romantic asset in making love to teen-age boys.

New Era. Establishment of prison paper at Leavenworth. A discussion of the paper and its influence.

O.E. Library League. The story of one of the greatest reformative steps in the entire history of American prisons.

Christmas. The story of the beginning of what later grew into the greatest instrumentability of goodwill between officials and inmates that ever existed in any prison. A movement that stretched over two decades. The discussion is completed under the sub-title, The Yule Log, Chapter VIII.

CHAPTER V. "*America's Greatest Penologist*"

A study of how a well-meaning egotist took over the best-fed, best-disciplined and best-behaved prison in the country and in nine short months, simply by trying to please everybody, reduced it to chaos and bloodshed.

While the detail of Stroud's views on reformation are merely outlined in the table of contents, his theory is based upon the prisoner's desire to create. "This force can, if properly handled", he states, "be turned into the greatest reformative force yet discovered." Of his serious interest in the subject there could be small doubt.

Self-educated and the author of two books, he had learned to write with clarity and force. He was a kind of left-handed authority in the penal field because of his unprecedented span of confinement in four Federal institutions.

The view of a prisoner-scientist might conceivably hold interest for a country whose prison problem had not shrunk, but grown.

The relentless muzzling of Stroud cemented his determination to lay his work at any cost before the public.

The thinking expressed in one of his letters was characteristic and also premonitory:

From my sixth year I have never had any fear of death, probably because most of my life has been so miserable that I did not care, but I have been fighting all my life. No amount of work, no amount of careful planning has ever been too great a price. On more occasions than you will ever know about, when I had shoved all of my other chips into the pot and found that they were not enough, I have shoved my life in too, without hesitation, and on more than one occasion I have come very close to losing it. But I have never whined about it or begged for quarter. I have never turned back from a position once taken in my whole life, and I never shall.

In May, 1951, an Iowa bird-lover wrote to the Federal Bureau, citing Stroud's work, and inquired whether he was still considered dangerous. In the absence of James V. Bennett, A. H. Conner, Acting Director, answered.

It is undoubtedly true that Stroud's work on the diseases of birds has been most helpful to the bird breeders of the world. It is unfortunate that his adjustment in our care degenerated so that it became necessary to transfer him to the prison at Alcatraz. As you know, Mr. Stroud was originally convicted for murder and became eligible to parole some years ago. The U.S. Board of Parole has considered his application for parole on a number of occasions, but has not indicated that he is ready for release to the community.

Between attacks of sickness, Stroud prepared an appeal on his court action from the Circuit Court to the United States Supreme Court. Warden Swope allowed him to receive from his brother records of other court cases for completing his brief. He required many court docket numbers from cases whose names he remembered. These were supplied by his tireless brother, L. G. Marcus.

Stroud was determined to get the entire brief printed, rather than to submit it in *forma pauperis* as a destitute prisoner. His brother Marcus agreed to foot the bill.

Stroud wrote the entire petition of some 30,000 words in pen and ink in six days, including a table of contents, exhibits and numerous annotated and analysed references.

On July 2, 1951, he turned the manuscript over to the Associate Warden with a written request that it be mailed to Marcus for printing and forwarding to the Supreme Court.

Two weeks later the petition was returned to him with one typed original and four carbon copies. If he would sign these, they would be sent to the Supreme Court. But, the official cautioned, he would not be allowed to have his petition printed. Both Stroud and the officials knew such a legal document in printed form might attract attention. Stroud then wrote the following letter to the Clerk of the United States Supreme Court:

I wish to call your attention to the following facts, some of which have been mentioned before:

Section 41 of Title 8 grants to all persons the equal benefit of the laws. Amendment 1 of the Constitution secures to all persons the right to petition Congress for the redress of grievances. Paragraph 2 of Rule 38 of the rules of your Court provides that the petitioner for certiorari shall file with your court 40 copies of his petition and supporting brief, printed in accordance with terms of rule 28.

The rule also requires the serving of the respondent and his attorney, in this case, the Solicitor-General of the U.S.

There is no provision which permits any litigant to proceed in any other manner, excepting those proceeding in *forma pauperis* or upon special permission from your court to proceed upon typewritten papers.

I am not proceeding in *forma pauperis* and I have not and shall not ask for permission to proceed on typewritten papers, and I have paid all fees in to your court.

Your rules nor the law make no provision as by whom I may have my printing done, nor as to how many copies of my petition I may have printed, so long as the printing is done in compliance with Rule 26.

After outlining the circumstances of the warden's refusal to send the petition to his brother, the prisoner resumed:

I have signed the copies and am returning them to the Associate Warden herewith, so that it cannot be said that any of the obstruction was my fault. But I still insist that he and the respondent herein are in contempt of your court for blocking the orderly presentation of this case in the manner and form provided for by law.

I also insist that I have a legal and constitutional right under the sections cited above to have my petition printed and to receive exactly the same consideration that is accorded any other litigant before your court. I still wish to have my petition and brief printed by my agent, and I believe that the processes of this court are powerful enough to accord me that right. If they are not, and if they are not available to me even in a prison cell, our government has fallen into a sorry mess.

It is my desire to have 120 copies of my petition and brief printed, and a copy sent to every member of the Judiciary Committee of both Houses of Congress, which is my right under the 1st Amendment and it is my desire and intention to exercise it. Therefore I again ask you to call this letter to the attention of the presiding justice and to convey to him my desire to have such appropriate process issued under the seal of your Court as to secure to me the rights of which I am attempting to avail myself. As a man in prison, at the complete mercy and will of the respondent, I am making this request in the only manner and form available to me, but I believe that is legally sufficient. In that respect, I call your attention to this Court's opinion in Steffler *v.* U.S. I do not have the volume and page number, but it was in the October Term of 1943 and 1944. Thanking you for past favours, I am

Sincerely yours,
Robert Stroud, No. 594 Alcatraz.

Following receipt of the above letter, the brief was printed.

The seventy-six-page, bound document was duly laid in front of the United States Supreme Court. Stroud's dreams and hopes, his brother's money and endless study and work went into the Petition. It was among the most comprehensive briefs ever written by a convict.

Concerning his release and plans, Stroud wrote:

He [appellant Stroud] wants to be free, but the only freedom he wants or would accept is that of carrying on his work under his own name and under more favourable conditions than prison can afford. . . . It has been my plan for many years to form, as soon as I am released, a corporation under the laws of Nevada to be known as Stroud Laboratory, Inc.; an educational and research institution devoted to the study of avian genetics, physiology, pathology and therapeutics and education in those fields, under the direction of Robert Stroud. . . .

Exhausted, Stroud waited for October and the reaction of the high court.

The Supreme Court declined to review the case. The Circuit Court's decision stood.

Stroud was now over sixty. He had endured a decade alone on the Rock. The juices of his body, so fierce in his youth, had run dry. His consuming thought now was to find some way to get his manuscript before the public.

Despite his Promethean endurance, a querulous note began to creep into Stroud's letters. After an intense gall-bladder attack, he wrote:

. . . I am very tired, and I don't think I have much farther to go. But I do hope to leave behind me something that will last as long as our civilization lasts.

The real thing that has kept me in prison is not that statement of my mother. It has been used many times to hurt me, but what keeps me in is that I am not a compromiser. I never condone what I think is wrong, and I never forget anything. They know that if I ever get out and have the opportunity, I will make that Bureau over; and they know I have the organizing ability to do it.

Shortly after this he wrote again:

My other work is going pretty fast now. I have the first book ready for the printer, and am halfway through the rewriting of the second one. They will be powerful works and they will occupy the same position in penological literature as my other book does in bird literature. Book IV is over half done. I consider those books a whole lot more valuable than I am. I will not be able to complete the whole project. I know that now.

Then he penned several strange lines:

The point about my books is not that I will kill myself writing them; but that may be the price-tag attached to accomplishing what I have set out to accomplish. And to me, accomplishment is the only justification for existence.

As he groped for some way to outwit his keepers, an odd notion came to Stroud. For the next weeks, each time he had a gall-bladder attack, he would take the glass of water but would save the pills, suffering the pain.

One morning, Stroud selected a piece of onion-skin paper and printed a message on it in minute letters. After signing and dating it, he folded it until it made a small square. From a slit in the mattress he drew out a tiny polished metal tube. He slid the paper into the tube and returned it to the mattress.

One afternoon in December, 1951, Stroud carried a glass of water to his bedside. He brought out the tiny tube and swallowed it quickly, washing it down with a little water. Then he swallowed his cache of pills.

He walked over to the window and took a lingering look at the land rising through the mist. He saw a seagull and drowsily watched it fly away. "Even the birds avoid this unspeakable place," he muttered. He padded over to his bed. Soon he was still.

The guard with the evening meal tray knocked at the door, waited, shrugged and moved away.

Toward morning, the count guard unlocked the door, looked

in, closed the door—and paused. He peered in again. He did not like the motionless position of the prisoner. He went back in and flashed his light on Stroud's face. There was no response except slow stertorous breathing.

The guard ran for the doctor. The doctor took a careful look and moved fast.

Stroud was injected with stimulants and his stomach was pumped.

"The old man has great strength," the doctor said. "He's been frustrated for so many years he has an over-responsive adrenal gland. Another hour and he would have gone."

When Stroud regained consciousness he found himself unable to move. There was a guard posted by him sitting in a chair.

Stroud was in a strait jacket.

His first thought was for his manuscript. His eyes started wildly as he scanned the room. It was picked clean and bare. There were no boxes of manuscript, no materials, nothing.

"Where is—it?" he asked faintly.

"Where is what?"

The prisoner shut his eyes. The warden had confiscated everything.

Then he remembered the tube. He waited for the guard to leave and then called for the male nurse who had befriended him.

"This is bad—very bad, Stroud," said the tall, ascetic man gently.

"Did they—find anything else?"

"Yes, they recovered the tube in your stool. It made them mad."

The small metal tube had contained a legal document. Stroud, expecting his body to be shipped to a San Francisco morgue for inquest, had made out a paper willing his prison manuscript to the care of the coroner for forwarding to a legal friend, asking it be made public.

"How long will they keep me in this?" asked Stroud, glancing down at the white canvas which pinioned him, cutting off all movement.

"Oh, maybe a couple of weeks," the nurse replied. "Then you'll be put in muffs."

"I thought I'd said goodbye to this place."

"You nearly did. A guard just had a hunch . . ."

Later the friendly chaplain came to visit Stroud. The old prisoner was chalk-pale. He looked like a mummy, with his arms strapped across under the canvas hospital-type strait jacket. He rose from the bed and slid his feet into slippers. He bowed to the chaplain. His folded-over arms and close-cropped head made him look like an old mandarin.

"Does that thing bother you much?" asked the chaplain.

Stroud smiled thinly. He bent over. His eyes centred on his left thigh. "There's a bandage there where I cut myself last week. I'm over it now."

"You tried twice?"

"I showed them they couldn't hold me by force."

The chaplain's mouth fell open. "You mean you can slip a strait jacket?"

"Sure. Turn around a minute."

The chaplain hesitated. Then he moved to the far side of the bare room and looked away. He could hear small rustling sounds.

"All right!" Stroud said.

The chaplain swung around nervously. Stroud's hands were free.

"Where did you learn that?"

"From my brother. He used to do it on the stage . . ."

"You—almost killed yourself," said the minister, casually. "I'm glad it didn't happen that way—for your sake."

Stroud looked at him. His old hands trembled and his eyes took on a glitter.

"I'm an old man now. I don't know what follows after death, but I have always taken my chances. I could die, but that wouldn't get the manuscript out."

"What are your plans now?" the chaplain asked.

"I'll have to keep working. By the way, did the papers get wind of this?"

"Not that I saw."

"It was all for nothing then. Well"—the old convict stirred—"I'd better get my hands back in."

The chaplain looked away until the prisoner called to him. Stroud was a cross-armed mandarin in white again.

Later that month the strait-jacket was removed and Stroud's hands were placed in "muffs" for several weeks—canvas mittens fastened with straps.

Despite his isolation, Stroud continued to reveal an amazing knowledge of conditions inside and events outside his stone home. Allowed no newspapers, no exercise, no radio, seeing no visitors except his brother, and required to eat alone, he watched with weary bitterness the censored events inside the Rock.

In July, 1950, a riot had erupted in the mess hall. The tear-gas bombs suspended from the ceiling were ignored. Prisoners overturned tables and beat spoons against their chairs.

In April, 1951, a guard had been sentenced to five years in prison for smuggling letters, money, alcohol and drugs. An assistant United States Attorney said the traffic reflected large-scale operations, and termed conditions in Alcatraz "very explosive".

Then the prison barber plunged a knife through the neck of a convict who came for a haircut. For the murder he was sentenced to an additional ten to thirty years. Interviewed, he told reporters that "goof balls" were still available on the Rock.

In April, 1952, another food riot broke out. Twenty prisoners were placed in solitary. They put detergent in the coffee and soaked meat with kerosene. Later in April, prisoners in the shops set fire to their work gloves. A Washington official flew out to inspect the Rock.

Prison Bureau chiefs were attacking their fearsome prison in public statements, and printing booklets in praise of it. The warden requested funds for building more gun ports.

Several senators moved to abolish the island bastille. But the Federal Bureau was a part of the prosecuting arm of the government—an historic stone in the path of its best penologists in their effort to effect a basic change in outlook. In an era of inquisition, fear and unrest, the Rock as a symbol appeared to satisfy some hunger in the public.

Stroud's efforts through legal means to place his prison manuscript before the public had met with failure. The requests of attorneys met a blank wall. Nor was Stroud able to have his work returned to him. Some prison officials now deny its existence. Does Stroud's enormous tome contain material of value to the public? Is it the mad raving of a prison-crazed mind, or an explosive charge of prison facts strapped to the deck of the Rock? This is known only to the men who keep the men of Alcatraz.

Incongruously, Stroud's *Digest of Bird Diseases* was now circulating briskly in public libraries. It was advertised in *All-Pets Magazine*, whose owner, Frank Dittrich, had purchased the copyright. The edition was now dwindling in supply after ten years, and he contemplated a new and revised edition.

"Even today", Dittrich revealed, "Mr. Stroud's book is still considered the number-one bird disease volume in the world. Its popularity has increased greatly in the past few years due to the unprecedented expansion of the bird industry. There is a great need for a new, revised edition."

Dittrich inquired of Stroud's brother and agent, L. G. Marcus, whether the old prisoner might wish to revise his book. Stroud told his brother he would be glad of the opportunity to do so.

The publisher then wrote to the warden of Alcatraz. Revision of the book would entail letting the prisoner have a small library, writing materials and permission to correspond with several leading avian scientists. The warden took the matter up with his Washington superior. The request was refused.

The bewildered publisher wrote to his senators and congressmen. They inquired of the Federal Prison Bureau and received such overwhelmingly negative reports on Stroud that the lawmakers were dumbfounded.

A congressman's inquiry about the matter received this answer from the Bureau's Director, J. V. Bennett:

Both the Warden and I have given this matter a great deal of consideration and in view of our experience with Stroud and his general attitude now, we cannot permit him to undertake any such project. Stroud has been in our custody since 1909 when he was sentenced for a murder committed in Alaska. Some years later, he received an additional sentence for an assault with a weapon on another prisoner and later received a death sentence for killing a guard at Leavenworth which was commuted to life in 1920. All these years, he has required constant custodial supervision and has been a source of apprehension to us for his own safety as well as for the safety of others. While at Leavenworth many years ago, Stroud became interested in birds and slowly he accumulated a collection of birds, expanded his cell into a laboratory and built up a supply of drugs, medicines, scalpels and other laboratory instruments. Although we permitted this, we watched it with a great deal of concern and I can assure you that our concern was justified when we decided to transfer him to Alcatraz in 1942. The story of a man like Stroud being interested in birds is of course an appealing one, but we are dealing with a very difficult individual who has been a constant source of trouble and agitation since he has been in our institutions, involving incidentally a very considerable expense to the Government.

Under the circumstances, I am convinced that it would be decidedly inadvisable to permit Stroud to engage in any such project. I hope that information gives you sufficient background on this case so that you may know what is involved. I am returning the letter you requested.

In 1953, one of the world's eminent penologists asked a policy-making Bureau official why the old prisoner was not allowed to revise his bird book.

"Stroud is merely trying to increase his nuisance value," the official said.

It was the same official who once stated: "The aim of the Federal system is to fill the inmate's time with useful activity, to create conditions that make for normal and reasonable living."

By 1953 Stroud had exhausted the library's readable works in English. Looking through the library catalogue he discovered a collection of French volumes someone had donated. He secured permission to get a French-English dictionary and grammar. Before long he was laboriously translating French classics. In June, 1953, he wrote:

I am getting along very well with French. The French have a unique, formalized way of saying things, and one letter or one two-lettered word often means as much as a whole English phrase. In a play by Molière, two women are gossiping about a third one. "She has not been able to teach herself how to forget that she is no longer an infant." Which I thought was about as neat a description as I had ever read, especially when it only takes about seven words to say all that in French. I am learning things about style that will greatly improve my own writing.

Victor Hugo, Stroud complained, drove him to the dictionary many times; and Zola wrote as he, Stroud, still hoped to.

Six months later he wrote to Fred Daw, an eighty-year-old bird fancier. Daw, one of the three people allowed to correspond with Stroud, had been a loyal friend for twenty-six years to a man he had never seen.

. . . We have known each other a long time, Fred. We have always got on well, which just goes to show that we are not such old cranks as some people would make us out to be. *I wish you could read French, Fred.* I would have you read *Le Voyage* from *Fleurs du Mal*. by Charles Baudelaire. The translation loses the flavour. This fellow was very bitter at life, and he had reason to be, but it was that very bitterness that made him one of the greatest poets who ever lived. I have a bunch of his poems that I have copied and am learning by heart. In the one mentioned he says in one verse:

> It is bitter to know what one learns from travel; that the world is small and monotonous, that yesterday, today, tomorrow and forever, it makes us see our own image; an oasis of horror in a desert of ennui.

Can you beat that for a figure of speech?

Love and best wishes, as ever.

Bob, No. 594.

What writing could afford greater comfort to a life prisoner than a noted poet's distaste for travel?

In the world of the H-bomb, the man who went to jail in the age of the kerosene lamp watched time drag toward his sixty-sixth birthday. His infirmities were carefully treated, and he lived on. To the slivers of his sanity, Stroud clung with desperate hope.

His muffled outcry was heard every month by L. G. Marcus, now a Sacramento businessman, whose desperate effort to help his tortured brother now amounted to decades of time and a fortune in money.

Stroud was a man on a Rock, a Prometheus pledged to endless rebellion against the punitive vengeance inherent in the structure, attitude and emotional weather of prisons.

Under the leadership of the Director, under whose supervision and control Stroud was held, the Federal Prison Bureau had achieved an enormous prestige and power. Praised by penal authorities the world over for its new prisons without walls, and the humane improvements in their operation, the Bureau set standards for the state prisons, and admonished their commissioners and wardens to improve their own penal empires. The Bureau dominated the literature and journalism of the correctional field, and made any penologist think twice before daring to give it offence.

And yet, the attitude of many Federal prison officials, present or retired, revealed that their indomitable prisoner, Stroud, had begun to exert a curious influence.

In the Bureau's information booklet about Alcatraz, Stroud, under the name of "Jack", is the only prisoner whose life and record are outlined; and these are called "a typical case history".

In the Bureau's book of *Correctional Institution Design and Construction*, Stroud, under the name of "X", is again a "Typical Case", the only prisoner dwelt upon in a 300-page book of architecture devoted to prison ground plans, layout and equipment for detention facilities.

None of the résumés mention that their inmate had so much as seen a canary.

Was it unnerving to the keeper, holding power over this prisoner, to watch him suffer unbroken in his thirty-eighth solitary year? Has any other Federal convict been confined alone for more than a decade?

Each new day Stroud endured in the chalice of the Rock, which held within its fog-shrouded rim its futureless inmates, a place where lay terror for the mind; which ate into the vitals of the keepers and the kept alike, unnerving their decency, making survival contingent upon ruthless force, steep routine, and counting . . . The guards become prisoners themselves, and everyone counting, counting, the prisoners counting the hours and the guards counting the prisoners and the warden counting the counts.

In 1955 Stroud watched the fading vapour trail of a jet plane across the sky. The sun was falling fast. Soon, as he had for years, he would watch the fog roll in with the dusk, and see bright banks of neon kindle and glow behind the fog, opening the night life of the West Coast's most cultured city.

He is an old man now, ailing and spent. His birds, once the lively companions of his solitude, are now the small dead ghosts of memory. His prison writings confiscated, his iron spirit obscured in stone, he waits for pardon or death, his spirit still unbroken.

Robert Stroud still hopes, still dreams. He hopes the President may choose to intervene in his behalf. He dreams of making a ten-acre sanctuary for birds, if a pardon comes. He does not know the real name of Alcatraz. It is the *Isla de Los Alcatraces*, or Island of Pelicans. They used to call it Bird Island.

EPILOGUE

PUBLISHER'S NOTE

The author's concern for Robert Stroud continued after publication of *Birdman of Alcatraz* in 1955 and he helped to form a committee which campaigned for the prisoner's release. Thomas E. Gaddis was preparing a second volume of biography, including material that was suppressed from the first, when he died in 1984. Here his daughter contributes an epilogue outlining the origins of the book and the considerable impact made by its publication. She also describes her father's further efforts on Stroud's behalf and traces the prisoner's personal story until his death in 1963.

EPILOGUE

by Phyllis E. Gaddis

When my father's literary agent, Bertha Klausner, suggested to him that he investigate the story of Robert Stroud, a chain of events was started which resulted in a world-wide attempt to free the prisoner.

After hearing the first few intriguing details of the case, my father set to work, only to find that the more he knocked on government doors, the tighter they closed—which only increased his determination. When he had enough information for an article, great pressure was evidently brought to bear by the prison authorities to prevent publication in any magazine. But Bertha Klausner finally sold it to the American magazine, *Cosmopolitan*, in 1951 and (aided by a cover featuring Marilyn Monroe) it increased the public interest in Stroud's situation. My father continued to work for over three years, in an improvised office in our garage, to complete the book. He had already visited the island of Alcatraz but once he had generated interest in Robert Stroud's case he was not allowed to visit it again until the prisoner had long since left, and the prison itself was dissolved.

News of the article astounded the Prison Bureau executives. They had, after all, refused to allow my father to see Stroud, or his file. A Beverly Hills lawyer, Stanley Furman, became involved and was allowed to visit Stroud for three hours. Though difficult legally, it was finally established that Furman could become Stroud's attorney. Two important changes were accomplished initially by the lawyer. After Furman learned that the prisoner had been required to use a bedpan for eight years because there were no facilities in his cell, he consulted the Warden and a toilet was installed. The other agreement was for Stroud to enjoy a small sense of freedom—the facility after many years to exercise, alone, in the open air of the prison exercise yard. Radio permission, however, was not granted.

Stroud's mailing list remained the same: two relatives and his lawyer. He was not allowed to communicate with my father. On one visit to the prisoner, Furman received a copy of his *Digest of Birds* as a gift from the grateful Stroud. Bob had written him a long note in the front pages of the book, thanking him for his efforts. But before leaving the prison Furman was required by the Warden to remove the inscription with a razor blade, before he had even had a proper chance to read it.

My father wrote other books after *Birdman of Alcatraz*, detailing the lives of other prisoners, but the story of Robert Stroud was closest to his heart. What has happened since the original publication of this book reflects two life dramas: not only that of the aging scientist-prisoner Stroud, but that of my father who, along with many, many others, attempted to rectify what was felt to be one of the most unjust legal treatments of a human being in prison. While Stroud was never given clemency or his freedom, his situation was to change drastically over the years, due to strenuous efforts on his behalf and despite the resistance of the prison authorities.

Unfortunately, Stroud was never officially allowed to read his own biography, but through the prison grapevine a copy of this book became available to him, and he no doubt realized that though he was alone in his cell, there were others outside who cared about his existence.

When *Birdman of Alcatraz* was published, a public outcry ensued, which led to the formation of the Committee for Release of Robert F. Stroud. Heading the list were such well-known authorities as Arthur Koestler, who had experienced solitary confinement as well as the threat of a death sentence, Negley Teeters, noted sociologist, Victor Weybright, head of New American Library, Walter Wanger, a film producer, and many others.

Thousands of letters were written, through the efforts of the committee's bulletins, to President Eisenhower and other federal officials. Senators and congressmen made inquiries, which were routed to the Federal Prison Bureau. Some people received detailed letters from James Bennett, head of the Bureau. Others received form letters.

As awareness of the committee increased, letters poured in from all over the world offering help and money; from as far away as Casablanca, where a *Comité International pour la Création d'une Cour de Justice Internationale pour la Protection des Personnes Privées* was created in regard of the rights of prisoners, Stroud included. And in France, a committee was formed by the President of the French Society of Friends of Animals, for the purpose of giving moral support for release of the prisoner; a law, "the law Robert Stroud", was introduced to the French legislature, permitting long-term prisoners to have animals and take care of them while incarcerated. Stroud's birds had been taken away from him fifteen years before.

Christmas cards flowed in for the prisoner. They were shown to him but he was not allowed to keep more than a few. One of them was from myself, aged twelve. About the same time, legal papers concerning a pardon were being prepared by the Friends of Robert Stroud, to be accompanied by a Petition to the President of the United States. The original petition was refused by the Pardon Attorney and Stroud was understandably disturbed.

During the process of legal appeals to the Parole Board, offers came in to the committee for free housing of the prisoner upon release. Stroud expressed appreciation on hearing of this, but he was concerned about his ability to be among people again. He hoped for a quiet situation, and specifically mentioned a worry that he wouldn't be able to handle cutlery at a dining-room table in public after so many years alone.

In 1958, Stroud's attorney submitted to the President a Petition for Executive Clemency, which allows a president to pardon criminals upon changed circumstances. It was determined by the Pardon Attorney, Cozart, that a petition was not viable while Stroud was subject to the discretion of the Board of Parole—though Stroud had been eligible for parole since 1937 and had been turned down every year. Furman made plans to leave for Washington, but Stroud mentioned in a letter that he'd heard of a Supreme Court decision concerning double jeopardy (where legally one may not be tried twice for the same crime) in the case of *Green* v. *US*. The high court had freed Green because he was twice put in jeopardy of life for the same offence. Stroud immediately prepared a writ of habeus corpus claiming that since his first trial had given him life imprisonment, the second trial, which had given him a death sentence, could only have given him the same life imprisonment.

Though Green had received the court's decision to his favour, Judge Frankfurter entered a dissenting opinion, expressing his dissatisfaction with double jeopardy in this case. But he stated that if Green were to be released, then so should Robert Stroud. Stroud's attorney asked for reconsideration from the Supreme Court on Stroud's behalf. It was denied.

Around the same time, Stroud's case was under consideration again by the Parole Board, with a full board of seven people. One of the members interviewed Stroud personally, asking whether he would consider a conditional parole based on an agreement to relinquish all efforts in his manuscript about the prison system. Stroud asked to see his lawyer.

Meanwhile, several producers had shown interest in creating a film based on my father's biography of Stroud. One major producer applied for an option, but evidently the Federal Prison Bureau brought intense pressure on the company, which had currency investments overseas that could be blocked. Another company took an option, but could not get any screenwriters to create a successful script about a man kept alone in a room for four decades.

Producers then tried to extend the option to make the life of Robert Stroud into an Alaskan epic, utilizing only the earlier part of Stroud's adult life. My father refused this approach, as there was much more in Stroud's story that needed to be told.

Eventually, a film company finalized a concept of the film. Bennett, head of the Prison Bureau, refused to allow any federal prison to open its doors or files for the making of the film, so the producer spent $150,000 for construction of sets of both

Leavenworth Prison and Alcatraz on the studio lot.

The final screenplay, written by Guy Trosper, was offered to actor Burt Lancaster. According to my father's recollections, Burt had only one question—how soon could the project get underway. In 1960, he had received an Academy Award as best actor, and he was to be nominated again for his role as Robert Stroud in the film of *Birdman of Alcatraz*, a part which required him to age from 22 to 69.

My father was engaged as technical advisor for the film, and travelled in his station wagon with all the essentials. Our family received missives detailing his duties and experiences. Accuracy in physical details of the set was essential to the validity of the film, and that included whether or not a shaving cream tube existed in 1923 and what exactly a solitary prisoner's eating utensils looked like.

A brains trust of material was organized by contacting members of the "Grey Brotherhood"—former prisoners, in this case from Leavenworth and Alcatraz; men who had shunned publicity and were now citizens in good standing, grateful to be leading straight lives away from the Big Houses where they had spent so many years. Even a retired prison guard who had known Stroud was found; he contributed greatly, though he refused any remuneration.

My father was actually given a screen test for the part of himself, author-investigator of Stroud's life, but we learned that he failed because he was not "real" enough, and the part was given to an actor who could do it well, Edmund O'Brien.

An authentic duplication of the isolation cell on Alcatraz was created, with the added problems of room for cameras and crew. Burt studied birds while the crews continued to work, bringing in a complete prison steam laundry from the year 1912. This was put into operation in the studio, rusty pipes and all, just for one scene early in the film. It was only on screen for about 90 seconds.

The completed motion picture, with a powerful performance by Burt Lancaster, was released by United Artists in 1962.

Stroud, aware of the growing interest in his situation since the publication of this book, had strong hopes for changes in his life. He was buoyed up by the efforts of his lawyer and the committee. Though much pressure was made to get him off the Rock, Stroud had severe doubts about parole at this point. His life had become a pattern of prison procedure. But his failing health, and perhaps a sheer yearning to get to a warmer spot than the foggy climate of the bay of San Francisco, argued with his reluctance to accept a possible transfer to a prison hospital in Springfield, Missouri. In prison existence, there is seldom warning of changes. A knock on Stroud's door delivered the news that the Warden was offering him the transfer to Springfield. After conferring with his lawyer, Stroud agreed to the move from the Rock, and in the summer of 1959 he was indeed released from Alcatraz.

Suddenly, after so many years, Bob Stroud was no longer in complete isolation. He had a key to his own room for the first time since 1909, over fifty years before. He wrote of the experience:

> I have seen my first TV program, but I've been too interested in people to spend time with it . . . I probably walk three miles a day and feel like a million . . . the yard is a beautiful park . . . I've seen more people and spoken more words than in forty years . . . imagine what a pleasure it was to lie on the grass for the first time since 1914 . . . it is most amazing to see many of the most controversial things I have advocated [concerning prison reform] practiced here as a matter of course . . . I could live a happy and useful life here in this hospital . . . I have seen pitiful cases where an hour's talk at the bedside of a lonely and suffering human being can give a new hope, and where hope is impossible, much courage.

Shortly after his arrival in Springfield, Stroud received word that a Federal judge had consented to hear his case. Stroud's legal petition was made on the grounds of cruel and unusual punishment as well as the technical case of double jeopardy.

Word that a film of his biography was under negotiation encouraged him, and he renewed his legal efforts for release. In the fall of 1959, he petitioned the US District Court at Topeka, Kansas, to suspend his life sentence and free him. Stroud knew that the US Supreme Court had widened its interpretation of the constitutional safeguard against double jeopardy in court trials. And he had strong hopes that the screening of the film would help achieve the rights and freedom he had lost in Alaska back in 1909.

Stroud's petition, based on the case of *Green* v. *US*, was received. Federal Judge Walter Huxman of the Kansas District Court agreed to hear Stroud's petition. Since Huxman wanted to see the prisoner in person, old Bob Stroud had a trip to Topeka. Bent, gaunt, but determined, this man, hands manacled, was escorted down a public street for the first time since 1920.

Judge Huxman was told Stroud was no longer in solitary confinement, and the US attorney assured the court that the government no longer contended it could impose solitary confinement as part of his sentence.

The Judge ruled that the original solitary confinement order in 1922 was illegal, but since Stroud was no longer in solitary, the matter was moot.

"There are features in the case that challenge the imagination and even shock the court," Judge Huxman stated, "but what is done is done."

Old Bob Stroud, then, heard that his banishment to solitary was illegal, but that nothing could be done about it. He appealed to the Supreme Court, but was refused review in terms of the double jeopardy situation. He returned to his prison hospital, and redoubled his efforts as a librarian. He began working on a plan to improve the binding of heavily used prison books, using plastic for support.

Meanwhile, Stroud and his attorney began civil suit to wrest from the Prison Bureau the release of his manuscript concerning the prison system. Apparently, the increased public attention began to disturb Stroud's equilibrium, since for so many years he had been used to very restricted contact with other people. He reported that it was becoming more difficult to relate to his fellow inmates. I do wonder at how well he was able to adjust to the great changes from solitude to this prison hospital, and human interaction. He certainly seemed to become acquainted with a few of his fellow inmates, including Morton Sobell, the so-called "atom spy", who was given a sentence of thirty years at the time that Julius and Ethel Rosenberg were condemned and executed in the electric chair at Sing Sing prison in New York.

At the breakfast table, Stroud and Sobell enjoyed a burgeoning casual relationship; they avoided political discussions, relating more to their similar experiences in prison life. They were amongst imprisoned activists who were against the draft for the Vietnam War. Obviously, Stroud was now meeting the world through his inmates, a world that he had not been allowed contact with for many, many years.

Stroud continued with legal actions, including a petition to stop the Prison Bureau from interfering with his legal corresponding rights. A prisoner is legally allowed confidential contact with his attorney, but Stroud's correspondence with Furman was being read before he received it.

In the summer of 1961, in preparation for the film's release, our family took a long tour of the United States in an unusual combination of simple camping alternated with fancy hotels—my father was to be in certain cities for press conferences. In between those cities we drove through miles of mud, baking desert and accumulating road tar in our old station wagon before rolling into a fancy hotel—receiving judgemental glances at our bedraggled appearance from the hotel personnel. Once ensconced in the suite, we were treated like royalty, and my father continued his job of letting more of the world know about Robert Stroud.

As we travelled east, an important stop was Missouri. Dad hoped to visit Stroud in his prison hospital, and on a summer-stormed day he parked the car in front of the prison and escorted me in with him, leaving me in the lobby while he consulted the Warden. His request to visit Stroud was denied, and we returned to our motel.

It was not until the prisoner later stood in a courtroom that the two men were finally to meet.

In April 1962, Stroud's attorney petitioned to Kansas City, which produced an ordering by the judge for Stroud to appear in court. The legal situation was complicated, but involved release of Stroud's prison manuscript as well as other legal proceedings, including a plea about cruel and unusual punishment and definition of the rights of prisoners.

My father and mother sat in the first row behind the defence table, where attorney Stanley Furman was seated. Stroud appeared in the court, accompanied by two guards, and waved to a man he had never before met, but seemed to know—my father.

Furman noticed, after Stroud was seated at the defence table, that the guards had moved away and that the Judge had not yet entered the courtroom. He thought of bringing Thomas Gaddis up to meet the prisoner. At almost the same time, my mother was whispering to my father about a chance to introduce himself. Furman left the defence table and opened the small gate that divides formal court space from the public space behind, and ushered my father up to the defence table to meet Stroud. The guards were still at a distance, and Robert Stroud and Thomas Gaddis shook hands. The guards returned, ushering my father back to his seat, and the Judge entered. This was the only moment the two men ever met.

Stroud's case was not successful. He returned to the prison hospital and his health began to fail. In 1962 Attorney General Robert F. Kennedy announced he could not recommend commutation of Stroud's sentence. The following year, the prisoner's final application for his release was turned down with no comment from the Federal Board of Prisons.

Bob Stroud returned to his hospital room, which he had mentioned in correspondence as having complete toilet facilities, two big windows and hot water in one minute at any hour of the day or night.

But Stroud was feeling poorly. Though his work continued at the hobbyshop and the library, his hands were bothering him and he complained of continued eye problems. In his weakening health, he became more reflective: about the more active life he had led before, ironically, in prison (his manuscript on prison reform, and of course, his earlier extended study of bird diseases); and about his continuing efforts on his own behalf from studies of legal documents in the library. He had hopes of good return from yet another legal challenge for his rights, and the return of his prison document.

It was 1963, and he had been alive for 73 years. But his health was failing, his hands were shaking and the spots before his eyes felt wider and more intense.

He continued his efforts for parole, using his perfect record since 1916 as a basis, and he had high hopes of retrieving his manuscript about the prison system from the Prison Bureau files.

But at 5.30 a.m. on November 21, 1963, his fellow inmate, Morton Sobell, went to Stroud's room and found him dead. Fifty-four of Stroud's 73 years of life were spent in prison. Robert Stroud was buried beside relatives in Metropolis, Illinois.

This book has been published in 15 languages, including a

braille edition for the UK. Stroud's death would have been a front-page story had it not been overshadowed by events in Dallas, Texas, on the following day—the assassination of President Kennedy.

My sister and I grew up with Robert Stroud—he was a presence in our home. We had received birthday cards from this man we had never met. We had seen a large scrapbook that a class of grade-school children had created for the prisoner, with imaginative crayon drawings of birds flying free in country settings, reflecting Stroud's hope for the development of enormous aviaries. Stroud had sent us hand-tooled purses made in prison, signed with "RS" stamped in the leather.

Months before Stroud died, he also sent a hand-tooled billfold to an eighth grader, Dennis Norton, evidently a bird fancier. To this young boy, who had circulated a Petition for Executive Clemency for the aging prisoner, Stroud wrote a lengthy letter, which in part read:

> There is just one thing about your note that I do not like. You say that you know that you will never reach the heights in your studies that I have reached in mine. Now I do not like to see a young person sell himself short. Modesty may be all right on occasion, but in my opinion it is often a virtue of dubious value. Always tell yourself that you are as good as anyone that breathes; that you have two hands and a brain, and a little time in which to use them. But they are enough, and no one has any more. And if you train and force them to serve you well, you can reach any height to which you aspire. But to waste any of them is to betray yourself...
>
> I hope that you never make some of the terrible mistakes I have made or see some of the phases of life I have seen, but if you could, for one moment, see some of the men who are ten, fifteen and even twenty years my junior, you would understand what I mean and why it is that I always think of this place as the final port of wasted lives. And, Dennis, if there is any greatness or virtue in my life, it is not my work with birds. It is the fact that I have never joined that group. I have demonstrated time and again that no man is or even can be defeated until he, himself, quits fighting ... I have spent a lot of time locked up, but ... I have never served time ...

because I have made that time serve me, and I have never been able to find enough of it to do all the things that I wanted to do...

There will be times, however, when the whole bottom will seem to have fallen out of your life ... and when those times come, just say to yourself, "well, here goes nothing", fix a smile upon your lips that will not come off even if the whole world totters, clench your teeth and keep right on going ... you will be able to reach heights of accomplishments that I could not even dream of, and you will learn that the happiness, for which everyone is searching, is something to be found only within yourself. Not in your surroundings. And always remember that these suggestions come to you from a man who has seen the worst life has to offer and has made the best of it, who has ten times in his life had doctors tell him that he could not survive, and three times has heard a judge fix the day and hour of his death. Yet, who has outlived all of them and who knows by experience that the only thing that can ever defeat you is yourself.

P.E.G.
July 1985